THE
TOP
TEN

WRITERS PICK THEIR
FAVORITE BOOKS

Edited by J. Peder Zane

W. W. NORTON & COMPANY
New York • London

Manufacturing by Courier Westford
Book design by Anna Oler

Library of Congress Cataloging-in-Publication Data

The top ten : writers pick their favorite books /
edited by J. Peder Zane.—1st ed.
p. cm.
Includes indexes.
ISBN-13: 978-0-393-32840-0 (pbk.)
ISBN-10: 0-393-32840-6 (pbk.)
1. Authors, American—Books and reading. 2. Authors—Books and reading.
3. Best books. I. Zane, J. Peder.
Z1039.A87T67 2007
028'.9—dc22

2006032473

W. W. Norton & Company, Inc., 500 Fifth Avenue, New York, N.Y. 10110
www.wwnorton.com

W. W. Norton & Company Ltd.,
Castle House, 75/76 Wells Street, London W1T 3QT

1 2 3 4 5 6 7 8 9 0

THE
TOP
TEN

Also edited by J. Peder Zane

Remarkable Reads: 34 Writers and Their Adventures in Reading

To Janine,
My number one.

To our daughters,
Olivia, Annabel, and Amelia.
Oh, what awaits you!

CONTENTS

INTRODUCTION
J. PEDER ZANE

This book began with a dream.

I'm on a deserted island—lots of sand, single palm tree, you know the drill. Food and fresh water seem pretty scarce but what I *really* need is a good book. Suddenly, one drops from the sky. Thud! As I bend to lift it, I hear another thud. Then another. And another until I can't see the tree for all the books, which have turned my little isle into a Tower of Biblio-Babel.

Buried in books I'm awash in confusion: Where to begin?

Boom, I'm awake and I decipher my dream lickety-split. That sense of overwhelming possibility was all too familiar—it's the same feeling I get whenever I step into a megastore bursting with thousands of titles or click into an online retailer offering access to millions of works.

This is the yin and yang of the modern reader: opportunity and befuddlement.

We live in a Golden Age—never before have so many books been within such easy reach. But when anything is possible, choice becomes torture. What to pick? Where to start? This one?

That one? How about this—and that? What will I like? *What's worth my time?*

Help!

In response, various voices have emerged—from Oprah Winfrey to the book club craze she sparked—to provide readers direction as they navigate this book-rich world.

But these sources take us only so far. They offer signposts but not detailed road maps to the land of literary possibilities. *The Top Ten* fills this gap. Part Rand-McNally, part Zagat's, part cultural Prozac, it takes the anxiety out of bibliophilia by offering a comprehensive and authoritative guide to the world's best books.

Its premise is simple: Who knows more about great books than great writers? Where previous surveys have queried small groups of authors, *The Top Ten* draws from the responses of 125 leading British and American authors who were asked "to provide a list, ranked, in order, of what you consider the ten greatest works of fiction of all time—novels, story collections, plays, or poems."

There were no limits. The participants could pick any work, by any writer, from any time period. Though *The Top Ten* focuses on fiction, a few writers insisted on including works of nonfiction and, well, it's *their* list.

After awarding ten points to each first-place pick, nine to second-place picks, and so on, the results were tabulated to create the Top Top Ten list—the very best of the very best.

It was a horse race straight out of Lewis Carroll: *Anna Karenina's* out front, *Madame Bovary's* on her shoulder, *Lolita* is starting to make a move, and here comes *Moby-Dick* charging hard from the outside.

However, *The Top Ten* is not trying to anoint a canon. Its message is not: Here are the only ten books you need to read. Instead it points you toward the many fine books awaiting your discovery, highlighting a multitude of books, *each and every one of which is worth your time.*

The lists name 544 separate titles, ranging from the plays of Kenneth Koch to the mysteries of Georges Simenon to the poetry of Joy Harjo to the novels of Stephen King and Jane Austen. If you start today and read a book a week, it will take eleven and a half years to read them all.

That sounds daunting, but think of it like this: *The Top Ten* offers eleven and a half klunker-free years of reading pleasure; 544 books, *each of which is considered to be among the ten greatest books ever written.*

Best of all, it passes the telephone book test: Close your eyes, open the book, place your finger on the page. Read that book you're pointing to: *It's a winner!*

One book readers may want to spend some time with is *The Top Ten* itself, which is both a guide to great books—including brief descriptions of every work listed—and a wellspring of surprising statistics that can make literature seem like baseball.

Where to start? Begin with the lists themselves, which spark mind games (the good kind) both large and small.

Taking a big-picture view in his essay on the Top Top Ten list, Sven Birkerts observes that the biggest vote getters suggest the qualities that writers consider to be the essence of great writing. "The collective preference," he writes, "is clearly for memorable character-driven dramas of love and death delineated in sensuous, nuanced prose."

In another essay, David Orr suggests a more personal approach—using the lists as windows into their creators' literary sensibilities.

Notice how some writers identified books that are clearly models for their own writings, while others selected works that seem straight out of literary left field. Some created "objective" lists filled with time-honored classics; others took a more "subjective" approach, choosing less-celebrated works that hold a high place in their own hearts. Robert Pinsky spoke for nearly everyone when he prefaced his list with these words: "Ten works of fiction that have been great *for me.*"

In fact, Pinsky's words were some of the mildest I heard from the contributors. As I collected their lists, I began to feel like a sadist—or at least a dentist—for the pain I was inflicting by forcing them to pick just ten books. "List sired by Necessity upon Despair," wrote Fred Chappell. "It is so *limited,*" sighed Susan Minot. "I know I'm forgetting ones I really love," Peter Carey fretted. "Lists, unless grocery shopping lists, are truly a *reductio ad absurdum,*" quipped Annie Proulx.

Mary Gaitskill gives full throat to these concerns in her essay on the difficulties of picking just ten books from a vast array of ever-changing favorites.

And yet, the list makers persevered because their discomfort was not as strong as their generous desire to pay tribute to works that inspired them, hoping that they might inspire others. As Reynolds Price so eloquently stated: "I don't offer these as the 'ten greatest novels.' . . . I do feel strongly, however, that there are few other substantial works of fiction from any culture known to me which equal these ten in the depth of their wisdom or the efficiency of their prose. . . . I offer them in the hope of widening their readership."

Furthermore, the constraints placed on each writer seem to vanish when we consider all 125 lists. Expansive and inclusive seem the best adjectives, prompting us to imagine various methods for organizing the results.

An appendix makes a preliminary stab at tabulating, ranking, collating, and cross-referencing these literary milestones. It includes two lists of the top ten authors—one based on whose books earned the most points, the other reflecting who had the greatest number of titles mentioned (Shakespeare in a landslide!).

Other tallies identify the top ten works of the twentieth century, the top ten American novels, the top ten mysteries and thrillers, and the top ten comic novels.

But that is just the beginning of fun and provocative avenues the lists might lead you down.

One of my favorite findings concerns the one-hit wonders. A total of 353 books appeared on only one list. Twenty-three of those solo acts earned the top slot. Put another way, there were twenty-three books that one writer considered his or her absolute favorite and that no other writer cast so much as a tenth-place vote for, although in fairness, tenth place is none too shabby in this competition.

Or consider *Waiting for Godot* by Samuel Beckett. The six points it earned puts it far down in the rankings, but those points came from three different voters, making it one of only ninety-seven works named on three or more lists.

It was feast or famine for the great nineteenth-century novels. While the best of them garnered huge vote totals, the century produced few also-rans. Among the books named on more than one list, eighty-seven were written during the twentieth century and only thirty-five during the nineteenth.

The 1920s proved the most popular decade, producing fifteen works named on two or more lists. This was followed by the 1930s and 1940s, which boasted fourteen titles each, and the 1950s and 1960s, which had twelve apiece. The leading decades of the nineteenth century were the 1850s and 1880s, which each produced seven works named on multiple lists.

Then, of course, there are rankings based on race, gender, and genre, books that are happy or sad; optimistic, pessimistic, or cynical; sexually frigid or lustily explicit. The parlor games are as fascinating as they are endless—I have only just begun to calculate literarily.

But *The Top Ten* is only a barker's voice seeking to draw you into the tent of great literature. It beckons you to close its pages and open those of another book, one that will entertain, enrich, and perhaps, transform you.

The Top Ten is not the only book you'd want to have on a deserted island. But it can help you navigate the literary floodwaters of our Golden Age, when books seem to drop from the sky like raindrops.

THE
TOP
TOP
TEN

THE TOP TOP TEN LIST

1. *Anna Karenina* by Leo Tolstoy
2. *Madame Bovary* by Gustave Flaubert
3. *War and Peace* by Leo Tolstoy
4. *Lolita* by Vladimir Nabokov
5. *The Adventures of Huckleberry Finn* by Mark Twain
6. *Hamlet* by William Shakespeare
7. *The Great Gatsby* by F. Scott Fitzgerald
8. *In Search of Lost Time* by Marcel Proust
9. The stories of Anton Chekhov
10. *Middlemarch* by George Eliot

ON THE TOP TOP TEN
SVEN BIRKERTS

A haruspex, as everyone knows—though I'll confess I looked it up just to be sure—*haruspicates*. He takes divination from entrails, reads the scatter of signs to discover the concealed play of forces and to determine the look of the future. I like the sound of that, the sense of importance it confers, even if looking for patterns and meanings in a ranked list of "greatest books" as nominated by living writers is not what the ancients had in mind. But still, the process does capture some sense of the spirit with which I approached my task. Yes, I told myself, we do live in an age of lists, of "best" this and "top" that, and there is a trendy aspect to many compilations, but why not take this one seriously? More than a hundred respected writers opining on greatness, answering the question by looking to their own literary obsessions—it has to tell us a good deal. The only question is *"What* does it tell us?"

As self-anointed haruspex, I start with my own reactions on receiving the results of the survey, a closely printed twelve-page list of titles. The inky phalanx of titles was as daunting as it was exhilarating, and before I gave free rein to my curiosity, before I even sharpened my pencil for the inevitable orgy of celebration and dissent, I caught myself grappling with the demon of skeptical relativism. I thought—in Latin, of course—*de gustibus disputandum non est*, there's no disputing tastes. We are all irrevocably, terminally subjective in our responses to art—it's how we're wired. We like what we like for hundreds of reasons, and there is no arguing for stable hierarchies. What could a list like the one in my hand offer besides a tabulation of errant subjectivities?

And yet, the more I considered, the more I had to allow that with a large enough sample—and certainly a pool of one hundred and twenty-five writers counts for something—certain convergences also had to be meaningful. That a significant number of these practitioners time and again put the same works on their lists of ten could not be an empty fact. If it didn't tell us about greatness, it certainly said something about how writers read, how pigs (I mean nothing pejorative here) grade for themselves the varieties of bacon.

Having settled that, I had to go right to the list. I couldn't resist—ranked lists of writers or books are my Achilles heel. I was entirely predictable in my behavior: I scanned the top ten "winners" right away, curious and also braced for disappointment. But hurrying down the roster, I first registered only clicks of confirmation—of course, of course, yes, right, check. I was surprised only at not being more surprised. I had not yet begun chiming in with my "But hey, what about—?" That would come in a few moments. My gut was in essential agreement. These were all great works, many of them ones I would have put on my sheet as well. *Anna Karenina, Madame Bovary, War and Peace, Lolita, The Adventures of Huckleberry Finn, Hamlet, The Great Gatsby, In Search of Lost Time,* Chekhov's stories, *Middlemarch* . . . I heard no protesting voice until I finally paused and looked away from the page. Then it came, of course. "Wait—where is Joyce, Woolf, Dostoevsky, Hemingway, Homer . . . ?" But then a quick glance at the titles on page 2 confirmed that they were all there, on deck, not so much excluded as slightly bested. *"De gustibus—"* I remembered, thinking of how no table set for ten could accommodate the available greatness in the room. And then I took up my pencil.

What a reader's sport! I tracked in sequence the hundreds and hundreds of titles, heartened by how many I knew, disheartened by how many I didn't know, at the same time jerking my head this way and that in approval and disagreement: I looked like a man overtaken by a cloud of midges. Indeed, if I were to somehow annotate this process, mapping in slow motion the ups and downs of my increasingly agitated sensibility—well, it wouldn't tell you anything except that all readers are partisans, yielding ground to no one, and that no two lovers of literature love it in the same way or for the same reasons. You would find me insisting on the proper place for my Malcolm Lowry, my Ford Madox Ford, my Marguerite Yourcenar, but it would be against your Toni Morrison, your Gabriel García Márquez, your Barbara Pym. By definition, no list is ever satisfactory. And by commodious vicus (*Finnegans Wake* did not make the list, but Chuck Palahniuk's *Fight Club* did) the chaos of jousting tastes brings me back to the ranking of the top ten, for here at least we have the mystery of consensus to ponder, to haruspicate upon. Or from.

The reader will notice a few things right away. Of the Decalogue, the group adjudged the "greatest," nine works are by men, one by a woman, George Eliot, who adopted a male *nom de plume* in order to make her literary way. Six belong to the nineteenth century, three to the early or middle years of the twentieth century, and Shakespeare's *Hamlet* is the anomaly, not only for its time period, but its genre as well. What else? What message, what truth? Well, push, pull, and parse as I will, I can only extract a few striking commonalities, at least such as might fit comfortably in the small frame I've been given. One is so obvious that we could risk looking right past: that these are brilliantly written, verbally sophisticated, challenging works of imagination. From the massed juggernaut paragraphs of Tolstoy and Proust, to the sable-brush verbal nuances of Flaubert, Nabokov, and Fitzgerald, our writers picked writers unsurpassed in their craft performance.

But, let's also note, the writers did not put *Ulysses* or *To the Lighthouse* in the highest place, not by consensus anyway. There was, very clearly, another consideration, another evaluative factor. What to call it? Passion, conflict, struggle, conscience . . . Staring at the list for a while, a fairly straightforward answer comes to mind. We might remember that Sigmund Freud long ago theorized all exis-tence as a primal combat between two immensely powerful drives, *Eros* and *Thanatos*, love and death. And whether we agree or disagree with the theory, we do have to allow that, if there is any common strain to be found in the authors' top ten choices, it has to be the dramatic interlocking of just these forces: the heat of erotic and romantic passion coupled with the fear and pity of the individual face to face with extinction. Not just the interlocking, but the vivid embodiment of the struggle in surpassingly vivid characters.

This is crucial. One thing that stands out so clearly in the list of top choices is the outsized vividness of the characters, what might be called their psychological and emotional throw weight. They are our representatives in the world of life imagined: Prince Andrei and Natasha, Pierre, Anna and Vronsky, Levin and Kitty, Tom and Huck, Emma, Gatsby and Daisy, Hamlet, Ophelia, Humbert Humbert and Lolita, Dorothea Brooke and Causabon. Even to name them is to recall their compact human resonance. To read their lives is to be forced to reconsider our own. Which is, of course, part of the secret of their enormous appeal: they have the power to define and heighten our feelings to ourselves.

There is no disputing tastes, this we know. But there is also no disputing that collective preferences exist. The collective preference reflected in the list of greats is clearly for memorable character-driven dramas of love and death delineated in sensuous, nuanced prose. And presented in traditional modes.

This last fact is not surprising, but it *is* interesting in several ways. It declares that our writers, those who shape and mirror our collective imagination, are still deeply compelled by the old forms, by what might almost be considered the archetypes of earlier times, as if once expressed they are hardly to be improved upon. And it's true, the appetite for these narratives survives in the face of—and I'm sure because of—our new ways of living. For no doubt about it, we are all now charter members of the digital millennium, surrounded on every side with an invisible floss of distracting signals. But at the same time our emotional centers of gravity—or at least those of the writers who represent us—are still attuned to the expressions of an earlier, far less diffuse world. One way to read the list of greatest is to see it as countering the diffusion and narrative thinness of our present-day world. The choices argue for density and coherence, as well as for subjective—dare I say "romantic"?— intensities that some might deem outmoded. This is interesting. And for the haruspex it is also paradoxical. For in looking toward the future, as his ancient vocation dictates, he finds himself contemplating what look like the emblematic outlines of a fantasied past. What can he possibly conclude from that?

Sven Birkerts is the author of five books of essays and a memoir. He edits the journal AGNI at Boston University and is Briggs-Copeland lecturer at Harvard University.

THE
LISTS

ONLY TEN?

MARY GAITSKILL

The difficulties of choosing ten best books are obvious: When you last read a book has much to do with how large it looms on your radar. You may remember a book you read twenty years ago with such a surge of feeling that you must honor that surge (once removed from "urge") even if you aren't sure what you would think about the book now. Or you may barely remember a book you loved, not because it isn't great, but because your mind has absorbed and enfolded it in such a way that its piercing qualities are temporarily blunted or hidden, perhaps to become vivid again ten years from now when your mind performs one of its periodic seismic shifts, disgorging the story and its characters anew: Nana and Silk roaming the streets of Paris; Rabbit and Thelma in the tub; Ishmael fantasizing that he might reach out to tweak the imaginary nose of a whale as the *Pequod* careens around it. Based on memory, you sometimes can't tell if a book really was great or if it just hit the spot that needed hitting at the time. (Or not: Joyce's *Ulysses* is at the top of my list because I re-read it three years ago. If I hadn't, I would've remembered it as it appeared to my undergraduate mind—as an assignment.) There are all the authors you haven't read, which in my case are Balzac, Eliot, Shakespeare, and most of Dostoevsky, to shamefacedly name a few. Then there is the peculiar issue of proximity, which is the reason there are no contemporary authors on my list. It isn't that I can't think of any; John Updike, Philip Roth, Marilyn Robinson, and Haruki Murakami are only a few that might be considered great. But I can't see them clearly enough to judge their greatness. I can't see them for the same reason astronomers practice their business in isolation from the cities; there is too much artificial light. It is hard to separate the light of the book from the live beams of many fierce minds—themselves pale and seeping in the context of a violently lit modernity.

The books on my list (see page 66) are visible to me from hundreds of miles away: *Lolita*, so dense with feeling, thought, and beauty that you can't see it in all its dimensions at once any more than you could see an enchanted forest in its entirety; *Pale Fire*, a tragicomedy about the dream world shimmering under corporeal life, and the skulking hero's equally ardent and ridiculous attempt to find a bridge to that world through a misdirected love—a strange misconnection harboring an imaginary connection more real than reality; *Bleak House*, with its great rattletrap plot, steaming forward on a kinetic, dreamlike storm of characters and images that are made of words, but which transcend words to become conduits for essential forces; *To the Lighthouse*, a marvel of clarity and precision, yet suffused with a vague, iridescent verbal haziness that is gorgeous on the page; *Ulysses*, too beautiful and vast to describe in the space I have here. *Madame Bovary*; "Gusev"; *Peter Pan*; *Dead Souls*; *The Hunchback of Notre Dame*; the titles alone describe whole star systems that give off light strong enough to see hundreds of years away.

Some of my contemporaries and near-contemporaries have doubtless written books, that is to say, created stars, in close proximity to these. But at the present time they are invisible or only partially visible to me.

Mary Gaitskill has written the story collections Bad Behavior *and* Because They Wanted To *and the novels* Two Girls, Fat and Thin, *and* Veronica.

READING THE LISTS

DAVID ORR

If you're putting together a list of "the greatest books," you'll want to do two things: (1) out of kindness, avoid anyone working on a novel; and (2) decide what the word "great" means. The first part is easy, but how about the second? A short list of possible definitions of "greatness" might look like this:

1. "Great" means "books that have been greatest for me."
2. "Great" means "books that would be considered great by the most people over time."
3. "Great" has nothing to do with you or me—or people at all. It involves transcendent concepts like God or the Sublime.
4. "Great"? I like Tom Clancy.

As writers tend to be practical—at least, as regards writing—the list makers here generally have avoided adhering strictly to one approach. That's to their credit and our benefit. We learn more about literature from intuitions than calculations, and the intuitions of good authors are especially valuable because, as the poet James Richardson puts it, writers are "how books read each other." So what can these lists tell us about how these writers read great books, and how those great books, in turn, read them? For a representative example, let's consider the selections made by Judy Budnitz, a younger author known for fabular, dreamily deadpan short stories.

The first thing to notice about Budnitz's list is that it isn't an effort to capture all the eternal works of the West. There's no Homer, no Shakespeare, no Dante, no Chaucer—no roundup of Great Greats. But she also hasn't ignored the giants; at least four of her choices—Nabokov, Tolstoy, Isaac Babel, and Bruno Schulz—are picks that would look reasonable in any collection of All Stars. This is a common approach, and it speaks to the loyalty most writers feel to their craft heritage (and in a book like this, to their desire to look erudite alongside their peers). It's a hard pull to resist. Even David Foster Wallace's idiosyncratic selection of top-selling authors (see #4 above) includes C. S. Lewis, who's no less canonical for being wildly popular.

The best parts of Budnitz's list, however, are personal. Some of these elements are obvious—as a short story writer, she favors short fiction (four of her ten selections); as an Atlanta native, she likes Southerners (three of ten); and as a contemporary writer, she prefers more recent work (only Tolstoy predates the twentieth century).

But Budnitz's list also tells a less straightforward story about aesthetic and political affinities. Her more obscure picks are especially revealing in this regard. She's the only author here, for instance, to choose a book by Donald Barthelme, whose ludic, funny, and intensely smart stories are likely formal touchstones for her own work. Her selection of Richard Yates (who's enjoying a minor renaissance) and William Goyen (who remains largely unknown) tells us even more. Yates's work bears little technical resemblance to Budnitz's, but his attention to the ways in which dreams are diminished by neighborhood expectations would be attractive to Budnitz, whose stories, however oblique, are often social parables. Goyen, a Texan with a cascading, biblical prose style, would seem to be the odd man out here. Yet while Budnitz is more understated, more withholding, and decidedly more off-kilter, there is a soulfulness to her best writing—a willingness to relinquish control—that recalls the best of Goyen.

This is her most unusual pick, and it is likely the truest. And isn't that what we want from a "greatest books" list, that it show, as Goethe said genius always must, "the love of truth"?

David Orr, the 2004 recipient of the Nona Balakian Citation for Excellence in Reviewing from the National Book Critics Circle, lives in New York City.

THE WRITERS' PICKS

LEE K. ABBOTT

1. *Heart of Darkness* by Joseph Conrad
2. *The Adventures of Huckleberry Finn* by Mark Twain
3. *Nine Stories* by J. D. Salinger
4. *So Long, See You Tomorrow* by William Maxwell
5. *The Ponder Heart* by Eudora Welty
6. *Rabbit, Run* by John Updike
7. *Separate Flights* by Andre Dubus
8. *The Sound and the Fury* by William Faulkner
9. The stories of John Cheever
10. *One Hundred Years of Solitude* by Gabriel García Márquez

Lee K. Abbott is the author of seven collections of stories, most recently *All Things, All at Once: New and Selected Stories*.

SHERMAN ALEXIE

1. *Invisible Man* by Ralph Ellison
2. *Howl* by Allen Ginsberg
3. The poems of Emily Dickinson
4. *The Things They Carried* by Tim O'Brien
5. *Don Quixote* by Miguel de Cervantes
6. *Ceremony* by Leslie Marmon Silko
7. *She Had Some Horses* by Joy Harjo
8. *The Branch Will Not Break* by James Wright
9. *The Grapes of Wrath* by John Steinbeck
10. *Beloved* by Toni Morrison

Sherman Alexie is a writer, filmmaker, and Spokane/Coeur d'Alene Indian whose works include the story collection *The Lone Ranger and Tonto Fistfight in Heaven* and the novel *Reservation Blues*.

KATE ATKINSON

1. *Persuasion* by Jane Austen
2. *Alice's Adventures in Wonderland* by Lewis Carroll
3. *Pride and Prejudice* by Jane Austen
4. *Middlemarch* by George Eliot
5. *The Portrait of a Lady* by Henry James
6. *Slaughterhouse-Five* by Kurt Vonnegut
7. *Pricksongs & Descants* by Robert Coover
8. *Revolutionary Road* by Richard Yates
9. *The Adventures of Huckleberry Finn* by Mark Twain
10. *The Railway Children* by E. Nesbit

Kate Atkinson won the 1995 Whitbread Book of the Year Award for her first novel, *Behind the Scenes at the Museum*. Her works include the story collection *Not the End of the World* and the novel *One Good Turn*.

PAUL AUSTER

1. *Don Quixote* by Miguel de Cervantes
2. *War and Peace* by Leo Tolstoy
3. *Moby-Dick* by Herman Melville
4. *Crime and Punishment* by Fyodor Dostoevsky
5. *In Search of Lost Time* by Marcel Proust
6. *Ulysses* by James Joyce
7. *The Scarlet Letter* by Nathaniel Hawthorne
8. *The Castle* by Franz Kafka
9. *Molloy, Malone Dies,* and *The Unnamable* (trilogy) by Samuel Beckett
10. *Tristram Shandy* by Laurence Sterne

Paul Auster is a poet (*Disappearances: Selected Poems*), essayist (*Why Write*), novelist (*Brooklyn Follies*), screenwriter (*Smoke*), and translator (*The Notebooks of Joseph Joubert*).

MELISSA BANK

1. *Anna Karenina* by Leo Tolstoy
2. *Lolita* by Vladimir Nabokov
3. The stories of Ernest Hemingway
4. *East of Eden* by John Steinbeck
5. *The Great Gatsby* by F. Scott Fitzgerald
6. The stories of Raymond Carver
7. *Middlemarch* by George Eliot
8. *Washington Square* by Henry James
9. *The Remains of the Day* by Kazuo Ishiguro
10. *Nine Stories* by J. D. Salinger

Melissa Bank is the author of *The Girls' Guide to Hunting and Fishing* and *The Wonder Spot*. Her fiction has been translated into twenty-nine languages.

RUSSELL BANKS

1. *Don Quixote* by Miguel de Cervantes
2. *Moby-Dick* by Herman Melville
3. *The Adventures of Huckleberry Finn* by Mark Twain
4. *The Sound and the Fury* by William Faulkner
5. *The Odyssey* by Homer
6. *The Canterbury Tales* by Geoffrey Chaucer
7. *War and Peace* by Leo Tolstoy
8. *Madame Bovary* by Gustave Flaubert
9. *The Brothers Karamazov* by Fyodor Dostoevsky
10. *One Hundred Years of Solitude* by Gabriel García Márquez

Russell Banks has published fifteen books of fiction, including *Continental Drift*, *Cloudsplitter*, and *The Darling*. He is a member of the American Academy of Arts and Letters and currently serves as New York State Author.

JOHN BANVILLE

1. *Ill Seen, Ill Said* by Samuel Beckett
2. *Notes from Underground* by Fyodor Dostoevsky
3. *Ulysses* by James Joyce
4. *Doctor Faustus* by Thomas Mann
5. *Moby-Dick* by Herman Melville
6. *Lolita* by Vladimir Nabokov
7. *Austerlitz* by W. G. Sebald
8. *Dirty Snow* by Georges Simenon
9. *Gulliver's Travels* by Jonathan Swift
10. *Vanity Fair* by William Makepeace Thackeray

John Banville's novels include *The Book of Evidence*, *The Untouchable*, *Shroud*, and *The Sea*, which won the 2005 Man Booker Prize.

JULIAN BARNES

1. *Madame Bovary* by Gustave Flaubert
2. *Don Juan* by Lord Byron
3. *Persuasion* by Jane Austen
4. *Anna Karenina* by Leo Tolstoy
5. *Candide* by Voltaire
6. *The Custom of the Country* by Edith Wharton
7. *The Good Soldier* by Ford Madox Ford
8. *The Leopard* by Giuseppe Tomasi di Lampedusa
9. *Rabbit Angstrom: The Four Novels* by John Updike
10. *Amours de Voyage* by Arthur Hugh Clough

Julian Barnes is an English novelist (*Flaubert's Parrot, Arthur & George*), short story writer (*The Lemon Table*), and essayist (*Something to Declare*).

ANDREA BARRETT

1. *Paradise Lost* by John Milton
2. *War and Peace* by Leo Tolstoy
3. *Middlemarch* by George Eliot
4. *Metamorphoses* by Ovid
5. *Bleak House* by Charles Dickens
6. *Frankenstein* by Mary Shelley
7. *The Aeneid* by Virgil
8. *Moby-Dick* by Herman Melville
9. *Jane Eyre* by Charlotte Brontë
10. *The Radetzky March* by Joseph Roth

Andrea Barrett won a National Book Award for her story collection *Ship Fever*. Her other works include the novel *The Voyage of the Narwhal* and story collection *Servants of the Map*.

MADISON SMARTT BELL

1. *The Book of Leviathan* by Peter Blegvad
2. *1982, Janine* by Alasdair Gray
3. *Blood Meridian* by Cormac McCarthy
4. *The Beans of Egypt, Maine; Letourneau's Used Auto Parts;* and *Merry Men* (trilogy) by Carolyn Chute
5. *The Horse's Mouth* by Joyce Cary
6. *Death of the Fox, The Succession,* and *Entered from the Sun* (trilogy) by George Garrett
7. *Continental Drift* by Russell Banks
8. *Street of Lost Footsteps* by Lyonel Trouillot
9. *The Adventures of Huckleberry Finn* by Mark Twain
10. *The Conference of the Birds* by Farid ud-Din Attar

Madison Smartt Bell's works include a trilogy of novels on the Haitian Revolution, *All Souls' Rising, Master of the Crossroads,* and *The Stone That the Builder Refused.*

CHRIS BOHJALIAN

1. *The Divine Comedy* by Dante Alighieri
2. *Ulysses* by James Joyce
3. *Great Expectations* by Charles Dickens
4. *Anna Karenina* by Leo Tolstoy
5. *The Great Gatsby* by F. Scott Fitzgerald
6. *To Kill a Mockingbird* by Harper Lee
7. *Jane Eyre* by Charlotte Brontë
8. *The Adventures of Huckleberry Finn* by Mark Twain
9. *Invisible Man* by Ralph Ellison
10. *Les Misérables* by Victor Hugo

Chris Bohjalian is the author of ten novels, including *Of Two Minds*, *Before You Know Kindness*, and *Midwives*, an Oprah Book Club selection. His Web address is www.chrisbohjalian.com.

T. C. BOYLE

1. *Love Medicine* by Louise Erdrich
2. *The Remains of the Day* by Kazuo Ishiguro
3. *Fiskadoro* by Denis Johnson
4. *The Messiah of Stockholm* by Cynthia Ozick
5. *Lucy* by Jamaica Kincaid
6. *White Noise* by Don DeLillo
7. *Chronicle of a Death Foretold* by Gabriel García Márquez
8. *Ficciones* by Jorge Luis Borges
9. *V.* by Thomas Pynchon
10. The stories of John Cheever

T. C. Boyle's works include *T. C. Boyle Stories: The Collected Stories of T. Coraghessan Boyle* and the novels *Road to Wellville* and *Drop City*.

JUDY BUDNITZ

1. *Lolita* by Vladimir Nabokov
2. *Jesus' Son* by Denis Johnson
3. *All the King's Men* by Robert Penn Warren
4. *To Kill a Mockingbird* by Harper Lee
5. *Anna Karenina* by Leo Tolstoy
6. *Red Cavalry* by Isaac Babel
7. *The House of Breath* by William Goyen
8. *Revolutionary Road* by Richard Yates
9. *Sixty Stories* by Donald Barthelme
10. *The Street of Crocodiles* by Bruno Schulz

Judy Budnitz has written two story collections, *Flying Leap* and *Nice Big American Baby*, and a novel, *If I Told You Once*.

JAMES LEE BURKE

1. *The Sound and the Fury* by William Faulkner
2. *Dubliners* by James Joyce
3. *For Whom the Bell Tolls* by Ernest Hemingway
4. *All the King's Men* by Robert Penn Warren
5. The stories of Flannery O'Connor
6. The stories of Andre Dubus
7. *Mildred Pierce* by James M. Cain
8. *The Big Sky* by A. B. Guthrie, Jr.
9. *The Moon and Sixpence* by W. Somerset Maugham
10. *The Great Gatsby* by F. Scott Fitzgerald

James Lee Burke is the author of twenty-five published novels, many of them mysteries featuring Dave Robicheaux, who works for the sheriff's department in Burke's hometown of New Iberia, Louisiana.

PETER CAMERON

1. *The Outward Room* by Millen Brand
2. *The Professor's House* by Willa Cather
3. *Uncle Vanya* by Anton Chekhov
4. *The Evening of the Holiday* by Shirley Hazzard
5. *The Towers of Trebizond* by Rose Macaulay
6. *The Chateau* by William Maxwell
7. *Quartet in Autumn* by Barbara Pym
8. *Light Years* by James Salter
9. *What's for Dinner?* by James Schuyler
10. *A Voice Through a Cloud* by Denton Welch

Peter Cameron is the author of *The City of Your Final Destination* and *The Weekend*, among other books.

BEBE MOORE CAMPBELL

1. *The Catcher in the Rye* by J. D. Salinger
2. *Native Son* by Richard Wright
3. *Song of Solomon* by Toni Morrison
4. *Beloved* by Toni Morrison
5. *Invisible Man* by Ralph Ellison
6. *Madame Bovary* by Gustave Flaubert
7. *Moby-Dick* by Herman Melville
8. *The Color Purple* by Alice Walker
9. *An American Tragedy* by Theodore Dreiser
10. *Anna Karenina* by Leo Tolstoy

Bebe Moore Campbell's works include the novels *Singing in the Comeback Choir* and *72 Hour Hold* and the children's book *Sometimes My Mommy Gets Angry*.

ETHAN CANIN

1. The stories of John Cheever
2. *Notes from Underground* by Fyodor Dostoevsky
3. *Winesburg, Ohio* by Sherwood Anderson
4. *Open Secrets* by Alice Munro
5. *The Old Forest and Other Stories* by Peter Taylor
6. *Henderson the Rain King* by Saul Bellow
7. *American Pastoral* by Philip Roth
8. *At Play in the Fields of the Lord* by Peter Matthiessen
9. *Sacred Hunger* by Barry Unsworth
10. *Mr. Bridge* by Evan S. Connell

Ethan Canin is the author of five books of fiction, including the story collections *Emperor of the Air* and *The Palace Thief* and the novel *Carry Me Across the Water*. He teaches at the Iowa Writers' Workshop and is also a physician.

PHILIP CAPUTO

1. *The Oresteia* by Aeschylus
2. *Medea* by Euripides
3. *The Divine Comedy* by Dante Alighieri
4. *Macbeth* by William Shakespeare
5. *Madame Bovary* by Gustave Flaubert
6. *The Possessed* by Fyodor Dostoevsky
7. *Anna Karenina* by Leo Tolstoy
8. *Life on the Mississippi* by Mark Twain
9. *Heart of Darkness* by Joseph Conrad
10. *Absalom, Absalom!* by William Faulkner

Philip Caputo is a former U.S. Marine who won a Pulitzer Prize for his newspaper reporting. His thirteen books include the Vietnam memoir *A Rumor of War* and the novel *Acts of Faith*.

PETER CAREY

Here it is—no Joyce or T. S. Eliot or Kafka although they invented the river we swim in. No Bible either, which is impossible. *The Great Gatsby* is a perfect work of art and I cut it out. No Faulkner, although I owe him everything. No Chekhov, Munro—what sort of list is that?

1.   *Madame Bovary* by Gustave Flaubert
2.   *Tristram Shandy* by Laurence Sterne
3.   *Great Expectations* by Charles Dickens
4.   *Don Quixote* by Miguel de Cervantes
5.   *Middlemarch* by George Eliot
6.   *Anna Karenina* by Leo Tolstoy
7.   *Austerlitz* by W. G. Sebald
8.   *Love in the Time of Cholera* by Gabriel García Márquez
9.   *The Portrait of a Lady* by Henry James
10.   *Jane Eyre* by Charlotte Brontë

Peter Carey is an Australian writer who has twice won the Booker Prize, for his novels *Oscar and Lucinda* and *True History of the Kelly Gang*. His most recent novel is *Theft: A Love Story*. He lives in New York City.

MICHAEL CHABON

1. *Labyrinths* by Jorge Luis Borges
2. *Pale Fire* by Vladimir Nabokov
3. *Scaramouche* by Rafael Sabatini
4. *Moby-Dick* by Herman Melville
5. *Pride and Prejudice* by Jane Austen
6. *Tales of Mystery and Imagination* by Edgar Allan Poe
7. *In Search of Lost Time* by Marcel Proust
8. *Paradise Lost* by John Milton
9. *Love in the Time of Cholera* by Gabriel García Márquez
10. *The Long Goodbye* by Raymond Chandler

Michael Chabon's books include the novels *Wonder Boys* and *The Amazing Adventures of Kavalier & Clay*, which won a Pulitzer Prize. He is married to the novelist Ayelet Waldman.

FRED CHAPPELL

List sired by Necessity upon Despair:

All the very best stories are in poetry: Homer, Virgil, the Bible, Milton, Dante, Aeschylus, Sophocles, Shakespeare, and thus off limits. Too bad—but to include poetry would have made the job even more impossible, the list even more arbitrary.

These are not necessarily my favorite books. One of them, the Joyce, I haven't even read much of—only enough to persuade me that it is worth a lifetime of attention, one that I haven't got. The Balzac might have been supplanted by *Lost Illusions*, *Père Goriot*, *César Biroteau*, or a dozen others. But he had to be on the list. Austen and Wodehouse are not there because I couldn't decide among titles. Some of my real favorites don't make it: H. G. Wells, Olaf Stapledon, Twain—but they should. Ten—jeez!

1. *The Iliad* by Homer (This one is real. Everything else is just literature.)
2. *Don Quixote* by Miguel de Cervantes
3. *The Canterbury Tales* by Geoffrey Chaucer
4. *Gargantua and Pantagruel* by François Rabelais
5. *The Odyssey* by Homer
6. *The Aeneid* by Virgil
7. *Finnegans Wake* by James Joyce
8. *The Adventures of Huckleberry Finn* by Mark Twain
9. *Paradise Lost* by John Milton
10. *Tom Jones* by Henry Fielding

Fred Chappell is a poet (he won the Bollingen Prize for *Midquest*), novelist (*Farewell, I'm Bound to Leave You*), and critic (*A Way of Happening*) from North Carolina.

Appreciation of François Rabelais' *Gargantua and Pantagruel*
by Fred Chappell

The stories of the giant Gargantua and his giant son Pantagruel, of their birth, nurture, education, and heroic feats of arms; of Pantagruel's voyages through strange lands and exotic cultures in search of ultimate wisdom; of their companions Rondibilis, Frère Jean, and the irrepressible, inexpressible Panurge; of their arriving at last in the abode of the Priestess Bacbuc whose oracular Bottle utters the final truth they have sought—these stories are impossible to summarize and set in order.

It would be presumptuous even to try to do so, since one of the great themes of François Rabelais (1494?–1553) is glorious, raucous, exasperating, exhilarating, universal disorder. The author, a maverick cleric and observant physician, gave our modern world, at the moment of its birth in the Renaissance, its first comprehensive picture of what it was and what it could become. The world borrowed his name for its most treasured and common kind of humor: Rabelaisian, meaning rowdy, rude, satirical, unsparing, obscene, and sometimes cruel.

As Rabelais invented a new literary form, the exorbitant picaresque satire, he invented a new language to express it. His pages are a Babel of polyglot puns, monkish obscurities, legalisms, overblown fustian, and street demotic. Lists abound: diseases and cures, body parts, herbs, geographical oddities, and cusswords in droves.

Here is fantasy rooted in folktale, offering what only the great literary fantasies—*The Faerie Queene, The Tempest, Paradise Lost, Orlando Furioso, The Time Machine*, and a few others—can: a vision of humanity in its relationship with the cosmos and with eternity. At the same time, it presents an earthy panorama of daily concerns and relationships. Unique among the great visionary works, *Gargantua and Pantagruel* is the only slapstick comedy. Among all comedies, it is one of the best.

SANDRA CISNEROS

1. *The Time of the Doves* by Mercè Rodoreda
2. *The Ten Thousand Things* by Maria Dermout
3. *Stones for Ibarra* by Harriet Doerr
4. *The Burning Plain and Other Stories* by Juan Rulfo
5. *Good Morning, Midnight* by Jean Rhys
6. *La Flor de Lis* by Elena Poniatowska
7. *Borderlands/La Frontera* by Gloria Anzaldúa
8. *The Book of Embraces* by Eduardo Galeano
9. *Dreamtigers* by Jorge Luis Borges
10. *Maud Martha* by Gwendolyn Brooks

Sandra Cisneros writes novels (*The House on Mango Street, Caramelo*), short stories (*Woman Hollering Creek*), poetry (*My Wicked, Wicked Ways, Loose Woman*), and children's books (*Hairs/Pelitos*). She is a MacArthur Fellow.

Appreciation of Elena Poniatowska's
La Flor de Lis
by Sandra Cisneros

The little hand serving me coffee is also the hand that wrote the exquisite novel *La Flor de Lis* (1988). It seems absurd a writer of such worth should bother serving coffee to anyone, but it's precisely this humility, this willingness to serve others, whether it be coffee, or novels, or testimonies, or tamales, that makes Elena Poniatowska a writer as well loved by cab drivers as by professors. The title alludes to France, but if you're hip to Mexico City, you'll know La Flor de Lis is also the famous tamale restaurant in la colonia Condesa.

La Flor de Lis is a love story about mother and motherland, about love of México *lindo y querido* (pretty and best), a culture where mothers are revered as goddesses, and a goddess, la Virgen de Guadalupe, is revered because she is "the" mother.

It's a fairy tale told in reverse. Daughters of royalty flee France under siege from World War II, and in the course of their childhood and adolescence in Mexico, we witness the discovery of what it means to belong to a culture, what it means to fall in love, and what, after all, it means to be a woman, because the story is steeped in the body of a woman, in the body of that country.

Nowhere else have I read anyone describe the joy of scrubbing a courtyard with a bucket of suds and a broom. But it's *el zócalo*, the central plaza of Mexico City that the narrator wants to scrub out of *puro amor*. And that ultimately sums up how a writer like Elenita became Elena Poniatowska. What we do for love, after all, is the greatest work we can do.

PEARL CLEAGE

1. *One Hundred Years of Solitude* by Gabriel García Márquez
2. *A Streetcar Named Desire* by Tennessee Williams
3. *Their Eyes Were Watching God* by Zora Neale Hurston
4. *To Kill a Mockingbird* by Harper Lee
5. *A Raisin in the Sun* by Lorraine Hansberry
6. *Gorilla, My Love* by Toni Cade Bambara
7. *Tropic of Cancer* by Henry Miller
8. *Hedda Gabler* by Henrik Ibsen
9. *China Men* by Maxine Hong Kingston
10. *The Grapes of Wrath* by John Steinbeck

Pearl Cleage is the author of five novels, a dozen plays, a book of poetry, and two books of essays. Her novels include *What Looks Like Crazy on an Ordinary Day*, *Some Things I Never Thought I'd Do*, and *Baby Brother's Blues*.

MICHAEL CONNELLY

1. *The Great Gatsby* by F. Scott Fitzgerald
2. *The Day of the Locust* by Nathanael West
3. *To Kill a Mockingbird* by Harper Lee
4. *One Flew Over the Cuckoo's Nest* by Ken Kesey
5. *Catch-22* by Joseph Heller
6. *For Whom the Bell Tolls* by Ernest Hemingway
7. *The Long Goodbye* by Raymond Chandler
8. *Slaughterhouse-Five* by Kurt Vonnegut
9. *The Public Burning* by Robert Coover
10. *Mildred Pierce* by James M. Cain

Michael Connelly is an Edgar Award writer whose novels include *The Lincoln Lawyer*, *Blood Work*, and the best-selling series of Harry Bosch novels.

DOUGLAS COUPLAND

1. *Answered Prayers* by Truman Capote
2. *Slaughterhouse-Five* by Kurt Vonnegut
3. *The Ice Age* by Margaret Drabble
4. *Radiant Way* by Margaret Drabble
5. *Winesburg, Ohio* by Sherwood Anderson
6. *Play It as It Lays* by Joan Didion
7. *Fight Club* by Chuck Palahniuk
8. *Decline and Fall* by Evelyn Waugh
9. *Ask the Dust* by John Fante
10. *Breaking and Entering* by Joy Williams

Douglas Coupland has written nine novels, including *Generation X* and most recently, *jPod*. He lives in Vancouver, British Columbia.

JIM CRACE

1. *Things Fall Apart* by Chinua Achebe (for setting the record straight)
2. *Invisible Cities* by Italo Calvino (for his celebration of lying)
3. *Waiting for the Barbarians* by J. M. Coetzee (for its pessimism)
4. *Robinson Crusoe* by Daniel Defoe (for its optimism)
5. *Middlemarch* by George Eliot (for insight and wisdom)
6. *Invisible Man* by Ralph Ellison (for its call to arms)
7. *A Passage to India* by E. M. Forster (for its symphonic perfection)
8. *The Tin Drum* by Günter Grass (for his imaginative courage)
9. *Beloved* by Toni Morrison (for her emotional clarity)
10. The stories of Flannery O'Connor (for unerring narrative focus)

Jim Crace is the British author of nine novels, including *Quarantine* (a Whitbread Novel of the Year) and *Being Dead* (a National Critics Circle Award winner).

STANLEY CRAWFORD

1. *Gulliver's Travels* by Jonathan Swift
2. The plays of Molière
3. *Emma* by Jane Austen
4. *The Charterhouse of Parma* by Stendhal
5. *Middlemarch* by George Eliot
6. The stories of Anton Chekhov
7. *War and Peace* by Leo Tolstoy
8. *The Portrait of a Lady* by Henry James
9. *The Stranger* by Albert Camus
10. *Disgrace* by J. M. Coetzee

Stanley Crawford's writings include the novels *Log of the S.S. The Mrs. Unguentine*, *Gascoyne*, and *Petroleum Man*, and the memoir *A Garlic Testament: Seasons on a Small Farm in New Mexico*.

MICHAEL CUNNINGHAM

1. *King Lear* by William Shakespeare
2. *Madame Bovary* by Gustave Flaubert
3. *Leaves of Grass* by Walt Whitman
4. *To the Lighthouse* by Virginia Woolf
5. *The Great Gatsby* by F. Scott Fitzgerald
6. *Lolita* by Vladimir Nabokov
7. *Dubliners* by James Joyce
8. *As I Lay Dying* by William Faulkner
9. *The Turn of the Screw* by Henry James
10. The stories of Flannery O'Connor

Michael Cunningham won a Pulitzer Prize and PEN/Faulkner Award for his novel *The Hours*. His other writings include the novel *Specimen Days* and the nonfiction work *Land's End: A Walk Through Provincetown*.

EDWIDGE DANTICAT

1. *Their Eyes Were Watching God* by Zora Neale Hurston
2. *The Stranger* by Albert Camus
3. *Germinal* by Émile Zola
4. *Invisible Man* by Ralph Ellison
5. *One Hundred Years of Solitude* by Gabriel García Márquez
6. *Beloved* by Toni Morrison
7. *Night* by Elie Wiesel
8. *The Color Purple* by Alice Walker
9. *The Trial* by Franz Kafka
10. *Masters of the Dew* by Jacques Roumain

Edwidge Danticat was born in Haiti and moved to the United States when she was twelve. Her books include *Breath, Eyes, Memory; The Dew Breaker;* and *The Farming of Bones*, which won an American Book Award.

Appreciation of Jacques Roumain's
Masters of the Dew
by Edwidge Danticat

This novel charmed Langston Hughes and Mercer Cook so much that when they visited Haiti in the 1940s they decided to translate it. Theirs remains the only English translation. This is the plot: A Haitian young man goes to Cuba to cut sugarcane in the 1930s. When he returns to his village in rural Haiti, he finds that a drought has ravaged the entire area and a Romeo and Juliet–type feud between the two most powerful families stands in the community's way of finding a solution.

Like Romeo, the young man, Manuel, falls in love with the stunning daughter of the family that despises his and a battle ensues that results in tragedy, with some measure of hope. (To say much more would be giving away too much of the plot of this slim volume.) The book has often been called a peasant novel, but it is also an environmental novel, as well as a love story.

I read this book when I was ten years old; it was the first novel in which I recognized people I knew living in circumstances similar to my life and my world. It was also the first time that I realized books could not only help us escape but hold a mirror to our lives, to help us examine a problem and ponder—along with the characters—a possible solution. It was my first engagée or socially engaged novel, one that showed me that the novel could have many roles, that fiction could be used for different purposes without losing its artistic merit. It made me want to write the types of books that could inform and entertain as well as help others live, through a powerful narrative, a heartbreaking, painful, and even redemptive experience.

ROBB FORMAN DEW

1. *The Man Who Loved Children* by Christina Stead
2. *War and Peace* by Leo Tolstoy
3. *Tender Is the Night* by F. Scott Fitzgerald
4. *Little Women* by Louisa May Alcott (May seem silly, but it was my first experience of death—I was ten years old.)
5. *Macbeth* by William Shakespeare
6. *Pride and Prejudice* by Jane Austen
7. *All the King's Men* by Robert Penn Warren
8. *Mrs. Dalloway* by Virginia Woolf
9. *Alice's Adventures in Wonderland* by Lewis Carroll
10. *Catch-22* by Joseph Heller

Robb Forman Dew has written the novels *Dale Loves Sophie to Death*, *The Time of Her Life*, *Fortune Lives*, and *The Truth of the Matter*.

CHITRA DIVAKARUNI

1. *Bhagavadgita*
2. *Mahabharata*
3. *Galpo Guchho* by Rabindranath Tagore
4. *Anna Karenina* by Leo Tolstoy
5. *The Lord of the Rings* (trilogy) by J. R. R. Tolkein
6. *His Dark Materials* (trilogy) by Philip Pullman
7. *One Hundred Years of Solitude* by Gabriel García Márquez
8. *The Handmaid's Tale* by Margaret Atwood
9. The poems of Pablo Neruda
10. *The Power of Now: A Guide to Spiritual Enlightenment* by Eckhart Tolle

Chitra Divakaruni's novels include *The Mistress of Spices*, *Sister of My Heart*, and *Queen of Dreams*. Her honors include an American Book Award, an O. Henry Award, and an Allen Ginsberg Poetry Award.

EMMA DONOGHUE

1. *Clarissa* by Samuel Richardson
2. *Romeo and Juliet* by William Shakespeare
3. *Emma* by Jane Austen
4. *Great Expectations* by Charles Dickens
5. *The Poisonwood Bible* by Barbara Kingsolver
6. *Red Shift* by Alan Garner
7. *Les Liaisons Dangereuses* by Pierre Choderlos de Laclos
8. *Oldest Living Confederate Widow Tells All* by Allan Gurganus
9. *The Passion* by Jeanette Winterson
10. *Ulverton* by Adam Thorpe

Emma Donoghue is an Irish novelist (*Slammerkin*), short story writer (*Touchy Subjects*), playwright (*Ladies and Gentlemen*), and historian (*Passions Between Women: British Lesbian Culture, 1668–1801*).

MARGARET DRABBLE

1. *Antony and Cleopatra* by William Shakespeare
2. *Emma* by Jane Austen
3. *Madame Bovary* by Gustave Flaubert
4. *The Three Sisters* by Anton Chekhov
5. *The Aeneid* by Virgil
6. *The Divine Comedy* by Dante Alighieri
7. *Germinal* by Émile Zola
8. *The Golden Notebook* by Doris Lessing
9. *To the Lighthouse* by Virginia Woolf
10. *The Old Wives' Tale* by Arnold Bennett

Margaret Drabble has published seventeen novels, most recently *The Sea Lady*. She also edited the fifth and sixth editions of *The Oxford Companion to English Literature* (1985, 2000).

DAVID ANTHONY DURHAM

1. *Beloved* by Toni Morrison
2. *The Brothers Karamazov* by Fyodor Dostoevsky
3. *The Book of Laughter and Forgetting* by Milan Kundera
4. *Moby-Dick* by Herman Melville
5. *The Green House* by Mario Vargas Llosa
6. *Blood Meridian* by Cormac McCarthy
7. *The Amazing Adventures of Kavalier & Clay* by Michael Chabon
8. *The Famished Road* by Ben Okri
9. *Dune* by Frank Herbert
10. *Watership Down* by Richard Adams

David Anthony Durham is the author of the novels *Pride of Carthage*, *Walk Through Darkness*, and *Gabriel's Story*. His Web address is davidanthony durham.com.

Appreciation of Mario Vargas Llosa's
The Green House
by David Anthony Durham

I remember wandering through the world literature section of my university library, feeling a bit lost, recognizing few names. On the recommendation of my writing instructor I was searching for a Peruvian novelist named Mario Vargas Llosa. I found a coverless edition of *The Green House*, one with no blurbs, no review quotes, no author photo or biography. The surprises found inside, then, were complete and unforgettable.

With *The Green House* (1966), Vargas Llosa began to explore the ongoing battle that started the moment European culture collided with that of the Americas. The novel is populated by all segments of Peruvian society: indigenous Indians, people of Latin origins, immigrants cast ashore on Peru for myriad reasons—from nuns and Fathers to prostitutes and pimps. There's even a Brazilian rubber baron–warlord–leper of Japanese ancestry. It ranges from the depths of the rainforest to windblown desert outposts. It's a novel in which crimes are committed without remorse, conveyed with the brutal honesty of an author confronting the duplicitous exploitation tainting his nation.

The story is rendered in prose as varied as its cast: inner monologue, assimilated dialogue, objective third person, or an omniscient point of view, with multiple timelines, concurrent plots, and scenes repeated in layering montage. Honestly, it's rarely an easy read. One can see the influence of Faulkner, of Sartre and Flaubert, but the manner in which Vargas Llosa transmuted Western influences to enrich his tale remains remarkable. And, I wondered, if this Peruvian writer could do this, what else might be happening out there? By inspiring that question *The Green House* drew me into a much more complete world of literature. I've been grateful to Vargas Llosa ever since.

CLYDE EDGERTON

I've never been one for the Great Books idea because it seems almost, though not quite, like a Great Clothes idea. . . . Interaction with art is not objective, though there will be overlaps and that's what will be interesting—to see what books have "traveled" where, into what sets of imaginations, and so I go along for the fun of it.

1.   *Hamlet* by William Shakespeare
2.   *Don Quixote* by Miguel de Cervantes
3.   *The Canterbury Tales* by Geoffrey Chaucer
4.   *The Adventures of Huckleberry Finn* by Mark Twain
5.   *Light in August* by William Faulkner
6.   The stories of Flannery O'Connor
7.   *As I Lay Dying* by William Faulkner
8.   *Death of a Salesman* by Arthur Miller
9.   The stories of Ernest Hemingway
10. *Candide* by Voltaire

Clyde Edgerton is a former Air Force pilot whose books include the novels *Raney*, *Killer Diller*, and *Lunch at the Piccadilly* and the memoir *Solo: My Adventures in the Air*.

PERCIVAL EVERETT

1. *Tristram Shandy* by Laurence Sterne
2. *The Way of All Flesh* by Samuel Butler
3. *The Adventures of Huckleberry Finn* by Mark Twain
4. *Invisible Man* by Ralph Ellison
5. *Cane* by Jean Toomer
6. *A Clockwork Orange* by Anthony Burgess
7. *Death Comes for the Archbishop* by Willa Cather
8. *Angle of Repose* by Wallace Stegner
9. *Bluebeard* by Kurt Vonnegut
10. *Nights at the Circus* by Angela Carter

Percival Everett is the author of twenty books, including the novels *Wounded* and *Erasure*. He lives in Los Angeles with the novelist Danzy Senna.

KAREN JOY FOWLER

1. *Middlemarch* by George Eliot
2. *The Tempest* by William Shakespeare
3. *Don Quixote* by Miguel de Cervantes
4. *The Tale of Genji* by Shikibu Murasaki
5. *A Midsummer Night's Dream* by William Shakespeare
6. *Emma* by Jane Austen
7. *Jane Eyre* by Charlotte Brontë
8. *Mrs. Dalloway* by Virginia Woolf
9. *One Hundred Years of Solitude* by Gabriel García Márquez
10. *Dubliners* by James Joyce

Karen Joy Fowler is a Nebula Award–winning writer of science fiction/ fantasy (*Sarah Canary, Artificial Things: Stories*) and literary fiction (*The Jane Austen Book Club, Sister Noon*).

PAULA FOX

1. *War and Peace* by Leo Tolstoy
2. *In Search of Lost Time* by Marcel Proust
3. *Tender Is the Night* by F. Scott Fitzgerald
4. *Dubliners* by James Joyce
5. *Red Cavalry and Other Stories* by Isaac Babel
6. *Death Comes for the Archbishop* by Willa Cather
7. *The Mayor of Casterbridge* by Thomas Hardy
8. *Daniel Deronda* by George Eliot
9. *The Marquise of O— and Other Stories* by Heinrich von Kleist
10. *Death in Midsummer and Other Stories* by Yukio Mishima

Paula Fox has written six novels (*Desperate Characters*), two memoirs (*Borrowed Finery*), and twenty-two books for children, including the Newbery Award–winner *The Slave Dancer*.

Appreciation of Heinrich von Kleist's *The Marquise of O— and Other Stories*
by Paula Fox

Heinrich von Kleist was born in 1777 and killed himself thirty-five years later in a suicide pact with a young lady, after having been blessed, or cursed, with a formidable talent for writing. During his brief life he turned out eight plays, among which is the marvelous one-act *Robert Guiscard;* eight stories, including the novella *Michael Kohlaas;* and a long story, *The Marquise of O—*. He also wrote a philosophical discourse, "On the Puppet Theatre," a group of anecdotes, and some brilliant journalism.

Von Kleist was a true Romantic, yet he is utterly modern in the swiftness and depth of his perception of his subjects. Perhaps he didn't choose them—they chose him, as it often seems with such a writer, a kind of fatality of choice.

In *Michael Kohlaas* von Kleist writes of the passion for justice turning a man into an outlaw. In *The Beggarwoman of Locarno*, a three-page arrow of a short story, a man sets fire to his own house. *The Marquise of O—* begins with an advertisement, placed in journals by a widowed Marquise, that pleads for the father of the child she is carrying to come forward and marry her. She hasn't the faintest idea how her pregnancy came about.

And here's the remarkable opening line of "The Earthquake in Chile": "In Santiago, the capital of the kingdom of Chile, at the very moment of the great earthquake of 1647 in which many thousands of lives were lost, a young Spaniard by the name of Jeronimo Rugera, who had been locked up on a criminal charge, was standing against a prison pillar, about to hang himself."

There are other stories of so lyrical yet violent a nature that the reader is infected with a fever of interest and admiration; at least this reader.

JONATHAN FRANZEN

1. *The Brothers Karamazov* by Fyodor Dostoevsky
2. *War and Peace* by Leo Tolstoy
3. *The Trial* by Franz Kafka
4. *In Search of Lost Time* by Marcel Proust
5. *The Great Gatsby* by F. Scott Fitzgerald
6. *Absalom, Absalom!* by William Faulkner
7. *The Charterhouse of Parma* by Stendhal
8. *Lolita* by Vladimir Nabokov
9. *The Man Who Loved Children* by Christina Stead
10. *Independent People* by Halldór Laxness

Jonathan Franzen is the author of the novels *The Twenty-Seventh City*, *Strong Motion*, and *The Corrections*; an essay collection, *How to Be Alone*; and a memoir, *The Discomfort Zone*.

ALAN FURST

1. **The Seven Pillars of Wisdom* by T. E. Lawrence
2. *A Dance to the Music of Time* by Anthony Powell
3. *Man's Fate* by André Malraux
4. *Nightwood* by Djuna Barnes
5. **Black Lamb and Grey Falcon* by Rebecca West
6. *Darkness at Noon* by Arthur Koestler
7. *Red Cavalry* by Isaac Babel
8. **Homage to Catalonia* by George Orwell
9. *The Radetzky March* by Joseph Roth
10. *Kaputt* by Curzio Malaparte

*Works of nonfiction that should be read as fiction.

Alan Furst's historical spy novels include *Night Soldiers*, *Dark Star*, *The Polish Officer*, *The World at Night*, *Red Gold*, *Kingdom of Shadows*, *Blood of Victory*, and *Dark Voyage*.

MARY GAITSKILL

1. *Ulysses* by James Joyce
2. *Lolita* by Vladimir Nabokov
3. *Pale Fire* by Vladimir Nabokov
4. *Bleak House* by Charles Dickens
5. *Madame Bovary* by Gustave Flaubert
6. *To the Lighthouse* by Virginia Woolf
7. "Gusev," a single short story by Anton Chekhov
8. *Peter Pan* by J. M. Barrie
9. *Dead Souls* by Nikolai Gogol
10. *The Hunchback of Notre Dame* by Victor Hugo

Mary Gaitskill has written the story collections *Bad Behavior* and *Because They Wanted To* and the novels *Two Girls, Fat and Thin*, and *Veronica*.

G. D. GEARINO

1. *Candide* by Voltaire
2. *Henry V* by William Shakespeare
3. *The Sound and the Fury* by William Faulkner
4. *The Heart Is a Lonely Hunter* by Carson McCullers
5. *East of Eden* by John Steinbeck
6. *Hombre* by Elmore Leonard
7. *Oryx and Crake* by Margaret Atwood
8. *Montana 1948* by Larry Watson
9. *Rabbit Redux* by John Updike
10. *Love in the Time of Cholera* by Gabriel García Márquez

G. D. Gearino is the author of four novels, including *What the Deaf-Mute Heard*. He is a columnist for *The News & Observer* of Raleigh, North Carolina.

DENISE GESS

1. *Wuthering Heights* by Emily Brontë
2. *The Stranger* by Albert Camus
3. *Mrs. Bridge* by Evan S. Connell
4. *The Great Gatsby* by F. Scott Fitzgerald
5. *The Sheltering Sky* by Paul Bowles
6. *Dubliners* by James Joyce
7. *Beloved* by Toni Morrison
8. *Crime and Punishment* by Fyodor Dostoevsky
9. *Madame Bovary* by Gustave Flaubert
10. *Mrs. Dalloway* by Virginia Woolf

Denise Gess has written the novels *Good Deeds* and *Red Whiskey Blues* and, with William Lutz, the history *Firestorm at Peshtigo: A Town, Its People, and the Deadliest Fire in American History*.

GAIL GODWIN

1. *The Portrait of a Lady* by Henry James
2. *Emma* by Jane Austen
3. *The Secret Agent* by Joseph Conrad
4. *Anna Karenina* by Leo Tolstoy
5. *Middlemarch* by George Eliot
6. *The Power and the Glory* by Graham Greene
7. *The Death of the Heart* by Elizabeth Bowen
8. *A Portrait of the Artist as a Young Man* by James Joyce
9. *Seven Gothic Tales* by Isak Dinesen
10. *Atonement* by Ian McEwan

Gail Godwin's novels include *The Odd Woman*, *A Mother and Two Daughters*, *The Good Husband*, and *Queen of the Underworld*.

ARTHUR GOLDEN

1. *I, Claudius* by Robert Graves
2. *Lolita* by Vladimir Nabokov
3. *Don Quixote* by Miguel de Cervantes
4. *The Story of the Stone* (5 volumes) by Cao Xueqin
5. *The Catcher in the Rye* by J. D. Salinger
6. *Right Ho, Jeeves* by P. G. Wodehouse
7. *Lonesome Dove* by Larry McMurtry
8. *Eleven Kinds of Loneliness* by Richard Yates
9. *Leaves of Grass* by Walt Whitman
10. *The Adventures of Huckleberry Finn* by Mark Twain

Arthur Golden is the author of the novel *Memoirs of a Geisha*.

MARY GORDON

1. *The Good Soldier* by Ford Madox Ford
2. *The Diary of a Country Priest* by Georges Bernanos
3. *In Search of Lost Time* by Marcel Proust
4. *Dubliners* by James Joyce
5. *Pale Horse, Pale Rider* by Katherine Ann Porter
6. *King Lear* by William Shakespeare
7. *The Tempest* by William Shakespeare
8. *To the Lighthouse* by Virginia Woolf
9. *Persuasion* by Jane Austen
10. *Middlemarch* by George Eliot

Mary Gordon has published books of novellas (*The Rest of Life*), stories (*Temporary Shelter*), and essays (*Good Boys and Dead Girls*). Her novels include *Final Payments* and *Pearl*.

MICHAEL GRIFFITH

1. *Pale Fire* by Vladimir Nabokov
2. *Bleak House* by Charles Dickens
3. *One Hundred Years of Solitude* by Gabriel García Márquez
4. *Lolita* by Vladimir Nabokov
5. *Madame Bovary* by Gustave Flaubert
6. *The Tin Drum* by Günter Grass
7. *Dom Casmurro* by Joaquim Maria Machado de Assis
8. *Mrs. Dalloway* by Virginia Woolf
9. *Middlemarch* by George Eliot
10. *Outer Dark* by Cormac McCarthy

Michael Griffith is the author of the novel *Spikes* and the story collection *Bibliophilia*.

Appreciation of Joaquim Maria Machado de Assis's *Dom Casmurro*
by Michael Griffith

In 1878, nearing forty and afflicted by epilepsy and rickets, Machado, a successful but conventional Brazilian *romancier*, withdrew from Rio to convalesce. He returned not only rejuvenated but transformed; in coming decades he would write, among other works, three classic novels: *Posthumous Memoirs of Brás Cubas*, *Philosopher or Dog?*, and *Dom Casmurro*.

Dom Casmurro ("Lord Taciturn") is Bento Santiago, an affluent old man undone by jealousy. He believes that his wife, Capitu, betrayed him; his friend Escobar must be the real sire of Bento's son. Yet what's most remarkable here is not the story but the storytelling. There's its fragmented form (148 chapters in scarcely

250 pages); there's Machado's mixture of scathing satire with empathy for his narrator, whose autobiography is part legal brief, part *cri de coeur*, part special pleading, even (covertly, poignantly) part *mea culpa*. But Machado's signal feat is his pioneering handling of unreliable narration.

Though Bento prosecutes his case zealously, his evidence boils down to the oft-repeated fact that Capitu has "eyes like the tide." Bento may be deluded, even reprehensible, but we are not allowed to laugh at him, to think ourselves superior. He's like us. And if every narrator is subject to similar blindness and self-pity, how to trust *anyone?* The question would loom large in twentieth-century literature.

The reader, too, is implicated. Bento writes, "[E]verything is to be found outside a book that has gaps, gentle reader. This is the way I fill in other men's lacunae; in the same way you may fill in mine." *Reader, jury, do with me what you will.* Machado admits into his text radical postmodern ambiguity, years before its heyday, for what book does not have gaps, is not *made up of* gaps?

Allusive, psychologically penetrating, politically charged, darkly funny, *Dom Casmurro* links Sterne to Barthelme, Flaubert to Nabokov, and remains startlingly fresh.

ALLAN GURGANUS

1. *Robinson Crusoe* by Daniel Defoe
2. The stories of Anton Chekhov
3. *Middlemarch* by George Eliot
4. *Speak, Memory* by Vladimir Nabokov
5. *A Death in the Family* by James Agee
6. *Absalom, Absalom!* by William Faulkner
7. *The Importance of Being Earnest* by Oscar Wilde
8. *Vile Bodies* by Evelyn Waugh
9. *Emma* by Jane Austen
10. *The Tin Drum* by Günter Grass

Allan Gurganus lives in his native North Carolina and is the author of novels and short stories, including *Oldest Living Confederate Widow Tells All* and *The Practical Heart*.

BARRY HANNAH

1. *The Brothers Karamazov* by Fyodor Dostoevsky
2. *As I Lay Dying* by William Faulkner
3. *The Stranger* by Albert Camus
4. The stories of Flannery O'Connor
5. *Blood Meridian* by Cormac McCarthy
6. *The Adventures of Huckleberry Finn* by Mark Twain
7. *One Day in the Life of Ivan Denisovich* by Alexander Solzhenitsyn
8. *The Sun Also Rises* by Ernest Hemingway
9. *Airships* by Barry Hannah (Why not?)
10. *War and Peace* by Leo Tolstoy

Barry Hannah is a Mississippi writer whose works include the novels *Yonder Stands Your Orphan* and *Geronimo Rex* (winner of the William Faulkner Prize) and the story collection *Bats Out of Hell*.

DONALD HARINGTON

1. *Lolita* by Vladimir Nabokov
2. *A Death in the Family* by James Agee
3. *Sophie's Choice* by William Styron
4. *A Confederacy of Dunces* by John Kennedy Toole
5. *All the King's Men* by Robert Penn Warren
6. *The Sot-Weed Factor* by John Barth
7. *Love in the Time of Cholera* by Gabriel García Márquez
8. *Beloved* by Toni Morrison
9. *Tender Is the Night* by F. Scott Fitzgerald
10. *Some Other Place. The Right Place.* by Donald Harington

Donald Harington, who has written fourteen novels about the Ozark mountains of Arkansas, including *With* and *The Cockroaches of Stay More*, won the Robert Penn Warren Award for fiction from the Fellowship of Southern Writers.

JIM HARRISON

1. *The Possessed* by Fyodor Dostoevsky
2. *In Search of Lost Time* by Marcel Proust
3. *Wuthering Heights* by Emily Brontë
4. *Moby-Dick* by Herman Melville
5. *Ulysses* by James Joyce
6. *Independent People* by Haldór Laxness
7. *Absalom, Absalom!* by William Faulkner
8. *One Hundred Years of Solitude* by Gabriel García Márquez
9. *Tropic of Cancer* by Henry Miller
10. *The Stranger* by Albert Camus

Jim Harrison has written novels (*Legends of the Fall*, *The Summer He Didn't Die*), a memoir (*Off to the Side*), and a work of gastronomy (*The Raw and the Cooked: Adventures of a Roving Gourmand*).

KATHRYN HARRISON

1. *The Woman in the Dunes* by Kobo Abe
2. *The Master and Margarita* by Mikhail Bulgakov
3. *Life and Times of Michael K* by J. M. Coetzee
4. *David Copperfield* by Charles Dickens
5. *Stones for Ibarra* by Harriet Doerr
6. *The Lover* by Marguerite Duras
7. *Middlemarch* by George Eliot
8. *Madame Bovary* by Gustave Flaubert
9. *Midnight's Children* by Salman Rushdie
10. *The House of Mirth* by Edith Wharton

Kathryn Harrison has published six novels (*Thicker Than Water, Envy*), three memoirs (*The Kiss*), and a biography (*Saint Thérèse of Lisieux*).

Appreciation of Kobo Abe's
The Woman in the Dunes
by Kathryn Harrison

One day in August a man disappeared. The man was an entomologist and had set out into the desert with a canteen of water and a pack filled with the tools he used to collect specimens. It was his hope to discover an as yet unknown species of insect that lived in the sand dunes. Were he to find one, then he would be promised a kind of immortality: his name would be recorded and forever linked to the taxonomic identification of the bug—*his* bug.

Shifting sands, isolation, a quixotic attempt to defy mortal limits: even before the hero of Kobo Abe's *The Woman in the Dunes* has missed the last bus out of the desert, the reader knows he is lost to an existential quest. Abe, trained as a medical doctor, writes as a clinician, dispassionately and with exactitude. In the dunes his hero, Niki Jumpei, falls captive to the enigmatic woman from whom he seeks shelter for a night. Having descended into the sand pit where the woman lives, Jumpei discovers that there's no way out; he's trapped in a sinister village where each citizen becomes Sisyphus. Every day Jumpei must join the inhabitants in their necessary work: shoveling away the sand that threatens to bury them and their homes.

The Woman in the Dunes transcends the form of allegory—often lifeless and didactic—to engage its readers to the point of discomfort. It's a claustrophobic novel, subjecting us to Jumpei's mounting panic as he begins to suspect that he will never leave the sand pit, that meaningless striving is his, and our, inescapable fate.

KENT HARUF

1. *The Sound and the Fury* by William Faulkner
2. *Peasants and Other Stories* by Anton Chekhov
3. *Hamlet* by William Shakespeare
4. *The Hamlet* by William Faulkner
5. The stories of Ernest Hemingway
6. *The Adventures of Huckleberry Finn* by Mark Twain
7. The stories of Flannery O'Connor
8. *Waiting for Godot* by Samuel Beckett
9. *The Stranger* by Albert Camus
10. *The Grapes of Wrath* by John Steinbeck

Kent Haruf has written the novels *Where You Once Belonged*, *The Tie That Binds*, *Plainsong*, and *Eventide*.

ADAM HASLETT

1. *King Lear* by William Shakespeare
2. *Paradise Lost* by John Milton
3. *War and Peace* by Leo Tolstoy
4. *Absalom, Absalom!* by William Faulkner
5. *In Search of Lost Time* by Marcel Proust
6. *Middlemarch* by George Eliot
7. *Independent People* by Halldór Laxness
8. *Moby-Dick* by Herman Melville
9. *Long Day's Journey into Night* by Eugene O'Neill
10. *The Prelude* by William Wordsworth

Adam Haslett is the author of the story collection *You Are Not a Stranger Here*, which was a finalist for the Pulitzer Prize and the National Book Award.

ELIZABETH HAY

1. The stories of Anton Chekhov
2. *Mrs. Dalloway* by Virginia Woolf
3. *The Gate of Angels* by Penelope Fitzgerald
4. *The Rings of Saturn* by W. G. Sebald
5. *Disgrace* by J. M. Coetzee
6. *Persuasion* by Jane Austen
7. The stories of Alice Munro
8. *Jane Eyre* by Charlotte Brontë
9. *The Member of the Wedding* by Carson McCullers
10. *Break It Down* by Lydia Davis

Elizabeth Hay has written the novels *A Student of Weather* and *Garbo Laughs* and the story collection *Small Change*. She received Canada's Marian Engel Award for her body of work.

CARL HIAASEN

1. *Catch-22* by Joseph Heller
2. *The Adventures of Huckleberry Finn* by Mark Twain
3. *The Catcher in the Rye* by J. D. Salinger
4. *The Comedians* by Graham Greene
5. *Slaughterhouse-Five* by Kurt Vonnegut
6. *The Metamorphosis* by Franz Kafka
7. *The Big Sleep* by Raymond Chandler
8. *Ninety-two in the Shade* by Thomas McGuane
9. *A Good Man Is Hard to Find and Other Stories* by Flannery O'Connor
10. *Money* by Martin Amis

Carl Hiaasen is the author of twelve novels, including *Skinny Dip*, *Native Tongue*, and for young readers, *Hoot*. He is a columnist for *The Miami Herald*.

ALICE HOFFMAN

1. *Wuthering Heights* by Emily Brontë
2. *Great Expectations* by Charles Dickens
3. *The Catcher in the Rye* by J. D. Salinger
4. *Pride and Prejudice* by Jane Austen
5. *Beloved* by Toni Morrison
6. *The Sound and the Fury* by William Faulkner
7. *One Hundred Years of Solitude* by Gabriel García Márquez
8. The stories of Grace Paley
9. *Fahrenheit 451* by Ray Bradbury
10. *Grimm's Fairy Tales* by Wilhelm and Jacob Grimm

Alice Hoffman is the author of sixteen novels and two story collections, including *Practical Magic, Turtle Moon, Blackbird House, The Ice Queen,* and most recently, *Skylight Confessions.*

A. M. HOMES

1. *The Homecoming* and *The Birthday Party* by Harold Pinter
2. *The American Dream, The Zoo Story,* and *Who's Afraid of Virginia Woolf* by Edward Albee
3. *Bullet Park* by John Cheever
4. *Disturbing the Peace* by Richard Yates
5. *Manchild in the Promised Land* by Claude Brown
6. *A Severed Head* by Iris Murdoch
7. *The Loved One* by Evelyn Waugh
8. *Flat Stanley* by Jeff Brown
9. *Crime and Punishment* by the big D
10. *Lolita* by the big N

A. M. Homes's books include the novels *This Book Will Save Your Life, Music for Torching,* and *The End of Alice* and the story collection *Things You Should Know.*

ANDREW HUDGINS

1. The Bible
2. *The Odyssey* by Homer
3. *The Divine Comedy* by Dante Alighieri
4. *The Canterbury Tales* by Geoffrey Chaucer
5. *Hamlet* by William Shakespeare
6. *Tom Jones* by Henry Fielding
7. *Gulliver's Travels* by Jonathan Swift
8. *Middlemarch* by George Eliot
9. *Absalom, Absalom!* by William Faulkner
10. *The Great Gatsby* by F. Scott Fitzgerald

Andrew Hudgins is the author of one book of criticism and six books of poetry, including *Ecstatic in the Poison.*

Appreciation of the Bible
by Andrew Hudgins

The Bible is both a holy book and a work of supreme fiction; those of us who read it both ways are doubly blessed. One does not need to believe in God to hear the majesty of the story that begins, "In the beginning, God created the heaven and the earth. And the earth was without form, and void; and darkness was upon the face of the deep. And the Spirit of God moved upon the face of the waters. And God said, Let there be light: and there was light." A great story itself, the Bible is also the source of great stories, by geniuses from Dante to Dostoevsky, Faulkner to Thomas Mann, and the poetry of the Psalms echoes through great poetry from William Blake to Walt Whitman to T. S. Eliot.

One does not have to believe Jesus is the Son of God to understand that his parables are penetrating works of fiction that embody complex truths about human nature. One need not believe Adam and Eve existed to see Genesis is, whatever else it is, a philosophically sophisticated and psychologically acute story about people's innate response to authority, even loving authority. And it is perfectly possible to believe Moses and King David are fictional, and yet find true to life the Bible's stories of these flawed men who succeed greatly, if only partially, while failing God time and again.

And what of Jesus—a god entering history as a man and living as a mortal? True or not true, "the greatest story ever told," in the majesty of its telling and the power of its message, has taught an entire culture how to think about love, suffering, and transcendence, and it has fundamentally colored the language by which we talk about everything.

JOHN IRVING

1. *Great Expectations* by Charles Dickens
2. *Tess of the D'Urbervilles* by Thomas Hardy
3. *Moby-Dick* by Herman Melville
4. *The Scarlet Letter* by Nathaniel Hawthorne
5. *David Copperfield* by Charles Dickens
6. *The Mayor of Casterbridge* by Thomas Hardy
7. *The Tin Drum* by Günter Grass
8. *One Hundred Years of Solitude* by Gabriel García Márquez
9. *Fifth Business* by Robertson Davies
10. *Madame Bovary* by Gustave Flaubert

John Irving is a novelist whose works include *The World According to Garp*, *A Prayer for Owen Meany*, *The Cider House Rules*, and *Until I Find You*.

HA JIN

1. *Anna Karenina* by Leo Tolstoy
2. *The Brothers Karamazov* by Fyodor Dostoevsky
3. *War and Peace* by Leo Tolstoy
4. The late stories of Anton Chekhov
5. *Swann's Way* by Marcel Proust
6. *Absalom, Absalom!* by William Faulkner
7. *Silence* by Shusaku Endo
8. *Pnin* by Vladimir Nabokov
9. *A Bend in the River* by V. S. Naipaul
10. *Heat and Dust* by Ruth Prawer Jhabvala

Ha Jin was born in China and emigrated to the United States as an adult. He won a National Book Award and PEN/Faulkner Award for his novel *Waiting*, and the Flannery O'Connor Award for Short Fiction for *Oceans of Words*.

HEIDI JULAVITS

1. *The Arabian Nights: Tales from a Thousand and One Nights*
2. *Daniel Deronda* by George Eliot
3. *The Decameron* by Giovanni Boccaccio
4. *The Stranger* by Albert Camus
5. *The Pillow-Book of Sei Shōnagon*
6. *Nothing, Doting,* and *Blindness* by Henry Green
7. *How German Is It* by Walter Abish
8. *A House for Mr. Biswas* by V. S. Naipaul
9. *Ask the Dust* by John Fante
10. *The Assistant* by Bernard Malamud

Heidi Julavits is the author of three novels, most recently *The Uses of Enchantments*. She is a founding editor of *The Believer* magazine.

KEN KALFUS

1. *The Odyssey* by Homer
2. *Hamlet* by William Shakespeare
3. *War and Peace* by Leo Tolstoy
4. *Ulysses* by James Joyce
5. *The Magic Mountain* by Thomas Mann
6. *Ficciones* by Jorge Luis Borges
7. *Rabbit, Run* by John Updike
8. *Dead Souls* by Nikolai Gogol
9. *Native Son* by Richard Wright
10. *The Grapes of Wrath* by John Steinbeck

Ken Kalfus is the author of four books, including his most recent novel *A Disorder Peculiar to the Country*.

THOMAS KENEALLY

1. *Wuthering Heights* by Emily Brontë
2. *Treasure Island* by Robert Louis Stevenson
3. *The Scarlet Letter* by Nathaniel Hawthorne
4. *Great Expectations* by Charles Dickens
5. *War and Peace* by Leo Tolstoy
6. *A Portrait of the Artist as a Young Man* by James Joyce
7. *Mrs. Dalloway* by Virginia Woolf
8. *The Great Gatsby* by F. Scott Fitzgerald
9. *Voss* by Patrick White
10. *The Tin Drum* by Günter Grass

Thomas Keneally is an Australian historian (*The Great Shame: And the Triumph of the Irish in the English Speaking World*) and novelist who won the Booker Prize for his historical novel of the Holocaust, *Schindler's List*.

A. L. KENNEDY

1. *The Confidence-Man: His Masquerade* by Herman Melville
2. *The Strange Case of Dr. Jekyll and Mr. Hyde* by Robert Louis Stevenson
3. *The Third Policeman* by Flann O'Brien
4. *The Prime of Miss Jean Brodie* by Muriel Spark
5. *Tristram Shandy* by Laurence Sterne
6. *Lanark: A Life in Four Books* by Alasdair Gray
7. *The Book of Evidence* by John Banville
8. *The Lost Father* by Mona Simpson
9. *Sergeant Getulio* by João Ubaldo Ribeiro
10. *Closely Watched Trains* by Bohumil Hrabal

A. L. Kennedy is a Scottish writer whose short story collections include *Original Bliss* and *Indelible Acts* and whose most recent novel is titled *Paradise*.

Appreciation of Flann O'Brien's
The Third Policeman
by A. L. Kennedy

The Third Policeman is that rare and lovely thing—a truly hallucinatory novel, shot through with fierce logic and intellectual rigor. It is a lyrical, amoral, funny nightmare: the most disciplined and disturbing product of an always interesting writer. Our protagonist is "the poor misfortunate bastard"—a drinker, philosopher, and obsessive bibliophile. His sins grow with him, making a logical progression from book theft to burglary and murder—all this against a heightened version of poor, rural Ireland: a setting layered with absurd but weirdly recognizable detail. He then stumbles into a potentially fatal alternative reality: a haunting, teasing Irish countryside of parlors and winding roads from which it seems impossible to return.

Beneath the music of O'Brien's prose there is always a savage understanding of our failings, the pressures of poverty, greed, and fear. And there is always the dark humor that both excuses and condemns us. Our hero (who develops an entirely separate soul, called Joe) drifts into a weird landscape of jovially menacing policemen (who may or not may not be bicycles) and of inexplicable objects and mechanisms that operate beneath nature's skin. His imprisonment and threatened execution seem even more troubling because they are nonsensical, perhaps even kind. Slowly it becomes clear that, among other things, this novel is about hell—a much-deserved, amusing, irrational, and entirely inescapable hell. Because, for O'Brien, hell is not only other people—it is ourselves.

Beyond this, *The Third Policeman* is genuinely indescribable: a book that holds you like a lovely and accusing dream. Read it and you'll never forget it. Meet anyone else who has read it and you'll find yourselves repeating sections of its melodious insanity within moments. Meet anyone who hasn't read it and you'll tell them they must. Which will be the truth.

SUE MONK KIDD

1. *The Awakening* by Kate Chopin
2. *A Doll's House* by Henrik Ibsen
3. *To Kill a Mockingbird* by Harper Lee
4. *Wuthering Heights* by Emily Brontë
5. *Alice's Adventures in Wonderland* by Lewis Carroll
6. *The Bell Jar* by Sylvia Plath
7. *Oedipus the King* by Sophocles
8. *The Scarlet Letter* by Nathaniel Hawthorne
9. *Thirteen Stories* by Eudora Welty
10. *The Color Purple* by Alice Walker

Sue Monk Kidd is the author of two novels, *The Secret Life of Bees* and *The Mermaid Chair*, and an essay collection, *The Dance of the Dissident Daughter: A Woman's Journey from Christian Tradition to the Sacred Feminine.*

HAVEN KIMMEL

1. The Gospel of Mark
2. *The Aeneid* by Virgil
3. *Hamlet* by William Shakespeare
4. *The Dead* by James Joyce
5. *To the Lighthouse* by Virginia Woolf
6. *Selected Tales and Sketches* by Nathaniel Hawthorne
7. *The Adventures of Huckleberry Finn* by Mark Twain
8. *Invisible Man* by Ralph Ellison
9. *Beloved* by Toni Morrison
10. *Little, Big* by John Crowley

Haven Kimmel is the author of two memoirs, *A Girl Named Zippy* and *She Got Up Off the Couch*, and two novels, *The Solace of Leaving Early* and *Something Rising (Light and Swift).*

STEPHEN KING

1. *The Golden Argosy* edited by Van H. Cartmell and Charles Grayson
2. *The Adventures of Huckleberry Finn* by Mark Twain
3. *The Satanic Verses* by Salman Rushdie
4. *McTeague* by Frank Norris
5. *Lord of the Flies* by William Golding
6. *Bleak House* by Charles Dickens
7. *1984* by George Orwell
8. *The Raj Quartet* by Paul Scott
9. *Light in August* by William Faulkner
10. *Blood Meridian* by Cormac McCarthy

Stephen King's dozens of best-selling works include the novels *Carrie*, *Cujo*, *Misery*, and *Cell*. A resident of Maine, he received the National Book Foundation's Medal for Distinguished Contribution to American Letters.

Appreciation of *The Golden Argosy*
by Stephen King

I first found *The Golden Argosy* in a Lisbon Falls (Maine) bargain barn called The Jolly White Elephant, where it was on offer for $2.25. At that time I only had four dollars, and spending over half of it on one book, even a hardcover, was a tough decision. I've never regretted it.

Originally published in 1947 and reissued in 1955—but not updated or reprinted since—*The Golden Argosy* is an anthology of roughly fifty-five short stories. The editors made no pretensions to "quality fiction," but simply tried to publish the best-loved stories published in the nineteenth and twentieth centuries, up to the post–World War II period.

Though it is in terrible need of updating (there is no Raymond Carver, for instance, no Joyce Carol Oates, because such writers came along too late for inclusion), it remains an amazing resource for readers and writers, a treasury in the true sense of the word, covering everything from sentimental masterpieces such as Bret Harte's "The Outcasts of Poker Flat" to realistic character studies such as "Paul's Case" by Willa Cather.

Every reader will find glaring omissions (Dorothy Parker's "Big Blonde," for instance), but you've got your Faulkner classic ("A Rose for Emily"), your Hemingway ("The Killers"), and your Poe ("The Gold-Bug"). It includes "The Rich Boy," in which F. Scott Fitzgerald famously observes "the rich are different from you and me," and overlooked gems from writers such as Sherwood Anderson ("I'm a Fool") and John Collier ("Back for Christmas").

The Golden Argosy taught me more about good writing than all the classes I've ever taken. It's the best $2.25 I ever spent.

WALTER KIRN

1. The stories of Flannery O'Connor
2. *The Killer Inside Me* by Jim Thompson
3. *Norwood* by Charles Portis
4. *Under the Volcano* by Malcolm Lowry
5. *Lolita* by Vladimir Nabokov
6. *The Postman Always Rings Twice* by James M. Cain
7. *Jesus' Son* by Denis Johnson
8. *Miss Lonelyhearts* by Nathanael West
9. *The Adventures of Huckleberry Finn* by Mark Twain
10. *Portnoy's Complaint* by Philip Roth

Walter Kirn is a frequent contributor to *The New York Times Book Review* whose novels include *Thumbsucker, Mission to America*, and *Up in the Air*.

WALLY LAMB

1. *The Odyssey* by Homer
2. *Don Quixote* by Miguel de Cervantes
3. *King Lear* by William Shakespeare
4. *Tom Jones* by Henry Fielding
5. *The Adventures of Huckleberry Finn* by Mark Twain
6. *Sister Carrie* by Theodore Dreiser
7. *The Great Gatsby* by F. Scott Fitzgerald
8. *The Grapes of Wrath* by John Steinbeck
9. The stories of Flannery O'Connor
10. *One Hundred Years of Solitude* by Gabriel García Márquez

Wally Lamb is the author of two novels, *She's Come Undone* and *I Know This Much Is True*, and the editor of the anthology of essays by women at York Correctional Institution, *Couldn't Keep It to Myself*.

DAVID LEAVITT

1. *In Search of Lost Time* by Marcel Proust
2. *Middlemarch* by George Eliot
3. *The Good Soldier* by Ford Madox Ford
4. *Pale Fire* by Vladimir Nabokov
5. *The Emigrants* by W. G. Sebald
6. *A Legacy* by Sybille Bedford
7. *The Importance of Being Earnest* by Oscar Wilde
8. *A Far Cry from Kensington* by Muriel Spark
9. *The Beginning of Spring* by Penelope Fitzgerald
10. The stories of Grace Paley

David Leavitt's books include the novels *The Lost Language of Cranes* and *While England Sleeps* and a volume of short fiction, *Collected Stories*.

Appreciation of Sybille Bedford's *A Legacy*
by David Leavitt

A Legacy, Sybille Bedford's remarkable first novel, might most simply be described as the story of two houses. "One was outrageously large and ugly," Bedford tells us in the opening paragraph; "the other was beautiful. They were a huge Wilhelminian town house in the old West of Berlin, built and inhabited by the parents of my father's first wife, and a small seventeenth-century château and park in the South, near the Vosges, bought for my father by my mother."

So Bedford sets us down, with remarkable velocity and confidence, right in the middle of the world to which she is going to devote the next 360 pages. This is the world of Germany before the Second World War. The owners of the Wilhelminian townhouse are Jews; the heroine's father is a Catholic aristocrat living in a sort of splendid rural poverty. As she is "bundled to and fro" between these two houses, our narrator—a version of Bedford herself—describes for us not just the struggle of her own growing up, but the complex intermingling of three very different families, as well as the rumblings of social and political change that underlie and ultimately disrupt the domestic and marital dramas in which she is enmeshed.

Because Bedford published *A Legacy* in 1956, her knowledge of what was to come invests the novel with an air of fragility and foreboding. The prose is stunning; raised in a mire of European languages, Bedford clung to English as a life raft, and she shows her gratitude by employing her adopted language with a grace and agility to rival Henry James's. Yet what is perhaps most astonishing about this astonishingly rich novel—more memorable, for me, even than E. M. Forster's *Howards End*, the other great English novel about houses—is the deftness with which its author reconciles two literary virtues that in other hands might seem irreconcilable: intimacy and grandeur.

JONATHAN LETHEM

1. *Great Expectations* by Charles Dickens
2. *The Trial* by Franz Kafka
3. *The Man Who Loved Children* by Christina Stead
4. *The Red and the Black* by Stendhal
5. *A Dance to the Music of Time* by Anthony Powell
6. *Alice's Adventures in Wonderland* and *Through the Looking Glass* by Lewis Carroll
7. *The Black Prince* by Iris Murdoch
8. *New Grub Street* by George Gissing
9. *Tristram Shandy* by Laurence Sterne
10. *Crime and Punishment* by Fyodor Dostoevsky

Jonathan Lethem's novels include *The Fortress of Solitude* and *Motherless Brooklyn*, which won a National Book Critics Circle Award. His book of personal essays is titled *The Disappointment Artist*.

MARGOT LIVESEY

1. *Jane Eyre* by Charlotte Brontë
2. *Sunset Song* by Lewis Grassic Gibbon
3. *Parade's End* by Ford Madox Ford
4. *The Fountain Overflows* by Rebecca West
5. *Invisible Cities* by Italo Calvino
6. *Memoirs of Hadrian* by Marguerite Yourcenar
7. *Lolita* by Vladimir Nabokov
8. *A Simple Heart* by Gustave Flaubert
9. The stories of Mavis Gallant
10. The stories of William Trevor

Margot Livesey grew up in Scotland and is a writer in residence at Emerson College in Boston. Her novels include *Banishing Verona* and *Eva Moves the Furniture*.

Appreciation of Rebecca West's
The Fountain Overflows
by Margot Livesey

I don't know why I waited so long to read *The Fountain Overflows*. There was a copy in the library of my Scottish school; after all, the novel sold 40,000 copies in 1956, the year it was published. Perhaps it was even in my father's library, squeezed between, say, Aldous Huxley's *Chrome Yellow* and Evelyn Waugh's *Decline and Fall*, two novels I adored. The book was around but the truth is I didn't want to read it, in part because I associated it with *Black Lamb and Grey Falcon*, West's massive tome about pre–World War II Yugoslavia, which I didn't want to read even more. I finally succumbed only a few years ago at the urging of a dear friend.

Some books, much lauded on publication, rapidly gather dust, but luckily for me *The Fountain Overflows* remains as lustrous and passionate as when West penned the last page. The novel tells the story of the Aubrey family living in Edwardian London. Mr. Aubrey is a charismatic and unreliable journalist; Mrs. Aubrey, a former pianist, is an awkward woman of immense moral intelligence. Around these two orbit the Aubrey children: the musical Mary and Rose, the awful Cordelia who wants to be musical, and the beloved Richard Quinn. The story is told by Rose.

One scene captures for me West's genius. A man comes to complain to Mrs. Aubrey about her husband having an affair with his wife. After she has done her best to cheer him up, Mrs. Aubrey takes refuge in *Madame Bovary* and, by the time her husband arrives home, is absorbed in the novel. Together they praise and criticize Flaubert. Only then does she recall what brought her to pick up the novel in the first place. "I am really very heartless," she cried, rising to her feet. "But art is so much more real than life. Some art is much more real than some life, I mean."

And this is exactly how I feel about *The Fountain Overflows;* it is more real, and more pleasurable, than most life.

DAVID LODGE

1. *The Odyssey* by Homer
2. *Hamlet* by William Shakespeare
3. *The Canterbury Tales* by Geoffrey Chaucer
4. *Ulysses* by James Joyce
5. *Emma* by Jane Austen
6. *Middlemarch* by George Eliot
7. *Anna Karenina* by Leo Tolstoy
8. *Tristram Shandy* by Laurence Sterne
9. *Madame Bovary* by Gustave Flaubert
10. *Alice's Adventures in Wonderland* by Lewis Carroll

David Lodge is an English novelist and critic whose most recent books are the novel about Henry James, *Author, Author* (2004), and a nonfiction account of the creation and reception of that work, *The Year of Henry James*.

NORMAN MAILER

I find that the books I think of as great were read when I was still a young and unpublished writer, with the exception of *Buddenbrooks* and *Labyrinths*.

1. *Anna Karenina* by Leo Tolstoy
2. *War and Peace* by Leo Tolstoy
3. *Crime and Punishment* by Fyodor Dostoevsky
4. *The Brothers Karamazov* by Fyodor Dostoevsky
5. *Pride and Prejudice* by Jane Austen
6. *U.S.A.* (trilogy) by John Dos Passos
7. *Moby-Dick* by Herman Melville
8. *The Red and the Black* by Stendhal
9. *Buddenbrooks* by Thomas Mann
10. *Labyrinths* by Jorge Luis Borges

Norman Mailer has won a Pulitzer Prize and National Book Award for a work of nonfiction, *Armies of the Night*, and a Pulitzer Prize for a novel, *The Executioner's Song*.

THOMAS MALLON

1. *Vanity Fair* by William Makepeace Thackeray
2. *Tristram Shandy* by Laurence Sterne
3. *Madame Bovary* by Gustave Flaubert
4. *Crime and Punishment* by Fyodor Dostoevsky
5. *Jude the Obscure* by Thomas Hardy
6. *Hard Times* by Charles Dickens
7. *The Golden Bowl* by Henry James
8. *Jacob's Room* by Virginia Woolf
9. *Eugénie Grandet* by Honoré de Balzac
10. *Rabbit Redux* by John Updike

Thomas Mallon is the author of seven novels, including *Henry and Clara*, *Bandbox*, and the forthcoming *Fellow Travelers*.

BEN MARCUS

1. *Crime and Punishment* by Fyodor Dostoevsky
2. *Macbeth* by William Shakespeare
3. *The Odyssey* by Homer
4. *The Trial* by Franz Kafka
5. *Impressions of Africa* by Raymond Roussel
6. *The Waves* by Virginia Woolf
7. *Correction* by Thomas Bernhard
8. *Stories and Texts for Nothing* by Samuel Beckett
9. *The Metamorphoses* by Ovid
10. *Everything That Rises Must Converge* by Flannery O'Connor

Ben Marcus is the author of a story collection, *The Age of Wire and String*, and a novel, *Notable American Women*.

VALERIE MARTIN

1. *Hamlet* by William Shakespeare
2. *Madame Bovary* by Gustave Flaubert
3. *Lolita* by Vladimir Nabokov
4. *The Makioka Sisters* by Junichiro Tanizaki
5. *Resurrection* by Leo Tolstoy
6. The stories of Anton Chekhov
7. *Persuasion* by Jane Austen
8. *The Portrait of a Lady* by Henry James
9. *Disgrace* by J. M. Coetzee
10. *Waiting for Godot* by Samuel Beckett

Valerie Martin, a winner of the Kafka Prize and the Orange Prize, has written seven novels, including *Mary Reilly* and *Property*, three collections of short fiction, and a biography of St. Francis of Assisi, *Salvation*.

BOBBIE ANN MASON

1. *Hamlet* by William Shakespeare
2. *Lolita* by Vladimir Nabokov
3. *The Great Gatsby* by F. Scott Fitzgerald
4. *A Portrait of the Artist as a Young Man* by James Joyce
5. *The Rime of the Ancient Mariner* by Samuel Taylor Coleridge
6. *The Sun Also Rises* by Ernest Hemingway
7. *The Adventures of Huckleberry Finn* by Mark Twain
8. *Parade's End* by Ford Madox Ford
9. *Moby-Dick* by Herman Melville
10. *Emma* by Jane Austen

Bobbie Ann Mason's books include *Nancy Culpepper: Stories* and *An Atomic Romance: A Novel*. Her memoir *Clear Springs* was nominated for a Pulitzer Prize. She is writer in residence at the University of Kentucky.

DENNIS McFARLAND

1. *The Ambassadors* by Henry James
2. *The Fountain Overflows* by Rebecca West
3. *Howards End* by E. M. Forster
4. The stories of Flannery O'Connor
5. *The Regeneration Trilogy* by Pat Barker
6. The stories of John Cheever
7. *The Master* by Colm Tóibín
8. *Going to Meet the Man* by James Baldwin
9. *Tennessee Williams: Plays 1937–1955*
10. *Dubliners* by James Joyce

Dennis McFarland is the best-selling author of five novels, including *Prince Edward* and *Singing Boy*. He lives in the Boston area with his family.

PATRICK McGRATH

1. *Moby-Dick* by Herman Melville
2. *Heart of Darkness* by Joseph Conrad
3. *Lord Jim* by Joseph Conrad
4. *Wuthering Heights* by Emily Brontë
5. *Ship of Fools* by Katherine Ann Porter
6. *Brideshead Revisited* by Evelyn Waugh
7. *The Great Gatsby* by F. Scott Fitzgerald
8. *Death in Venice* by Thomas Mann
9. *Anna Karenina* by Leo Tolstoy
10. *War and Peace* by Leo Tolstoy

Patrick McGrath is the author of two story collections and six novels, including *Spider, Asylum,* and *Port Mungo*.

ERIN McGRAW

1. The Pentateuch
2. *Othello, The Moor of Venice* by William Shakespeare
3. *The Divine Comedy* by Dante Alighieri
4. *The Canterbury Tales* by Geoffrey Chaucer
5. *Madame Bovary* by Gustave Flaubert
6. *The Power and the Glory* by Graham Greene
7. *The Brothers Karamazov* by Fyodor Dostoevsky
8. *Absalom, Absalom!* by William Faulkner
9. *The Great Gatsby* by F. Scott Fitzgerald
10. The stories of Flannery O'Connor

Erin McGraw is the author of four books of fiction, including the story collections *Lies of the Saints* and, most recently, *The Good Life*.

DAVID MEANS

1. *The Brothers Karamazov* by Fyodor Dostoevsky
2. *Independent People* by Halldór Laxness
3. *A Sportsman's Notebook* by Ivan Turgenev
4. The stories of Anton Chekhov
5. *The Trial* by Franz Kafka
6. *The Sound and the Fury* by William Faulkner
7. *Dubliners* by James Joyce
8. *Swann's Way* by Marcel Proust
9. *Ulysses* by James Joyce
10. *A Personal Matter* by Kenzaburō Ōe

David Means has published three story collections, *A Quick Kiss of Redemption*, *Assorted Fire Events* (winner of a *Los Angeles Times* Book Prize), and *The Secret Goldfish*.

CLAIRE MESSUD

1. *Pride and Prejudice* by Jane Austen
2. *In Search of Lost Time* by Marcel Proust
3. *The Portrait of a Lady* by Henry James
4. *Madame Bovary* by Gustave Flaubert
5. *Anna Karenina* by Leo Tolstoy
6. *The Possessed* by Fyodor Dostoevsky
7. *Confessions of Zeno* by Italo Svevo
8. *A House for Mr. Biswas* by V. S. Naipaul
9. *The Loser* by Thomas Bernhard
10. *Oscar and Lucinda* by Peter Carey

Claire Messud has written a collection of novellas, *The Hunters*, and three novels, *The Last Life*, *When the World Was Steady*, and *The Emperor's Children*.

LYDIA MILLET

1. *JR* by William Gaddis
2. *Mrs. Dalloway* by Virginia Woolf
3. *The Voyage of the 'Dawn Treader'* by C. S. Lewis
4. *The Lorax* by Dr. Seuss
5. *Woodcutters* by Thomas Bernhard
6. *War with the Newts* by Karel Čapek
7. *Auto-da-Fé* by Elias Canetti
8. *Red the Fiend* by Gilbert Sorrentino
9. *Masquerade and Other Stories* by Robert Walser
10. *Molloy* by Samuel Beckett

Lydia Millet is the author of several novels, including *Oh Pure and Radiant Heart* and *My Happy Life*, which won the 2003 PEN USA Award for Fiction.

Appreciation of Gilbert Sorrentino's
Red the Fiend
by Lydia Millet

Gilbert Sorrentino's most accessible, straightforward, and flawless novel, *Red the Fiend* (1989), explores the practical and psychic tribulations of young Red. He's a dirty urchin full of frustrated want and suppressed rage who lives in a working-class Brooklyn neighborhood (circa 1940) with his weak-willed mother and grandfather and, most important, his bitterly cruel, tyrannical grandmother. She makes his misery her first priority, calculating every move to maximize his exquisitely perfect emotional torment; for his part Red gradually learns to parry each of her sly thrusts with an equally sly one of his own. Eventually, he derives the lion's share of his meager joy in life from the daily toil of returning her loathing and attempting to give as bad as he gets. In brutal simplicity, with recourse to uniquely effective listing devices, the precise and beautiful prose lays bare the excruciating particularities of Red's pain and shame and makes palpably real his journey from, if not innocence, at least relative neutrality toward craftiness and deft manipulation. With the grace and rigor of thought and language that earned Sorrentino's reputation as a master of stylistic play and cold humor, *Red the Fiend* describes in direct terms this increasingly dangerous battle of wills as it rises to its unbearable boiling point. No other novel in recent memory evokes the desolation of lovelessness with such blunt passion.

SUSAN MINOT

1. *Anna Karenina* by Leo Tolstoy
2. *To the Lighthouse* by Virginia Woolf
3. *Lolita* by Vladimir Nabokov
4. *The Sound and the Fury* by William Faulkner
5. *The Age of Innocence* by Edith Wharton
6. *Tender Is the Night* by F. Scott Fitzgerald
7. *Mansfield Park* by Jane Austen
8. The stories of Ernest Hemingway
9. The stories of J. D. Salinger
10. The stories of Anton Chekhov

Susan Minot is the author of novels (*Monkeys*, *Folly*, *Evening*, and *Rapture*); a collection of poems (*Poems 4 A.M.*), and stories (*Lust & Other Stories*).

DAVID MITCHELL

I just wrote these down while I was eating my breakfast cereal. Sometimes first instincts can be "truer" than lengthy deliberation. I've instituted a wild card at the end of the list. The wild card denotes a book that I can't in all honesty claim is greater or weightier or of more significance to the marching ballroom of literature than the items on the main list, but that I badly want to be read more.

1. *The Duel* by Anton Chekhov (A novella, I know, but I would save it from a burning house before everything else I've ever read.)
2. *1984* by George Orwell
3. *Heart of Darkness* by Joseph Conrad
4. *Sense and Sensibility* by Jane Austen
5. *The Master and Margarita* by Mikhail Bulgakov
6. *As I Lay Dying* by William Faulkner
7. *Tom Jones* by Henry Fielding
8. *Labyrinths* by Jorge Luis Borges
9. *W, or The Memory of Childhood* by Georges Perec
10. *The Makioka Sisters* by Junichiro Tanizaki
Wild Card: *Lolly Willowes* by Sylvia Townsend Warner

David Mitchell has written the novels *Ghostwritten, number9dream, Cloud Atlas,* and *Black Swan Green*.

LORRIE MOORE

1. *Madame Bovary* by Gustave Flaubert
2. *Dubliners* by James Joyce
3. *The Iliad* by Homer
4. *The Decameron* by Giovanni Boccaccio
5. *Troilus and Criseyde* by Geoffrey Chaucer
6. *Romeo and Juliet* by William Shakespeare
7. *Jane Eyre* by Charlotte Brontë
8. *Washington Square* by Henry James
9. *Middlemarch* by George Eliot
10. *Open Secrets* by Alice Munro

Lorrie Moore is the author of three story collections (*Birds of America*), two novels (*Anagrams*), and a children's book (*The Forgotten Helper*). She teaches at the University of Wisconsin in Madison.

JOYCE CAROL OATES

1. *Crime and Punishment* by Fyodor Dostoevsky
2. *Ulysses* by James Joyce
3. *The Sound and the Fury* by William Faulkner
4. The poems of Emily Dickinson
5. The stories of Franz Kafka
6. *The Red and the Black* by Stendhal
7. *The Rainbow* by D. H. Lawrence
8. *Women in Love* by D. H. Lawrence
9. *Moby-Dick* by Herman Melville
10. *The Adventures of Huckleberry Finn* by Mark Twain

Joyce Carol Oates is the author of more than one hundred books, including novels, collections of stories, plays, and children's books, as well as poems, essays, and criticism. Her numerous honors include a 1970 National Book Award for the novel *Them*.

STEWART O'NAN

1. *Hamlet* by William Shakespeare
2. *Macbeth* by William Shakespeare
3. The stories of Anton Chekhov
4. *Anna Karenina* by Leo Tolstoy
5. *Heart of Darkness* by Joseph Conrad
6. *The Tempest* by William Shakespeare
7. *To the Lighthouse* by Virginia Woolf
8. *Winesburg, Ohio* by Sherwood Anderson
9. *Alice's Adventures in Wonderland* by Lewis Carroll
10. *Parables and Paradoxes* by Franz Kafka

Stewart O'Nan is the author of ten novels, including *Snow Angels, A Prayer for the Dying*, and *The Good Wife*.

ROBERT B. PARKER

1. *The Bear* by William Faulkner
2. *The Great Gatsby* by F. Scott Fitzgerald
3. *Hamlet* by William Shakespeare
4. *The Adventures of Huckleberry Finn* by Mark Twain
5. *The Maltese Falcon* by Dashiell Hammett
6. *The Love Song of J. Alfred Prufrock* by T. S. Eliot
7. *Dubliners* by James Joyce
8. *The Big Sleep* by Raymond Chandler
9. *U.S.A.* (trilogy) by John Dos Passos
10. *The Ambassadors* by Henry James

Robert B. Parker has written more than fifty novels, many featuring the street-smart Boston private eye Spenser.

ANN PATCHETT

1. *Anna Karenina* by Leo Tolstoy
2. *One Hundred Years of Solitude* by Gabriel García Márquez
3. *Lolita* by Vladimir Nabokov
4. *The Magic Mountain* by Thomas Mann
5. *The Great Gatsby* by F. Scott Fitzgerald
6. *So Long, See You Tomorrow* by William Maxwell
7. *The Good Soldier* by Ford Madox Ford
8. *Miss Lonelyhearts* by Nathanael West
9. *Persuasion* by Jane Austen
10. *The Human Stain* by Philip Roth

Ann Patchett has written the novels *The Patron Saint of Liars*, *Taft*, *The Magician's Assistant*, and *Bel Canto*, which won a PEN/Faulkner Award and the Orange Prize.

IAIN PEARS

1. *King Lear* by William Shakespeare
2. *The Fall* by Albert Camus
3. *The Bacchae* by Euripides
4. *Tinker, Tailor, Soldier, Spy* by John Le Carré
5. *The Deptford Trilogy* by Robertson Davies
6. *Pride and Prejudice* by Jane Austen
7. *Splendeurs et misères des courtisanes* by Honoré de Balzac
8. The Maigret series of detective novels by Georges Simenon
9. *Labyrinths* by Jorge Luis Borges
10. *Nice Work* by David Lodge

Iain Pears has written ten novels, including the *Instance of the Fingerpost* and *The Dream of Scipio*, as well as works on art history and economics.

Appreciation of Georges Simenon's
Maigret Detective Novels
by Iain Pears

The Maigret series of detective stories, written by the Belgian Georges Simenon, are part of that rare breed of books—the mass-market entertainment that also works as great literature. Simenon is the master of atmosphere; with the lightest of touches he is able to conjure up Paris in the 1940s and 1950s, a seedy, largely poor city of shabby concierges and downtrodden traveling salesmen, of cheap hotels and squalid nightclubs, of hissing steam radiators and grubby shirt collars.

Much of the narrative is liquor soaked—Maigret begins drinking after breakfast, interviews witnesses over brandy, and suspects over beer. Only rarely is a case concluded by unraveling clues; these are not whodunits. Rather, they are studies in character, of place, and of people. Simenon would have been a brilliant analyst. As often as not, the books end when Maigret (and through him, the reader) so understands the criminal that the suspect confesses all. Indeed, the reader is usually left sympathizing with the criminal, whose crime is reacting to limited choices and desperate circumstances.

The books are so compressed they could almost be short stories, but Simenon populates them with an extraordinary range of characters—the overweight, perpetually sweating Maigret, his eternally patient wife (more acute, in many ways, than her husband), his juniors, and the gallery of pimps and prostitutes, petty criminals, shopkeepers, bartenders, small tradesmen, and canal barge pilots who make up his world. There is no reveling in the grime of the underworld; most of the characters dream of better things and live a life of disappointment. Out of their lives, Simenon created some of the most enduring and compelling works of the twentieth century.

GEORGE PELACANOS

1. *All the King's Men* by Robert Penn Warren
2. *The Sun Also Rises* by Ernest Hemingway
3. *The Grapes of Wrath* by John Steinbeck
4. *Ask the Dust* by John Fante
5. *A Fan's Notes* by Frederick Exley
6. *The Long Goodbye* by Raymond Chandler
7. *True Grit* by Charles Portis
8. *Blood Meridian* by Cormac McCarthy
9. *Clockers* by Richard Price
10. *The Known World* by Edward P. Jones

George Pelacanos writes crime/noir novels set in and around his native city of Washington, D.C. They include *A Firing Offense*, *Drama City*, and *Hell to Pay*, which won a *Los Angeles Times* Book Award.

TOM PERROTTA

1. *Don Quixote* by Miguel de Cervantes
2. *Anna Karenina* by Leo Tolstoy
3. *Père Goriot* by Honoré de Balzac
4. *Howards End* by E. M. Forster
5. *The Good Soldier* by Ford Madox Ford
6. *My Ántonia* by Willa Cather
7. *Sister Carrie* by Theodore Dreiser
8. *The Great Gatsby* by F. Scott Fitzgerald
9. *Rabbit Angstrom* by John Updike
10. *Where I'm Calling From* by Raymond Carver

Tom Perrotta is the author of five works of fiction, including the novels *Election*, *Joe College*, and *Little Children*.

ARTHUR PHILLIPS

1. The stories of Franz Kafka
2. *Life: A User's Manual* by Georges Perec
3. *The Magic Mountain* by Thomas Mann
4. *Pale Fire* by Vladimir Nabokov
5. *Hamlet* by William Shakespeare
6. *In Search of Lost Time* by Marcel Proust
7. *War and Peace* by Leo Tolstoy
8. The stories of Anton Chekhov
9. *The Three Musketeers* by Alexandre Dumas
10. *The Odyssey* by Homer

Arthur Phillips is the author of the novels *Prague*, *The Egyptologist*, and *Angelica*.

Appreciation of Georges Perec's
Life: A User's Manual
by Arthur Phillips

The first miracle: A novel built from a strictly limited construction —the description of one single moment in a Paris apartment building—blossoms into an encyclopedia of stories and life spanning centuries, the globe, the history of literature. The second miracle: A moving, humane novel composed of implausible, even impossible parts. Perec's brainy puzzle-book somehow produces the exhilarating, alternating certainties that life is beautiful, cruel, sweet, meaningful.

Life's hundred and some tales about the residents of 11 rue Simon-Crubellier sometimes slow to Proustian crawls, and a reader's joy is in lounging, savoring every turn of phrase. A page later, though, Perec (almost audibly laughing) gallops us into insane plots of revenge, kleptomaniacal magistrates, intricate con games, a billionaire's entire life spent on a single project, and the heiress's egg collection, the destruction of which prompted the inaccurate painting, which later hung in . . .

Pictures within pictures, memories within memories, letters within letters, reflections of reflections, the novel represents the unachievable ambitions of the painter Valène, burning to accomplish on canvas what Perec actually did in text: a portrait of life in all its possibility, speed, variety, shimmer, impermanence, blindingly rich and achingly temporary.

Published in 1978, *Life* is infinitely entertaining, but it also can change how you see your surroundings; the wall between novel and world leaks. If Perec can imagine four paintings (and their histories) reproduced inside yet another painting, and the wallpaper against which that work hangs, and the life of the man who selected the wallpaper, then suddenly the world outside the book more proudly displays its own wondrous plumage, imagined by some creator even more ingenious than Perec. That all of his work (or Valène's, or Perec's) is so painfully transient only adds to its splendor, just as the lives led in the apartments at 11 rue Simon-Crubellier are both madly full and too quickly finished, forgotten.

ROBERT PINSKY

Ten works of fiction that have been great *for me*:

1. *The Odyssey* by Homer
2. The Books of Samuel
3. *King Lear* by William Shakespeare
4. *The Divine Comedy* by Dante Alighieri
5. *Ulysses* by James Joyce
6. *The Hamlet* by William Faulkner
7. *Alice's Adventures in Wonderland* and *Through the Looking Glass* by Lewis Carroll
8. *Dead Souls* by Nikolai Gogol
9. The stories of Isaac Babel
10. *A Connecticut Yankee in King Arthur's Court* by Mark Twain

Robert Pinsky's most recent books are *The Life of David* (prose) and *Jersey Rain* (poetry).

RICHARD POWERS

Age 5: *Harold and the Purple Crayon* by Crockett Johnson
Age 10: The Bible; *The Odyssey* by Homer (dead heat)
Age 15: *The Lord of the Rings* by J. R. R. Tolkien
Age 20: *Ulysses* by James Joyce
Age 25: *Moby-Dick* by Herman Melville
Age 30: *The Magic Mountain* by Thomas Mann
Age 35: *In Search of Lost Time* by Marcel Proust
Age 40: *Great Expectations* by Charles Dickens
Age 45: *My Ántonia* by Willa Cather
Age 50: Something wholly unforeseen, that will change all these
others, again

Richard Powers is the author of nine novels, including *The Gold Bug Variations*, *Gain*, and most recently, *The Echo Maker*.

REYNOLDS PRICE

Since books are not racehorses entered in identical events and bound for a common finish line, I don't offer these as the "ten greatest novels." The several attempts to come up with similar lists at the dawning of our latest millennium only proved the absurdity of such errands. I do feel strongly, however, that there are few other substantial works of fiction from any culture known to me which equal these ten in the depth of their wisdom or the efficiency of their prose (only three were originally written in a language other than English—*Madame Bovary* in French, *Anna Karenina* in Russian, and *Doctor Faustus* in German). I offer them in the hope of widening their readership, and I've listed them in the order of their first publication. They are all still in print. The fact that I've mentioned no novels of the recent past means only that I'm as yet uncertain of their durability, despite my conviction that American fiction, for instance, has never been richer than in the past fifty years.

1. *Madame Bovary* by Gustave Flaubert
2. *Great Expectations* by Charles Dickens
3. *Anna Karenina* by Leo Tolstoy
4. *Tess of the D'Urbervilles* by Thomas Hardy
5. *The Golden Bowl* by Henry James
6. *A Passage to India* by E. M. Forster
7. *The Sun Also Rises* by Ernest Hemingway
8. *To the Lighthouse* by Virginia Woolf
9. *Doctor Faustus* by Thomas Mann
10. *The Book of Ebenezer Le Page* by G. B. Edwards

Reynolds Price is a novelist (*Kate Vaiden*), short story writer (*The Collected Stories*), poet (*The Collected Poems*), memoirist (*Clear Pictures*), children's book writer (*A Perfect Friend*), and essayist (*Letter to a Man in the Fire: Does God Exist and Does He Care?*).

FRANCINE PROSE

1. *Anna Karenina* by Leo Tolstoy
2. *The Charterhouse of Parma* by Stendhal
3. *In Search of Lost Time* by Marcel Proust
4. The stories of Anton Chekhov
5. The stories of John Cheever
6. The stories of Mavis Gallant
7. *Moby-Dick* by Herman Melville
8. *Middlemarch* by George Eliot
9. *One Hundred Years of Solitude* by Gabriel García Márquez
10. *Crime and Punishment* by Fyodor Dostoevsky

Francine Prose's most recent works include the novel *A Changed Man*, the biography *Caravaggio: Painter of Miracles*, and the nonfiction work *Reading Like a Writer*.

Appreciation of Stendhal's
The Charterhouse of Parma
by Francine Prose

Opening *The Charterhouse of Parma* is like stepping into the path of a benevolent cyclone that will pick you up and set you down, gently but firmly, somewhere else. You can still feel the tailwind of inspiration, the high speed at which Stendhal wrote it, and you can't help admiring its assurance and audacity.

Stendhal marks the boundaries of the more traditional nineteenth-century novel, and then proceeds to explode them. Just as Fabrizio keeps discovering that his life is taking a different direction from what he'd imagined, so the reader keeps thinking that Stendhal has written one kind of book, then finding that it is something else entirely. Stendhal writes as if he can't see why everything—politics, history, intrigue, the battle of Waterloo, a love story, several love stories—can't be compressed into a single novel. The result is a huge canvas on which every detail is painted with astonishing realism and psychological verisimilitude.

First you are totally swept up in Fabrizio's peculiar experience of the Napoleonic wars, then moved by the Krazy Kat love triangle involving Fabrizio, Mosca, and Gina, and throughout, astonished by the accuracy of Stendhal's observations on love, jealousy, ambition, and of how the perception of biological age influences our behavior.

I love the way Stendhal uses "Italian" to mean passionate, and how he falls in love with his characters, for all the right reasons. One can only imagine how Tolstoy would have punished Gina, who is not only among the most memorable women in literature, but who is also scheming, casually adulterous, and madly in love with her own nephew. Each time I finish the book, I feel as if the world has been washed clean and polished while I was reading, and as if everything around me is shining a little more brightly.

ANNIE PROULX

I find this list of ten books project to be difficult, pointless, and wrong-headed. Just so you'll give it a rest, here is a list. One could, of course, quickly go on to put together list after list. Moreover, the lists would change from week to week as one's tastes change and as one reads more widely. It has not escaped me that nearly every newspaper, book review publication, and magazine are currently gripped by list fever. Lists, unless grocery shopping lists, are truly a *reductio ad absurdum*.

1. *The Odyssey* by Homer
2. *Wheat That Springeth Green* by J. F. Powers
3. *The Adventures of Tom Sawyer* by Mark Twain
4. *Ship of Fools* by Katherine Anne Porter
5. *The Master and Margarita* by Mikhail Bulgakov
6. *King Lear* by William Shakespeare
7. *Leaves of Grass* by Walt Whitman
8. The stories of William Trevor
9. *The Black Book* by Orhan Pamuk
10. The haiku of Matsuo Bashō

Annie Proulx won a PEN/Faulkner Award for her first novel, *Postcards*, and a Pulitzer Prize and National Book Award for her second novel, *The Shipping News*.

JONATHAN RABAN

1. *Our Mutual Friend* by Charles Dickens
2. *Emma* by Jane Austen
3. *Don Juan* by Lord Byron
4. *The Portrait of a Lady* by Henry James
5. *The Last Chronicle of Barset* by Anthony Trollope
6. *Middlemarch* by George Eliot
7. *Tristram Shandy* by Laurence Sterne
8. *The Adventures of Huckleberry Finn* by Mark Twain
9. *A Handful of Dust* by Evelyn Waugh
10. *Summer Lightning* by P. G. Wodehouse

Jonathan Raban is a British essayist, travel writer, and novelist, and winner of the 1996 National Book Critics Circle Award for *Bad Land*. His most recent book is the novel *Surveillance*.

IAN RANKIN

1. *King Lear* by William Shakespeare
2. *Catch-22* by Joseph Heller
3. *War and Peace* by Leo Tolstoy
4. *Crime and Punishment* by Fyodor Dostoevsky
5. *Ulysses* by James Joyce
6. *Bleak House* by Charles Dickens
7. *The Strange Case of Dr. Jekyll and Mr. Hyde* by Robert Louis Stevenson
8. *1984* by George Orwell
9. *Pride and Prejudice* by Jane Austen
10. *Moby-Dick* by Herman Melville

Ian Rankin is the Scottish author of the best-selling Inspector Rebus series. His books have won the Edgar and Gold Dagger awards.

ROXANA ROBINSON

1. *War and Peace* by Leo Tolstoy
2. The stories of Anton Chekhov
3. *To the Lighthouse* by Virginia Woolf
4. *Buddenbrooks* by Thomas Mann
5. *A Room with a View* by E. M. Forster
6. *The Raj Quartet* by Paul Scott
7. *The Leopard* by Giuseppe Tomasi di Lampedusa
8. *Rabbit at Rest* by John Updike
9. *The Transit of Venus* by Shirley Hazzard
10. *Disgrace* by J. M. Coetzee

Roxana Robinson is a novelist (*Sweetwater*), story writer (*A Perfect Stranger and Other Stories*), and biographer (*Georgia O'Keeffe: A Life*).

LOUIS D. RUBIN, JR.

1. *In Search of Lost Time* by Marcel Proust
2. *Ulysses* by James Joyce
3. *Absalom, Absalom!* by William Faulkner
4. *The Golden Apples* by Eudora Welty
5. *The Red and the Black* by Stendhal
6. *Don Quixote* by Miguel de Cervantes
7. *War and Peace* by Leo Tolstoy
8. *Tristram Shandy* by Lawrence Sterne
9. *Moby-Dick* by Herman Melville
10. *The Adventures of Huckleberry Finn* by Mark Twain

Louis D. Rubin, Jr., has published more than fifty books, including novels (*Surfaces of a Diamond*), criticism (*The Curious Death of the Novel*), and memoirs (*My Father's People: A Family of Southern Jews*), as well as works on boats, baseball, and trains.

Appreciation of the Stories of Eudora Welty
by Louis D. Rubin, Jr.

At first glance, the people Eudora Welty usually writes about seem unremarkable, as are the mostly Mississippi towns, cities, and countryside they live in.

To read her stories, however, such as "Why I Live at the P.O.," "Petrified Man," "Powerhouse," "Moon Lake," and "Kin," is to learn otherwise. Through them you enter the realm of the extraordinary, as revealed in the commonplace. Each of Welty's seemingly mundane people exhibits the depth, complexity, private surmise, and ultimate riddle of human identity. "Every-body to their own visioning," as one of her characters remarks.

There is plenty of high comedy. Few authors can match her eye for the incongruous, the hilarious response, the bemused quality of the way her people go about their lives. There is also pathos, veering sometimes into tragedy, and beyond that, awareness of what is unknowable and inscrutable.

Her most stunning fiction is the group of interconnected stories published in 1949 as *The Golden Apples*. These center on the citizenry of Morgana, Mississippi, over the course of some four decades. In "June Recital" German-born Miss Lottie Elisabeth Eckhart teaches piano to the young. These include Cassie Morrison, who carries on her teacher's mission, and Virgie Rainey, most talented of all, who in spite of herself absorbs "*the* Beethoven, as with the dragon's blood." In the closing story, "The Wanderers," Virgie sits under a tree not far from Miss Eckhart's grave and gazes into the falling rain, hearing "the magical percussion" drumming into her ears: "That was the gift she had touched with her fingers that had drifted and left her."

Welty's richly allusive style, alive to nuance, is not really like anyone else's. The dialogue (her characters talk *at* rather than *to* one another), the shading of Greek mythology and W. B. Yeats's poetry into the rhythms of everyday life in Morgana, the depth perception of a major literary artist, all make her stories superb.

JAMES SALTER

1. The Bible
2. *Aesop's Fables*
3. *A Thousand and One Nights* (first European translation by Antoine Galland)
4. The legends of King Arthur and the Knights of the Round Table
5. *Henry IV*, Parts I and II by William Shakespeare
6. *Madame Bovary* by Gustave Flaubert
7. *Dead Souls* by Nikolai Gogol
8. *Anna Karenina* by Leo Tolstoy
9. The stories of Isaac Babel
10. *Grimm's Fairy Tales* by Wilhelm and Jacob Grimm

James Salter, a former Air Force pilot, has published novels (*A Sport and a Pastime*), screenplays (*Downhill Racer*), memoirs (*Burning the Days*), and story collections (*Dusk and Other Stories*, which won a PEN/Faulkner Award).

GEORGE SAUNDERS

This was harder than I thought it would be. Because I found myself pondering the notion of Greatness: What good is it? Why even have such a concept? In the end I answered myself: We need a concept of greatness so we can know in what direction we should morally aspire. A book answers this question most eloquently, it seems to me, in its voice; that is, in its attitude toward the mayhem it observes. A book can be like the voice of God, telling us what to think of ourselves. These are, for me, the books that do this most valuably:

1. *Dead Souls* by Nikolai Gogol
2. *The Adventures of Huckleberry Finn* by Mark Twain
3. *War and Peace* by Leo Tolstoy
4. *Tristram Shandy* by Lawrence Sterne
5. *Hamlet* by William Shakespeare
6. *Red Cavalry* by Isaac Babel
7. The stories of Anton Chekhov
8. *Slaughterhouse-Five* by Kurt Vonnegut
9. *Waiting for Godot* by Samuel Beckett
10. *On the Road* by Jack Kerouac

George Saunders is the author of the short story collections *CivilWarLand in Bad Decline, Pastoralia,* and most recently, *In Persuasion Nation.*

CATHLEEN SCHINE

1. *Emma* by Jane Austen
2. *Leaves of Grass* by Walt Whitman
3. *War and Peace* by Leo Tolstoy
4. *Phineas Finn* by Anthony Trollope
5. *Our Mutual Friend* by Charles Dickens
6. *Quartet in Autumn* (and everything else) by Barbara Pym
7. *The Adventures of Huckleberry Finn* by Mark Twain
8. *Hateship, Friendship, Courtship, Loveship, Marriage* by Alice Munro
9. *The Makioka Sisters* by Junichiro Tanizaki
10. *Pictures from an Institution* by Randall Jarrell

Cathleen Schine is the author of six novels, including the international bestsellers *Rameau's Niece* and *The Love Letter*. She lives in New York City.

JIM SHEPARD

1. *Lolita* by Vladimir Nabokov
2. *One Hundred Years of Solitude* by Gabriel García Márquez
3. *The Trial* by Franz Kafka
4. The stories of Anton Chekhov
5. *The Leopard* by Giuseppe Tomasi di Lampedusa
6. *Dubliners* by James Joyce
7. The stories of Flannery O'Connor
8. The stories of Isaac Babel
9. *Waiting for the Barbarians* by J. M. Coetzee
10. *Memoirs of Hadrian* by Marguerite Yourcenar

Jim Shepard is the author of six novels, most recently *Project X*, and two story collections, most recently *Love and Hydrogen*.

ANITA SHREVE

1. *The Transit of Venus* by Shirley Hazzard
2. *The Line of Beauty* by Alan Hollinghurst
3. *The Scarlet Letter* by Nathaniel Hawthorne
4. *The Hours* by Michael Cunningham
5. *The Untouchable* by John Banville
6. *The Master* by Colm Tóibín
7. *Don't Let's Go to the Dogs Tonight* by Alexandra Fuller
8. *Lies of Silence* by Brian Moore
9. *Cal* by Bernard MacLaverty
10. *That Night* by Alice McDermott

Anita Shreve is a novelist whose books include *The Weight of Water*, *The Pilot's Wife*, and *A Wedding in December*.

ALEXANDER McCALL SMITH

1. *Anna Karenina* by Leo Tolstoy
2. *War and Peace* by Leo Tolstoy
3. *The Prime of Miss Jean Brodie* by Muriel Spark
4. *Kidnapped* by Robert Louis Stevenson
5. *Cry, the Beloved Country* by Alan Paton
6. *The Europeans* by Henry James
7. *Madame Bovary* by Gustave Flaubert
8. *One Hundred Years of Solitude* by Gabriel García Márquez
9. *The English Teacher* by R. K. Narayan
10. *To Kill a Mockingbird* by Harper Lee

Alexander McCall Smith is the African-born Scottish author of over sixty books, including his series of novels set in Botswana, *The No. 1 Ladies' Detective Agency*.

LEE SMITH

1. *The Dead* by James Joyce
2. *Kristin Lavransdatter* by Sigrid Undset
3. *The Sheltered Life* by Ellen Glasgow
4. *Absalom, Absalom!* by William Faulkner
5. *To the Lighthouse* by Virginia Woolf
6. The stories of Eudora Welty
7. The stories of Flannery O'Connor
8. *River of Earth* by James Still
9. *Jane Eyre* by Charlotte Brontë
10. *Madame Bovary* by Gustave Flaubert

Lee Smith has published eleven books of fiction, including the novels *Oral History*, *Fair and Tender Ladies*, and *The Last Girls*, and the story collection *News of the Spirit*.

ELIZABETH SPENCER

1. *Great Expectations* by Charles Dickens
2. *The Hamlet* by William Faulkner
3. *Joseph Andrews* by Henry Fielding
4. *The Red and the Black* by Stendhal
5. *The Golden Apples* by Eudora Welty
6. *On the Eve* by Ivan Turgenev
7. *Where Angels Fear to Tread* by E. M. Forster
8. *Cold Mountain* by Charles Frazier
9. *Tender Is the Night* by F. Scott Fitzgerald
10. *The Professor's House* by Willa Cather

Elizabeth Spencer is a five-time recipient of the O. Henry Prize for short fiction. Her books include *The Southern Woman: New and Selected Stories*, the novel *The Night Travelers*, and the memoir *Landscapes of the Heart*.

SCOTT SPENCER

1. *Lolita* by Vladimir Nabokov
2. *Madame Bovary* by Gustave Flaubert
3. *Great Expectations* by Charles Dickens
4. *The Adventures of Huckleberry Finn* by Mark Twain
5. *King Lear* by William Shakespeare
6. *The Power and the Glory* by Graham Greene
7. *Song of Solomon* by Toni Morrison
8. *Enemies, A Love Story* by Isaac Bashevis Singer
9. *Anna Karenina* by Leo Tolstoy
10. *Rabbit Angstrom* by John Updike

Scott Spencer has written eight novels, including *Endless Love, Waking the Dead, Men in Black, The Rich Man's Table,* and *A Ship Made of Paper.*

ADRIANA TRIGIANI

1. *Casa Guidi Windows* by Elizabeth Barrett Browning
2. *Jane Eyre* by Charlotte Brontë
3. *The Giving Tree* by Shel Silverstein
4. *Charlotte's Web* by E. B. White
5. *Bertha* and *George Washington Crosses the Delaware,* two plays by Kenneth Koch
6. *Blithe Spirit* by Noël Coward
7. *Death of a Salesman* by Arthur Miller
8. *Pride and Prejudice* by Jane Austen
9. *The Palm Beach Story, Sullivan's Travels,* and *The Lady Eve,* three screenplays by Preston Sturges
10. *When I Grow Too Old to Dream,* lyrics by Oscar Hammerstein

Adriana Trigiani is a playwright, television writer, filmmaker, and author of the best-selling novels *Big Stone Gap; Big Cherry Holler; Milk Glass Moon; Lucia, Lucia;* and *The Queen of the Big Time.*

SCOTT TUROW

1. *A Portrait of the Artist as a Young Man* by James Joyce, which first showed me that fiction could articulate what I took as wild and private dreams
2. *Anna Karenina* by Leo Tolstoy, because of the powerful and intimate rendition of these webbed lives
3. *Rabbit Angstrom* novels by John Updike, because of their acute observation and moral courage
4. *Herzog* by Saul Bellow, for its extraordinary language and intellectual power and for its observations of Chicago
5. *Tell Me a Riddle* by Tillie Olsen, for its inventiveness and power
6. *The Count of Monte Cristo* by Alexandre Dumas, for its spectacular plot
7. The works of William Shakespeare, for their miraculous language and extraordinary observations about humanity
8. *The Bear* by William Faulkner, for telling the quintessential American story from inside the American mind
9. *Tender Is the Night* by F. Scott Fitzgerald, an extremely contemporary book that anticipated much of our current preoccupation with gender
10. *The Thin Man* by Dashiell Hammett, for its elegance and perfect mystery

Scott Turow, a practicing attorney in Chicago, has written seven novels about the law, including *Presumed Innocent* and *Ordinary Heroes*, and the nonfiction works *One L* and *Ultimate Punishment*.

BARRY UNSWORTH

1. *The Oresteia* by Aeschylus
2. *The Mill on the Floss* by George Eliot
3. *Bleak House* by Charles Dickens
4. *Madame Bovary* by Gustave Flaubert
5. *The Idiot* by Fyodor Dostoevsky
6. *The Betrothed* by Alessandro Manzoni
7. *The Grapes of Wrath* by John Steinbeck
8. *The Confessions of Nat Turner* by William Styron
9. *A Curtain of Green* by Eudora Welty
10. *Rites of Passage* by William Golding

Barry Unsworth's novels include *Stone Virgin, Morality Play, The Songs of the Kings,* and *Sacred Hunger,* which was a joint winner of the 1992 Booker Prize.

VENDELA VIDA

1. *The Divine Comedy* by Dante Alighieri
2. *Crime and Punishment* by Fyodor Dostoevsky
3. *Pale Fire* by Vladimir Nabokov
4. *Clarissa* by Samuel Richardson
5. *Mrs. Dalloway* by Virginia Woolf
6. *The Decameron* by Giovanni Boccaccio
7. *Hedda Gabler* by Henrik Ibsen
8. *The Great Gatsby* by F. Scott Fitzgerald
9. *The Wind-Up Bird Chronicle* by Haruki Murakami
10. *A Heart So White* by Javier Marías

Vendela Vida, a founding editor of the literary journal *The Believer,* has written a novel, *And Now You Can Go,* and a book of nonfiction, *Girls on the Verge: Debutante Dips, Drive-bys, and Other Initiations.*

SUSAN VREELAND

1. *The Grapes of Wrath* by John Steinbeck
2. *Hamlet* by William Shakespeare
3. *To Kill a Mockingbird* by Harper Lee
4. *The Adventures of Huckleberry Finn* by Mark Twain
5. *All Quiet on the Western Front* by Erich Maria Remarque
6. *A Farewell to Arms* by Ernest Hemingway
7. *Mrs. Dalloway* by Virginia Woolf
8. *Ahab's Wife* by Sena Jeter Naslund
9. *A Portrait of the Artist as a Young Man* by James Joyce
10. *The Great Gatsby* by F. Scott Fitzgerald

Susan Vreeland's best-selling fiction on art-related themes, including *Girl in Hyacinth Blue*, *The Passion of Artemisia*, and *Life Studies*, has been translated into twenty-five languages.

DAVID FOSTER WALLACE

1. *The Screwtape Letters* by C. S. Lewis
2. *The Stand* by Stephen King
3. *Red Dragon* by Thomas Harris
4. *The Thin Red Line* by James Jones
5. *Fear of Flying* by Erica Jong
6. *The Silence of the Lambs* by Thomas Harris
7. *Stranger in a Strange Land* by Robert A. Heinlein
8. *Fuzz* by Ed McBain
9. *Alligator* by Shelley Katz
10. *The Sum of All Fears* by Tom Clancy

David Foster Wallace has published novels (*Infinite Jest*), story collections (*Oblivion*), and books of essays and reportage (*Consider the Lobster*).

ANTHONY WALTON

1. *The Oresteia* by Aeschylus
2. *Oedipus at Colonus* by Sophocles
3. *Madame Bovary* by Gustave Flaubert
4. *Crime and Punishment* by Fyodor Dostoevsky
5. *In Search of Lost Time* by Marcel Proust
6. *The Great Gatsby* by F. Scott Fitzgerald
7. *The Enigma of Arrival* by V. S. Naipaul
8. *The Iliad* by Homer
9. *Hamlet* by William Shakespeare
10. *Invisible Man* by Ralph Ellison

Anthony Walton is the author of *Mississippi: An American Journey* and an editor of *The Vintage Book of African-American Poetry*. He teaches at Bowdoin College.

JENNIFER WEINER

1. *Geek Love* by Katherine Dunn
2. *The Stand* by Stephen King
3. *Almost Paradise* and *Shining Through* by Susan Isaacs (equal favorites)
4. *A Tree Grows in Brooklyn* by Betty Smith
5. *Sheila Levine Is Dead and Living in New York* by Gail Parent
6. *Pearl* by Tabitha King
7. *Everybody Pays* by Andrew Vachss
8. *A Prayer for Owen Meany* by John Irving
9. *Rule of the Bone* by Russell Banks
10. *The Handmaid's Tale* by Margaret Atwood

Jennifer Weiner is the author of four novels, including *Good in Bed, Goodnight Nobody,* and *In Her Shoes,* and the story collection *The Guy Not Taken.*

ROBERT WILSON

1. *Embers* by Sándor Márai'
2. *The Great Gatsby* by F. Scott Fitzgerald
3. *The Old Man and the Sea* by Ernest Hemingway
4. *Heart of Darkness* by Joseph Conrad
5. *The Long Goodbye* by Raymond Chandler
6. *Our Mutual Friend* by Charles Dickens
7. *The Untouchable* by John Banville
8. *A Heart So White* by Javier Marías
9. *Love in the Time of Cholera* by Gabriel García Márquez
10. *London Fields* by Martin Amis

Robert Wilson, a British writer who shares his time between the U.K., Spain, and Portugal, writes police thrillers, including *A Small Death in Lisbon* (winner of the CWA Gold Dagger in 1999), *The Blind Man of Seville*, and *The Hidden Assassins*.

TOM WOLFE

1. *L'Assommoir* and *Nana* (tie) by Émile Zola
2. *Cousin Bette* by Honoré de Balzac
3. *Bel-Ami* by Guy de Maupassant
4. *Anna Karenina* by Leo Tolstoy
5. *The Grapes of Wrath* by John Steinbeck
6. *Appointment in Samarra* and *BUtterfield 8* (tie) by John O'Hara
7. *Sister Carrie* by Theodore Dreiser
8. *Studs Lonigan* by James T. Farrell
9. *Our Town* by Thornton Wilder
10. *Vile Bodies* by Evelyn Waugh

Tom Wolfe is a journalist (*The Electric Kool-Aid Acid Test*, *The Right Stuff*, *Hooking Up*) and novelist (*Bonfire of the Vanities*, *A Man in Full*, *I Am Charlotte Simmons*).

Appreciation of James T. Farrell's
Studs Lonigan Trilogy
by Tom Wolfe

To writers born after 1950, James T. Farrell (1904–79) is known, if at all, as a "plodding realist" who wrote a lot of dull, factual novels now as dead and buried as he is. To writers born from, say, 1925 to 1935, however, the very name James T. Farrell strums the heartstrings of youth. To be young and to read Farrell's first novel, *Studs Lonigan*! It made one tingle with exhiliration and wonder. How could anybody else understand your own inexpressible feelings so well?

A trio of novels published between 1932 and 1935, the *Studs Lonigan* trilogy is an account—"story" implies more plot than it actually has—of growing up in a lower-middle-class Irish-Catholic neighborhood in Chicago as Farrell did. He had the wit to make Studs a boy not like himself at all but like the sort of self-willed tough kid who probably made Farrell's own school days miserable by calling him "Goof" and pulling the goof's cap down over his eyes, eyeglasses and all. The book's opening lines stamp Studs's studied pose indelibly:

> Studs Lonigan, on the verge of fifteen, and wearing his first suit of long trousers, stood in the bathroom with a Sweet Caporal pasted in his mug. His hands were jammed in his trouser pockets, and he sneered. He puffed, drew the fag out of his mouth, inhaled and said to himself:
> "Well, I'm kissing the old dump goodbye tonight"—
> the old dump being a parochial junior high school.

I am convinced Farrell wrote those lines as a low-rent reprise to the far more famous lines James Joyce had opened *Ulysses* with eighteen years earlier: "Stately, plump Buck Mulligan came from the stairhead, bearing a bowl of lather on which a mirror and a razor lay crossed. A yellow dressing gown, ungirdled, was sustained gently behind him by the mild morning air. He held the bowl aloft and intoned:—*Introibo ad altare Dei.*"

Introibo ad altare Dei. For that bit of showboating by an Irish-Catholic intellectual in Dublin, Farrell had a good low-rent American raspberry: "Well, I'm kissing the old dump"—a Catholic school—"goodbye tonight."

Farrell, plodding realism and all, was quite conscious of Joyce and all other experimental writing of the early twentieth century. In *Studs Lonigan* he continually uses Joyce's most famous device, stream of consciousness, and in a more sophisticated way than the maestro. He just doesn't feel the need to keep prodding the reader with his elbow as if to say, "Be alert. This is experimental writing."

It is precisely through Joycean stream of conciousness that Farrell brings us beneath Studs's hide, which the fourteen-year-old boy keeps as thick as he can, and shows us the tenderness, the love, and the sense of beauty Studs will do anything to prevent the world, meaning the other boys his age on the block, from detecting.

To me, section IV of Chapter Four of the first novel, *Young Lonigan*, is one of the few sublime reflections of the *feeling* of *being in love* in all of literature. One scorching hot Chicago afternoon in early July when "life, along Indiana Avenue, was crawlingly lazy," Studs goes for a walk in Washington Park with the prettiest girl on the block, Lucy Scanlan. As the two fourteen-year-olds head for the park's wooded island, "Studs felt, knew, that it was going to be a great afternoon, different from every other afternoon in his whole life."

They cross the log bridge over onto the island and decide to climb up beneath the leafy dome of a huge oak tree and sit on a branch. Up in the tree it is as if they are removed from . . . the world . . . where Studs feels obliged to be so tough:

> The breeze playing upon them through the tree leaves was fine. Studs just sat there and let it play upon him, let it sift through his hair. . . . The wind seemed to Studs like the fingers of a girl, of Lucy, and when it moved through the leaves it was like a girl, like Lucy, running her hand over very expensive silk, like the silk movie actresses wore in the pictures. . . . They sat. Studs swinging his legs, and Lucy swinging hers, she chattering, himself not listening to it, only knowing that it was nice, and that she laughed and talked and was like an angel, and she was an angel playing in the sun. Suddenly, he thought of feeling her up, and he told himself he was a bastard for having such thoughts. He wasn't worthy of her, even of her fingernail, and he side-glanced at her, and he loved her, he loved her with his hands, and his lips, and his eyes, and his heart, and he loved everything about her, her dress, and voice, and the way she smiled, and her eyes, and her hair, and Lucy, all of her.

With that, Studs has enclosed himself in the cocoon of perfect love, sublime love. A century of psychologists and neuroscientists perfect in their rationalism—not to mention Studs's gottabe tough, therefore gottabe carnal, therefore gottabe perfectly cynical adolescent cohorts, such as the wonderfully named fourteen-year-old Weary Reilly—have taught us that such "sublime" moments are merely subliminal watts on the way to the one goal, which is no loftier than that of dogs in the park, namely, the old in and out.

But Studs consciously, or stream-of-consciously, rejects such . . . rationalism . . . dismisses the notion of "feeling her up" and reduces the world to two people or perhaps only one. "They sat." Farrell keeps repeating that sentence until it is like the ticking of a very big old clock. Studs and Lucy sat high up on a tree limb within a bower of leaves so thick, they shut out everything except the glittering surface of the lagoon and the sounds of children. There was no outside world. There was only Lucy, every perfect breath she breathed, every perfect morsel of her existence. Who, including any of the 20,000 attendees at the annual meeting of the Society for Neuroscience, can truthfully say that sublime feeling of two creatures dissolving into a single soul is not more thrilling than, in Rabelais's phrase, playing the two-backed beast?

> "He wanted the afternoon never to end, so that he and Lucy could sit there forever; her hands stole timidly into his, and he forgot everything in the world but Lucy. . . . And Time passed through their afternoon like a gentle, tender wind, and like death that was silent and cruel. . . . They sat, and about them their beautiful afternoon evaporated, split up and died like sun that was dying a red death in the calm sky."

This invocation of death—red, silent, and cruel—creates a mood of foreboding, if my own reaction to it is any measure. The next thing Studs knows, there are graffiti scrawled on walls along Indiana Avenue reading STUDS LOVES LUCY . . . LUCY IS CRAZY ABOUT STUDS . . . and others in that vein. Studs feels like a goof—the term boys used seventy years ago to mean dork—and hastily puts back on his bullet-proof vestments of gottabe tough, therefore gottabe carnal, therefore gottabe cynical. They had sat . . .

and that afternoon up in the tree, we eventually learn, was to be the last touch of the sublime in Studs Lonigan's short life.

The *Studs Lonigan* trilogy eventually totalled 919 pages. The life of every individual, sayeth the sage, runs along the line created by the intersection of two planes: personality and social setting. I can't think of any American novelist who ever drew that line more brilliantly than James T. Farrell in this trilogy. If this be "plodding realism," let every American novelist start plodding Studs-style, lest the American novel fall down in a heap and die, as it now seems wont to do.

MEG WOLITZER

1. *The Great Gatsby* by F. Scott Fitzgerald
2. *To the Lighthouse* by Virginia Woolf
3. *A Passage to India* by E. M. Forster
4. *Mrs. Bridge* by Evan S. Connell
5. *Dubliners* by James Joyce
6. *Madame Bovary* by Gustave Flaubert
7. *War and Peace* by Leo Tolstoy
8. *Hard Times* by Charles Dickens
9. *Goodbye, Columbus* by Philip Roth
10. *My Ántonia* by Willa Cather

Meg Wolitzer has written seven novels, including *The Position* and *The Wife*. Her short fiction has appeared in *Best American Short Stories* and *The Pushcart Prize*.

A GUIDE
TO THE
WORLD'S
BEST
BOOKS

NOTES ON THE BOOK DESCRIPTIONS

How to organize the descriptions of the 544 works of literature mentioned in all 125 Top Ten lists? Here is my method for that madness. The books are listed in order according to the total number of points they received: a first-place pick is worth ten points, and a tenth-place pick is worth one point. Books that received the same number of points are arranged alphabetically by author.

Entries begin with a bracketed number reflecting their vote total. Each description ends with a set of initials indicating who listed the book and the points they awarded it. The Index of Authors by Initials provides a key to these initials.

The specific story collections and novellas of several writers, including Raymond Carver, Anton Chekhov, Andre Dubus, Alice Munro, Flannery O'Connor, and Eudora Welty, are covered in omnibus descriptions, such as "The stories of Anton Chekhov" or "The stories of Andre Dubus." The point totals for these entries reflect all the votes received by the individual works combined.

Similarly, individual titles that are part of a series or grouping—such as the three works in Robertson Davies' *Deptford* trilogy, the four novels comprising John Updike's *Rabbit* series, and specific books or sections of the Bible—are addressed in single, all-encompassing entries.

(171) *Anna Karenina* by Leo Tolstoy (1877).

Anna's adulterous love affair with Count Vronsky—which follows an inevitable, devastating road from their dizzyingly erotic first encounter at a ball to Anna's exile from society and her famous, fearful end—is a masterwork of tragic love. What makes the novel so deeply satisfying, though, is how Tolstoy balances the story of Anna's passion with a second semiautobiographical story of Levin's spirituality and domesticity. Levin commits his life to simple human values: his marriage to Kitty, his faith in God, and his farming. Tolstoy enchants us with Anna's sin, then proceeds to educate us with Levin's virtue.

(MB 10) (JBarn 7) (CB 7) (JBud 6) (BMC 1) (PCap 4) (PC 5) (CD 7) (GG 7) (HaJ 10) (DLod 4) (NM 10) (PM 2) (CM 6) (SM 10) (SO'N 7) (TP 9) (RPri 8) (FP 10) (APat 10) (JSalt 3) (AMS 10) (SS 2) (ST 9) (TW 7)

(160) *Madame Bovary* by Gustave Flaubert (1857).

Of the many nineteenth-century novels about adulteresses, only *Madame Bovary* features a heroine frankly detested by her author. Flaubert battled for five years to complete his meticulous portrait of extramarital romance in the French provinces, and he complained endlessly in letters about his love-starved main character—so inferior, he felt, to himself. In the end, however, he came to peace with her, famously saying, *"Madame Bovary: c'est moi."* A model of gorgeous style and perfect characterization, the novel is a testament to how yearning for a higher life both elevates and destroys us.

(RB 3) (JBarn 10) (BMC 5) (PCap 6) (PC 10) (MCunn 9) (MD 8) (MGait 6) (DG 2) (MGri 6) (KHarr 3) (JI 1) (DLod 2) (TM 8) (VM 9) (EM 6) (CM 7) (LM 10) (RPri 10) (AMS 4) (LS 1) (JSalt 5) (SS 9) (BU 7) (AW 8) (MW 5)

(150) *War and Peace* by Leo Tolstoy (1869).

Mark Twain supposedly said of this masterpiece, "Tolstoy carelessly neglects to include a boat race." Everything else is included in this epic novel that revolves around Napoleon's invasion of Russia in 1812. Tolstoy is as adept at drawing panoramic battle scenes as he is at describing individual feeling in hundreds of characters from all strata of society, but it is his depiction of Prince Andrey, Natasha, and Pierre—who struggle with love and with finding the right way to live—that makes this book beloved. (PA 9) (RB 4) (AB 9) (SCraw 4) (RFD 9) (JF 9) (PF 10) (BH 1) (AHas 8) (HaJ 8) (KK 8) (TK 6) (NM 9) (PM 1) (APhil 4) (IR 8) (RR 10) (LDR 4) (GS 8) (CS 8) (AMS 9) (MW 4)

(131) *Lolita* by Vladimir Nabokov (1955).

"Lolita, light of my life, fire of my loins. My sin, my soul." So begins the Russian master's infamous novel about Humbert Humbert, a middle-aged man who falls madly, obsessively in love with a twelve-year-old "nymphet," Dolores Haze. So he marries the girl's mother. When she dies he becomes Lolita's father. As Humbert describes their car trip—a twisted mockery of the American road novel—Nabokov depicts love, power, and obsession in audacious, shockingly funny language. (MB 9) (JB 5) (JBud 10) (MCunn 5) (JF 3) (MGait 9) (AGold 9) (MGri 7) (DH 10) (AMH 1) (WK 6) (ML 4) (VM 8) (BAM 9) (SM 8) (APat 8) (JS 10) (SS 10)

(126) *The Adventures of Huckleberry Finn* by Mark Twain (1884).

Hemingway proclaimed, "All modern American literature comes from . . . 'Huckleberry Finn.' " But one can read it simply as a straightforward adventure story in which two comrades of convenience, the parentally abused rascal Huck and fugitive slave Jim, escape the laws and conventions of society on a raft trip down the Mississippi. Alternatively, it's a subversive satire in which Twain uses the only superficially naïve Huck to comment bitingly on the evils of racial bigotry, religious hypocrisy, and capitalist greed he observes in a host of other largely unsympathetic characters. Huck's climactic decision to "light out for the Territory ahead of the rest" rather than submit to the starched standards of "civilization" reflects a uniquely American strain of individualism and nonconformity stretching from Daniel Boone to *Easy Rider*.

(LKA 9) (KA 2) (RB 8) (MSB 2) (CB 3) (FC 3) (CE 7) (PE 8) (AGold 1) (BH 5) (KH 5) (CH 9) (HK 4) (SK 9) (WK 2) (WL 6) (BAM 4) (JCO 1) (RBP 7) (JR 3) (LDR 1) (GS 9) (CS 4) (SS 7) (SV 7)

(111) *Hamlet* by William Shakespeare (1600).

The most famous play ever written, *Hamlet* tells the story of a melancholic prince charged with avenging the murder of his father at the hands of his uncle, who then married his mother and, becoming King of Denmark, robbed Hamlet of the throne. Told the circumstances of this murder and usurpation by his father's ghost, Hamlet is plunged deep into brilliant and profound reflection on the problems of existence, which meditations delay his revenge at the cost of innocent lives. When he finally acts decisively, Hamlet takes with him every remaining major character in a crescendo of violence unmatched in Shakespearean theater.

(CE 10) (KH 8) (AHud 6) (KK 9) (HK 8) (DLod 9) (VM 10) (BAM 10) (SO'N 10) (RBP 8) (APhil 6) (GS 6) (SV 9) (AW 2)

(110) *The Great Gatsby* by F. Scott Fitzgerald (1925).

Perhaps the most searching fable of the American Dream ever

written, this glittering novel of the Jazz Age paints an unforgettable portrait of its day—the flappers, the bootleg gin, the careless, giddy wealth. Self-made millionaire Jay Gatsby, determined to win back the heart of the girl he loved and lost, emerges as an emblem for romantic yearning, and the novel's narrator, Nick Carroway, brilliantly illuminates the post–World War I end to American innocence.

(MB 6) (CB 6) (JLB 1) (MCon 10) (MCunn 6) (JF 6) (DG 7) (AHud 1) (TK 3) (WL 4) (BAM 8) (PM 4) (EM 2) (RBP 9) (TP 3) (APat 6) (VV 3) (SV 1) (AW 5) (RW 9) (MW 10)

(107) *In Search of Lost Time* by Marcel Proust (1913–27).
It's about time. No, really. This seven-volume, three-thousand-page work is only superficially a mordant critique of French (mostly high) society in the belle époque. Both as author and as "Marcel," the first-person narrator whose childhood memories are evoked by a crumbling madeleine cookie, Proust asks some of the same questions Einstein did about our notions of time and memory. As we follow the affairs, the badinage, and the betrayals of dozens of characters over the years, time is the highway and memory the driver.

(PA 6) (MC 4) (JF 7) (PF 9) (MG 8) (JH 9) (AHas 6) (HaJ 6) (DL 10) (DMe 3) (CM 9) (APhil 5) (RPow 1) (FP 8) (LDR 10) (AW 6)

(105) The stories of Anton Chekhov (1860–1904).
The son of a freed Russian serf, Anton Chekhov became a doctor who, between the patients he often treated without charge, invented the modern short story. The form had been overdecorated with trick endings and swags of atmosphere. Chekhov freed it to reflect the earnest urgencies of ordinary lives in crises through prose that blended a deeply compassionate imagination

with precise description. "He remains a great teacher-healer-sage," Allan Gurganus observed of Chekhov's stories, which "continue to haunt, inspire, and baffle."

(SCraw 5) (MGait 4) (AG 9) (KH 9) (EH 10) (HaJ 7) (VM 5) (DMe 7) (SM 1) (DM 10) (SO'N 8) (RR 9) (APhil 3) (FP 7) (GS 4) (JS 7)

(100) *Middlemarch* by George Eliot (1871–72).

Dorothea Brooke is a pretty young idealist whose desire to improve the world leads her to marry the crusty pedant Casaubon. This mistake takes her down a circuitous and painful path in search of happiness. The novel, which explores society's brakes on women and deteriorating rural life, is as much a chronicle of the English town of Middlemarch as it is the portrait of a lady. Eliot excels at parsing moments of moral crisis so that we feel a character's anguish and resolve. Her intelligent sympathy for even the most unlikable people redirects our own moral compass toward charity rather than enmity.

(KA 7) (MB 4) (AB 8) (PC 6) (JC 6) (SCraw 6) (KJF 10) (GG 6) (MG 1) (MGri 2) (AG 8) (KHarr 4) (AHas 5) (AHud 3) (DL 9) (DLod 5) (LM 2) (FP 3) (JR 5)

(91) *Don Quixote* by Miguel de Cervantes (1605, 1615).

Considered literature's first great novel, *Don Quixote* is the comic tale of a dream-driven nobleman whose devotion to medieval romances inspires him to go in quest of chivalric glory and the love of a lady who doesn't know him. Famed for its hilarious antics with windmills and nags, *Don Quixote* offers timeless meditations on heroism, imagination, and the art of writing itself. Still, the heart of the book is the relationship between the deluded knight and his proverb-spewing squire, Sancho Panza. If their misadventures illuminate human folly, it is a folly redeemed by

simple love, which makes Sancho stick by his mad master "no matter how many foolish things he does."
(SA 6) (PA 10) (RB 10) (PC 7) (FC 9) (CE 9) (KJF 8) (AGold 8) (WL 9) (TP 10) (LDR 5)

(88) *Moby-Dick* by Herman Melville (1851).

This sweeping saga of obsession, vanity, and vengeance at sea can be read as a harrowing parable, a gripping adventure story, or a semiscientific chronicle of the whaling industry. No matter, the book rewards patient readers with some of fiction's most memorable characters, from mad Captain Ahab to the titular white whale that crippled him, from the honorable pagan Queequeg to our insightful narrator/surrogate ("Call me") Ishmael, to that hell-bent vessel itself, the *Pequod*.
(PA 8) (RB 9) (JB 6) (AB 3) (BMC 4) (MC 7) (DAD 7) (JH 7) (AHas 3) (JI 8) (NM 4) (BAM 2) (PM 10) (JCO 2) (RPow 1) (FP 4) (IR 1) (LDR 2)

(87) *Great Expectations* by Charles Dickens (1860–61).

Dickens gives a twist to an ancient storyline—of the child of royal birth raised in humble surroundings. Looking back on his life, Pip describes his poor youth near marshes in rural England—his chance encounter with a murderous convict, his experiences with the strange Miss Havisham, who always wears a wedding dress, and his love for her beautiful adopted daughter Estella. As he approaches adulthood, Pip learns that he has a secret benefactor who arranges opportunities for him in London, wherein lies the tale, and the twist.
(CB 8) (PC 8) (EDon 7) (AH 9) (JI 10) (TK 7) (JL 10) (RPow 1) (RPri 9) (ES 10) (SS 8)

(85) *Ulysses* by James Joyce (1922).

Filled with convoluted plotting, scrambled syntax, puns, neologisms, and arcane mythological allusions, *Ulysses* recounts the misadventures of schlubby Dublin advertising salesman Leopold Bloom on a single day, June 16, 1904. As Everyman Bloom and a host of other characters act out, on a banal and quotidian scale, the major episodes of Homer's *Odyssey*—including encounters with modern-day sirens and a Cyclops—Joyce's bawdy mock-epic suggests the improbability, perhaps even the pointlessness, of heroism in the modern age.

(PA 5) (JB 8) (CB 9) (MGait 10) (JH 6) (KK 7) (DLod 7) (DMe 2) (JCO 9) (RPow 1) (RP 6) (IR 6) (LDR 9)

(81) *The Odyssey* by Homer (ninth century B.C.E.?).

Where *The Iliad* tells of war, *The Odyssey* is the story of survival and reconciliation following the ten-year battle with Troy. Where Achilles was defined by warrior brutality, Odysseus, King of Ithaca, is defined by his intelligence and wit. This epic poem follows Odysseus on his adventures as he struggles—against the threats of sea monsters and the temptation of the sirens' song—to be reunited with his son Telemachus, his faithful, clever queen Penelope, and their kingdom.

(RB 6) (FC 6) (AHud 9) (KK 10) (WL 10) (DLod 10) (BM 8) (RPow 1) (RP 10) (AP 10) (APhil 1)

(79) *Dubliners* by James Joyce (1916).

Although many of these largely autobiographical stories evoke themes of death, illness, and stasis, nearly all offer their characters redemption—or at least momentary self-knowledge—through what Joyce called "epiphanies," in which defeat or disappointment is transformed by a sudden, usually life-altering flash of awareness. The collection's emotional centerpiece is its concluding tale, "The Dead," which moves from a New Year's Eve party where guests muse about issues of the day—the Catholic church, Irish nationalism, Freddie Malins's worrying drunkenness—to a man's discovery of his wife weeping over a boy who died for love of her. A profound portrait of identity and loneliness, it is Joyce's most compassionate work.

(JLB 9) (MCunn 4) (KJF 1) (PF 7) (DG 5) (MG 7) (HK 7) (DMcF 1) (DMe 4) (LM 9) (RBP 4) (JS 5) (LS 10) (MW 6)

(72) *Crime and Punishment* by Fyodor Dostoevsky (1866).

In the peak heat of a St. Petersburg summer, an erstwhile university student, Raskolnikov, commits literature's most famous fictional crime, bludgeoning a pawnbroker and her sister with an axe. What follows is a psychological chess match between Raskolnikov and a wily detective that moves toward a form of redemption for our antihero. Relentlessly philosophical and psychological, *Crime and Punishment* tackles freedom and strength, suffering and madness, illness and fate, and the pressures of the modern urban world on the soul, while asking if "great men" have license to forge their own moral codes.

(PA 7) (DG 3) (AMH 2) (JL 1) (NM 8) (TM 7) (BM 10) (JCO 10) (FP 1) (IR 7) (VV 9) (AW 7)

(72) *King Lear* by William Shakespeare (1605).

Considered one of Shakespeare's four "core tragedies"—with *Hamlet*, *Othello*, and *Macbeth*—*King Lear* commences with Lear, having achieved great age but little wisdom, dividing his kingdom among his three daughters in return for their proclamations of love for him. Two of his daughters, evil to the core, falsely profess their love, while Cordelia, his good and true daughter, refuses his request. Enraged, Lear gives his kingdom to his evil daughters and banishes Cordelia. Lear pays a dear price for this rash act. The play systematically strips him of his kingdom, title, retainers, clothes, and sanity in a process so cruel and unrelenting as to be nearly unendurable.

(MCunn 10) (MG 5) (WL 8) (AHas 10) (IP 10) (RP 8) (AP 5) (IR 10) (SS 6)

(67) *Emma* by Jane Austen (1816).

The story of Miss Woodhouse—busybody, know-it-all, and general relationship enthusiast—is a comedy of manners deftly laced with social criticism. The charm largely inheres in Emma's imperfections: her slightly spoiled maneuverings, her highly fallible matchmaking, her inability to know her own heart. Emma teeters from lovable one moment to tiresome and self-centered the next. In writing her story, Austen found an ideal venue for her note-perfect, never-equaled archness.

(SCraw 8) (CS 10) (EDon 8) (MD 9) (KJF 5) (GG 9) (AG 2) (DLod 6) (BAM 1) (JR 9)

(66) *One Hundred Years of Solitude* by Gabriel García Márquez (1967).

Widely considered the most popular work in Spanish since *Don Quixote*, this novel—part fantasy, part social history of Colombia—sparked fiction's "Latin boom" and the popularization of magic realism. Over a century that seems to move backward and forward simultaneously, the forgotten and offhandedly magical village of Macondo—home to a Faulknerian plethora of incest, floods, massacres, civil wars, dreamers, prudes, and prostitutes—loses its Edenic innocence as it is increasingly exposed to civilization.

(LKA 1) (RB 1) (PCle 10) (ED 6) (CD 4) (KJF 2) (MGri 8) (AH 4) (JH 3) (JI 3) (WL 1) (APat 9) (FP 2) (JS 9) (AMS 3)

(63) *The Sound and the Fury* by William Faulkner (1929).

A modernist classic of Old South decay, this novel circles the travails of the Compson family from four different narrative perspectives. All are haunted by the figure of Caddy, the only daughter, whom Faulkner described as "a beautiful and tragic little girl." Surrounding the trials of the family itself are the usual Faulkner suspects: alcoholism, suicide, racism, religion, money, and violence both seen and unseen. In the experimental style of the book, Quentin Compson summarizes the confused honor and tragedy that Faulkner relentlessly evokes: "theres a curse on us its not our fault is it our fault."

(LKA 3) (RB 7) (JLB 10) (GDG 8) (KH 10) (AH 5) (DMe 5) (SM 7) (JCO 8)

(62) *To the Lighthouse* by Virginia Woolf (1927).

The Ramsays and their eight children vacation with an assortment of scholarly and artistic houseguests by the Scottish seaside. Mainly set on two days ten years apart, the novel describes the loss, love, and disagreements of family life while reaching toward the bigger question—"What is the meaning of life?"—that Woolf addresses in meticulously crafted, modernist prose that is impressionistic without being vague or sterile.

(MCunn 7) (MD 2) (MGait 5) (MG 3) (HK 6) (SM 9) (SO'N 4) (RPri 3) (RR 8) (LS 6) (MW 9)

(61) *The Brothers Karamazov* by Fyodor Dostoevsky (1880).

In perhaps the consummate Russian novel, Dostoevsky dramatizes the spiritual conundrums of nineteenth-century Russia through the story of three brothers and their father's murder. Hedonistic Dmitri, tortured intellectual Ivan, and saintly Alyosha embody distinct philosophical positions, while remaining full-fledged human beings. Issues such as free will, secularism, and Russia's unique destiny are argued not through authorial polemic, but through the confessions, diatribes, and nightmares of the characters themselves. An unsparing portrayal of human vice and weakness, the novel ultimately imparts a vision of redemption. Dostoevsky's passion, doubt, and imaginative power compel even the secular West he scorned.

(RB 2) (DAD 9) (JF 10) (BH 10) (HaJ 9) (NM 7) (EM 4) (DMe 10)

(56) *The Divine Comedy* **by Dante Alighieri (1321).**
Dante's poetic trilogy traces the journey of a man's soul from darkness (*The Inferno*) to the revelation of divine light (*Paradiso*) while providing commentary and gossip about the politics and prominent families of Florence. Led in his pilgrimage through the underworld and purgatory by the Greek poet, Virgil, Dante is escorted into paradise by his early beloved, Beatrice, while learning that, in order to ascend, he must be transformed.

(CB 10) (PCap 8) (MD 5) (AHud 8) (EM 8) (RP 7) (VV 10)

(55) The stories of Flannery O'Connor (1925–64).
Full of violence, mordant comedy, and a fierce Catholic vision that is bent on human salvation at any cost, Flannery O'Connor's stories are like no others. Bigots, intellectual snobs, shyster preachers, and crazed religious seers—a full cavalcade of what critics came to call "grotesques"—careen through her tales, and O'Connor gleefully displays the moral inadequacy of all of them. Twentieth-century short stories often focus on tiny moments, but O'Connor's stories, with their unswerving eye for vanity and their profound sense of the sacred, feel immense.

(JLB 6) (JC 1) (MCunn 1) (CE 5) (CH 2) (BH 7) (KH 4) (WK 10) (WL 2) (BM 1) (DMcF 7) (EM 1) (JS 4) (LS 4)

(54) *Tristram Shandy* **by Laurence Sterne (1759–67).**
Sterne promises the "life and opinions" of his protagonist. Yet halfway through the fourth volume of nine, we are still in the first

day of the hero's life thanks to marvelous digressions and what the narrator calls "unforeseen stoppages"—detailing the quirky habits of his eccentric family members and their friends. This broken narrative is unified by Sterne's comic touch, which shimmers in this thoroughly entertaining novel that harks back to *Don Quixote* and foreshadows *Ulysses*.
(PA 1) (PC 9) (PE 10) (ALK 6) (JL 2) (DLod 3) (TM 9) (JR 4) (LDR 3) (GS 7)

(52) *Pride and Prejudice* by Jane Austen (1813).

"It is a truth universally acknowledged, that a single man in possession of a good fortune must be in want of a wife," reads this novel's famous opening line. This matching of wife to single man—or good fortune—makes up the plot of perhaps the happiest, smartest romance ever written. Austen's genius was to make Elizabeth Bennet a reluctant, sometimes crabby equal to her Mr. Darcy, making *Pride and Prejudice* as much a battle of wits as it is a love story.
(KA 8) (MC 6) (RFD 5) (AH 7) (NM 6) (CM 10) (IP 5) (IR 2) (AT 3)

(52) *Wuthering Heights* by Emily Brontë (1847).

The author's only novel, published a year before her death, centers on the doomed love between Heathcliff, a tormented orphan, and Catherine Earnshaw, his benefactor's vain and willful daughter. Passion brings them together, but class differences, and the bitterness it inspires, keeps them apart and continues to take its toll on the next generation. *Wuthering Heights* tells you why they say that love hurts.
(DG 10) (JH 8) (AH 10) (TK 10) (SMK 7) (PM 7)

(50) The Bible.

See Andrew Hudgin's appreciation on page 78.
(AHud 10) (HK 10) (EM 10) (RPow 1) (RP 9) (JSalt 10)

(49) Pale Fire by Vladimir Nabokov (1962).
"It is the commentator who has the last word," claims Charles
Kinbote in this novel masquerading as literary criticism. The text
of the book includes a 999-line poem by the murdered American
poet John Shade and a line-by-line commentary by Kinbote, a
scholar from the country of Zembla. Nabokov even provides an
index to this playful, provocative story of poetry, interpretation,
identity, and madness, which is full to bursting with allusions,
tricks, and the author's inimitable wordplay.
(MC 9) (MGait 8) (MGri 10) (DL 7) (APhil 7) (VV 8)

(47) *Absalom, Absalom!* by William Faulkner (1936).
Weaving mythic tales of biblical urgency with the experimental
techniques of high modernism, Faulkner bridged the past and
future. This is the story of Thomas Sutpen, a rough-hewn striver
who came to Mississippi in 1833 with a gang of wild slaves from
Haiti to build a dynasty. Almost in reach, his dream is undone by
plagues of biblical (and Faulknerian) proportions: racism, incest,
war, fratricide, pride, and jealousy. Through the use of multiple
narrators, Faulkner turns this gripping Yoknapatawpha saga into a
profound and dazzling meditation on truth, memory, history, and
literature itself.
(PCap 1) (JF 5) (AG 5) (JH 4) (AHas 7) (AHud 2) (HaJ 5) (EM 3) (LDR 8)
(LS 7)

(45) *The Portrait of a Lady* by Henry James (1881).
James's *Portrait* is of that superior creature Isabel Archer, an
assured American girl who is determined to forge her destiny in
the drawing rooms of Europe. To this end, she weds the older and
more cultivated Gilbert Osmond, and eventually finds that she is
less the author of her fate than she thought. Throughout, James

gives us a combination of careful psychological refraction and truly diabolical plotting. The result is a book at once chilling and glorious.

(KA 6) (PC 2) (SCraw 3) (GG 10) (VM 3) (CM 8) (JR 7) (KA 6)

(44) *To Kill a Mockingbird* by Harper Lee (1960).
Tomboy Scout and her brother Jem are the children of the profoundly decent widower Atticus Finch, a small-town Alabama lawyer defending a black man accused of raping a white woman. Although Tom Robinson's trial is the centerpiece of this Pulitzer Prize–winning novel—raising profound questions of race and conscience—this is, at heart, a tale about the fears and mysteries of growing up, as the children learn about bravery, empathy, and societal expectations through a series of evocative set pieces that conjure the Depression-era South.

(CB 5) (JBud 7) (PCle 7) (MCon 8) (SMK 8) (AMS 1) (SV 8)

(43) *The Canterbury Tales* by Geoffrey Chaucer (1380s?).
Not so much a single poem as a gathering of voices ranging from bawdy to pious, this captivating work presents a panoramic view of medieval England. Vivid, direct, and often irresistibly funny, the tales are told by pilgrims making their way to Canterbury to visit the shrine of Saint Thomas Beckett. Each night another member of the party—a knight, a scholar, a miller—tells a story, and tale by tale, a portrait emerges of the diversity and delight of human possibility.

(RB 5) (CE 8) (AHud 7) (DLod 8) (EM 7) (FC 8)

(42) *Heart of Darkness* by Joseph Conrad (1899).
In a novella with prose as lush and brooding as its jungle setting, Phillip Marlowe travels to the Belgian Congo to pilot a trading

company's steamship. There he witnesses the brutality of colonial exploitation, epitomized by Kurtz, an enigmatic white ivory trader. To understand evil, Marlowe seeks out Kurtz, whom he finds amongst the natives, dying. After Kurtz laments his own depravity through his final, anguished words—"The horror! The horror!"—Marlowe must decide what to tell his widow back home. (LKA 10) (PCap 2) (PM 9) (DM 8) (SO'N 6) (RW 7)

(42) *Mrs. Dalloway* by Virginia Woolf (1925).

This masterpiece of concision and interior monologue recounts events in the life of Clarissa Dalloway, a delicate, upper-class London wife and mother, as she prepares for a party at her home on a single day in June 1923. In a parallel subsidiary plot, a shell-shocked World War I veteran Clarissa encounters spirals into suicide rather than submit to soul-stealing experimental psychotherapy. The novel explores questions of time, memory, love, class, and life choices through Woolf's intricate melding of points of view and powerful use of flashback.

(RFD 3) (KJF 3) (DG 1) (MGri 3) (EH 9) (TK 4) (LMill 9) (VV 6) (SV 4)

(41) *Invisible Man* by Ralph Ellison (1952).

This modernist novel follows the bizarre, often surreal adventures of an unnamed narrator, a black man, whose identity becomes a battleground in racially divided America. Expected to be submissive and obedient in the South, he must decipher the often contradictory rules whites set for a black man's behavior. Traveling north to Harlem, he meets white leaders intent on controlling and manipulating him. Desperate to seize control of his life, he imitates Dostoevsky's underground man, escaping down a manhole where he vows to remain until he can define himself. The book's famous last line, "Who knows, but that on the lower fre-

quencies I speak for you," suggests how it transcends race to tell a universal story of the quest for self-determination.
(SA 10) (CB 2) (BMC 6) (JC 5) (ED 7) (PE 7) (HK 3) (AW 1)

(40) *Bleak House* by Charles Dickens (1853).
Dickens is best known for his immense plots that trace every corner of Victorian society, and *Bleak House* fulfills that expectation to perfection. The plot braids the sentimental tale of an orphan unaware of her scandalous parentage with an ironic and bitterly funny satire of a lawsuit that appears to entail all of London. In doing so, the novel encompasses more than any other Dickens novel, shows the author's mature skills, and is the only Victorian novel to include an incident of human spontaneous combustion.
(AB 6) (MGait 7) (MGri 9) (SK 5) (IR 5) (BU 8)

(40) *The Trial* by Franz Kafka (1925).
The Trial is not just a book, but a cultural icon; Kafka is not just a writer but a mindset—"Kafkaesque." Here, Everyman Josef K is persecuted by a mysterious and sadistic Law, which has condemned him in advance for a crime of which he knows nothing. Modern anxieties are given near-archetypal form in this parable that seems both to foretell the totalitarian societies to come and to mourn our alienation from a terrible Old Testament God.
(ED 2) (JF 8) (JL 9) (BM 7) (DMe 6) (JS 8)

(40) *Beloved* by Toni Morrison (1987).
It's a choice no mother should have to make. In 1856, escaped slave Margaret Garner decided to kill her infant daughter rather than return her to slavery. Her desperate act created a national sensation. Where Garner's true-life drama ends, *Beloved* begins. In this Pulitzer Prize–winning novel, the murdered child, Beloved,

returns from the grave years later to haunt her mother Sethe. Aided by her daughter Denver and lover Paul D, Sethe confronts the all-consuming guilt precipitated by the ghostly embodiment of her dead child. Rendered in poetic language, *Beloved* is a stunning indictment of slavery "full of baby's venom."

(SA 1) (BMC 7) (JC 2) (ED 5) (DAD 10) (DG 4) (DH 3) (AH 6) (HK 2)

(39) *Jane Eyre* by Charlotte Brontë (1847).

Like *Wuthering Heights*, this is a romance set in the isolated moors of rural England the Brontës called home. Its title character is an exceptionally independent orphan who becomes governess to the children of an appealing but troubled character, Mr. Rochester. As their love develops, the author introduces a host of memorable characters and a shattering secret before sending Jane on yet another arduous journey.

(AB 2) (CB 4) (PC 1) (KJF 4) (EH 3) (ML 10) (LM 4) (LS 2) (AT 9)

(38) *The Stranger* by Albert Camus (1942).

The opening lines—"Mother died today. Or, maybe, yesterday. I can't be sure"—epitomize Camus's celebrated notions of "the absurd." His narrator, Meursault, a wretched little Algerian clerk sentenced to death for the murder, feels nothing: no remorse, love, guilt, grief, or hope. But he's not a sociopath; he's just honest. An embodiment of existential philosophy, he believes in no higher power and accepts that we are born only to die. Our only choice is to act "as if" life has meaning and thereby gain some freedom.

(SCraw 2) (ED 9) (DG 9) (BH 8) (KH 2) (JH 1) (HJ 7)

(36) *The Grapes of Wrath* by John Steinbeck (1939).

A powerful portrait of Depression-era America, this gritty social novel follows the Joad family as they flee their farm in the Oklahoma dust bowl for the promised land of California. While limping across a crippled land, Ma and Pa Joad, their pregnant daughter Rose of Sharon, and their recently paroled son Tom sleep in ramshackle Hoovervilles filled with other refugees and encounter hardship, death, and deceit. While vividly capturing the plight of a nation, Steinbeck renders people who have lost everything but their dignity.

(SA 2) (PCle 1) (KH 1) (KK 1) (WL 3) (GP 8) (BU 4) (SV 10) (TW 6)

(35) *All the King's Men* by Robert Penn Warren (1946).

In perhaps the most famous American political novel, Warren tracks the unsentimental education of Jack Burden, an upper-class, college-educated lackey to Willie Stark, the populist governor of Louisiana (whom Warren modeled on Huey Long). Burden spirals into self-loathing as he learns how political sausage is made, then finds a moral compass after Stark's assassination—all told in a bleak poetry that marries Sartre and Tennessee Williams.

(JBud 8) (JLB 7) (RFD 4) (DH 6) (GP 10)

(32) *The Good Soldier* by Ford Madox Ford (1915).

A novel made seminally modernist through an unreliable narration that is part cubist, part Freudian, it tells the story of the prissy and rather thick John Dowell and his wife Florence who repeatedly meet British soldier Edward Ashburnham and his wife over the years at various upper-crust European spas. Dowell's blindness to Edward and Florence's hidden-in-plain-sight affair finally lifts, but his class solidarity with the man he calls a "good soldier" endures—a tension that creates an exquisite portrait of denial and the death throes of Edwardian gentility.

(JBarn 4) (MG 10) (DL 8) (TP 6) (APat 4)

(32) *The Catcher in the Rye* by J. D. Salinger (1951).

After being dismissed from another prep school, Holden Caulfield—whose slangy, intimate narration defines this novel—has a series of misadventures in Manhattan before going home for Christmas. Haunted by the death of brother Allie, he wants what he cannot have—to snare the elusive Jane Gallagher, to run away with his sister Phoebe, to "catch" innocent youths before they fall into the "phony" world of adults. A timeless voice of adolescent rage and assurance, Holden may rank highest in the pantheon of antiestablishment heroes.

(BMC 10) (CH 8) (AH 8) (AGold 6)

(31) *Persuasion* by Jane Austen (1817).

Eight years ago, Anne Elliot was persuaded by a friend to break off her engagement to a handsome naval officer because he lacked wealth and name. Now twenty-seven, her romantic prospects a dim memory, she encounters him once again, only now he is a grand success. Can she rekindle his love?

(KA 10) (JBarn 8) (MG 2) (EH 5) (VM 4) (APat 2)

(31) *Macbeth* by William Shakespeare (1606).

The shortest of Shakespeare's tragedies, *Macbeth* runs along at breakneck speed, elevating Macbeth from Thane of Glamis to Thane of Cawdor to King of Scotland in two brief acts. It explores the psychology of ambition, abetted by supernatural forces, as Macbeth and his wife—one of the few successful marriages in the Shakespearean canon—engineer the murder of King Duncan and Macbeth's usurpation of the Scottish throne. The pleasures of kingship are rare and brief, however, as the past comes to haunt the future, in ways obscurely prophesied by three

witches, and Macbeth is brought down with a terrible swiftness matched only by the speed of his ascent.
(PCap 7) (RFD 6) (BM 9) (SO'N 9)

(30) The Oresteia by Aeschylus (458 B.C.E.).
Before Freud there was Aeschylus, who revealed the mind's darkest impulses through this trilogy of plays mapping the mad round of retaliations that bring down the royal house of Atreus. In the first play, the Greek King Agamemnon—who sacrificed his daughter Iphigenia to appease the gods before setting sail for the Trojan War—and his slave, Cassandra, are slain by his wife, Clytemnestra. In the second play, Clytemnestra is slain by her son, Orestes (egged on by his sister Electra to avenge their father's murder). In the final play, Orestes is freed from the Furies (or the curse) because, unlike the other characters—who search for scapegoats—he admits his own culpability, ending the cycle of violence through personal responsibility.
(PCap 10) (BU 10) (AW 10)

(30) The Scarlet Letter by Nathaniel Hawthorne (1850).
Hester Prynne is a sinner in the hands of seventeenth-century Puritans. Forced to wear the letter "A" for adultery, she is publicly disgraced and shunned. Despite her condemnation, Hester refuses to reveal the identity of her lover. Her husband, Roger Chillingworth, returns unexpectedly and seeks revenge. Chillingworth is a torment to the guilt-stricken minister, Arthur Dimmesdale, as is Pearl, the child born of Hester and Dimmesdale's adultery. Ultimately, it is the fallen lovers, not the Puritans, who come to understand the nature of sin and redemption.
(PA 4) (JI 7) (TK 8) (SMK 3) (AS 8)

(29) *Alice's Adventures in Wonderland* **by Lewis Carroll (1865).**
Young Alice follows a worried, hurrying White Rabbit into a
topsy-turvy world, where comestibles make you grow and shrink,
and flamingoes are used as croquet mallets. There she meets
many now-beloved characters, such as the Mad Hatter, the
Cheshire Cat, and the Queen of Hearts, in this linguistically
playful tale that takes a child's-eye view of the absurdities of adult
manners.
(KA 9) (RFD 2) (SMK 6) (JL 5) (DLod 1) (SO'N 2) (RP 4)

(28) *The Red and the Black* **by Stendhal (1830).**
Stendhal inaugurated French realism with his revolutionary collo-
quial style and the famous pronouncement, "A novel is a mirror
carried along a highway." Julien Sorel, the tragic antihero, rises
from peasant roots through high society. In his character, the
"red" of soldiering and a bygone age of heroism vies with the
"black" world of the priesthood, careerism, and hypocrisy.
(JL 7) (NM 3) (JCO 5) (LDR 6) (ES 7)

(28) *Rabbit Angstrom—Rabbit, Run* **(1960),** *Rabbit Redux* **(1971),**
Rabbit Is Rich **(1981),** *Rabbit at Rest* **(1990)—by John Updike.**
Read as four discrete stories or as a seamless quartet, the *Rabbit* novels are a tour de force chronicle, critique, and eloquent appreciation
of the American white Protestant middle-class male and the swiftly
shifting culture around him in the last four decades of the twentieth
century. From his feckless youth as a promising high school athlete
and unready husband and father in *Rabbit, Run;* through vulgar
affluence, serial infidelity, and guilt as a car dealer in *Rabbit Redux;* to
angry bewilderment over 1970s social upheaval in *Rabbit Is Rich,* the
meaningfully named Rabbit Angstrom gamely tries to keep up with

it all, to be a good guy. But the world is too much with, and for, Rabbit, who staggers through literal and metaphorical heart failure before finally falling in *Rabbit at Rest*.

(LKA 5) (JBarn 2) (GDG 2) (KK 4) (TM 1) (TP 2) (RR 3) (SS 1) (ST 8)

(27) The stories of Isaac Babel (1894–1940).

"Let me finish my work" was Babel's final plea before he was executed for treason on the orders of Josef Stalin. Though incomplete, his work is enduring. In addition to plays and screenplays, some in collaboration with Sergei Eisenstein, Babel made his mark with *The Odessa Stories*, which focused on gangsters from his native city, and even more important, the collection entitled *Red Cavalry*. Chaos, bloodshed, and mordant fatalism dominate those interconnected stories, set amid the Red Army's Polish campaign during the Russian Civil War. Babel, himself a combat veteran, embodied the war's extremes in the (doubtless autobiographically based) war correspon- dent–propagandist Kiril Lyutov and the brutally violent Cossack soldiers whom he both fears and admires. Several mas- terpieces herein (including "A Letter," "My First Goose," and "Berestechko") anticipate Hemingway's later achievement, and confirm Babel's place among the great modernist writers.

(JBud 5) (PF 6) (AF 4) (RP 2) (JSalt 2) (GS 5) (JS 3)

(27) *Tender Is the Night* by F. Scott Fitzgerald (1934).

The heartbreaking, semiautobiographical story of two expatriate Americans living in France during the 1920s: a gifted young psy- chiatrist, Dick Diver, and the wealthy, troubled patient who becomes his wife. In this tragic tale of romance and character, her lush lifestyle soon begins to destroy Diver, as alcohol, infidelities, and mental illness claim his hopes. Of the book, Fitzgerald wrote, "*Gatsby* was a tour de force, but this is a confession of faith." (RFD 8) (PF 8) (DH 2) (SM 5) (ES 2) (ST 2)

(27) *A Portrait of the Artist as a Young Man* by James Joyce (1916). In this semiautobiographical novel, hero Stephen Dedalus rejects the world of his youth—Ireland in its provincialism, nationalism, Catholicism, and sexual guilt—for art. From its stream of consciousness technique to its descriptions of expatriate life in Paris, *Portrait* inspired nearly all the touchstones of twentieth-century modernism, the most important of which is the artist as a misunderstood god.
(GG 3) (TK 5) (BAM 7) (ST 10) (SV 2)

(26) *Catch-22* by Joseph Heller (1962).
After flying forty-eight missions, Yossarian, a bomber pilot in World War II, is going crazy trying to find an excuse to be grounded. But the military has a catch, Catch 22, which states, (a) a sane man must fight, unless (b) he can prove he is insane, in which case (a) must apply—for what sane person doesn't want to avoid fighting? This novel is a congery of appallingly funny, logical, logistical, and mortal horrors. It defined the cultural moment of the 1960s, when black humor became America's pop idiom.
(MCon 6) (RFD 1) (CH 10) (IR 9)

(26) *Slaughterhouse-Five* by Kurt Vonnegut (1969).
Part science fiction, part war story, this is the story of Billy Pilgrim, a former World War II prisoner of war who survived the firebombing of Dresden, as did Vonnegut himself. Abducted by visitors from the planet Trafalmadore, Pilgrim comes "unstuck in time" and is thus able to revisit key points in his life and even his

future. Written at the height of the Vietnam War, this muscular satire reveals the absurdity and brutality of modern war.
(KA 5) (MCon 3) (DC 9) (CH 6) (GS 3)

(24) The stories of John Cheever (1912–82).
Seemingly confined to recording the self-inflations and petty hypocrisies of suburban WASPs, Cheever's short fiction actually redefined the story form, mixing minimalism and myth to create uniquely American tragicomedy. A master of the ambiguous ending, Cheever could also be direct: In "The Swimmer," a man dreams of his family as he blithely "swims" home through his neighbors' backyard pools, only to collapse at the door of his empty, locked house.
(LKA 2) (TCB1) (EC 10) (DMcF 5) (FP 6)

(24) *Paradise Lost* by John Milton (1667).
Recasting the biblical story of Adam and Eve's fall from grace, this epic poem details Satan's origins, his desire for revenge, his transformation into the serpent, and his seduction of Eve. The poem extends our understanding of Christian myth in lush and challenging language. Though Milton seeks to explain "the ways of God to man," he gives Satan—"Better to reign in hell than serve in heaven"—the best lines.
(AB 10) (MC 3) (FC 2) (AHas 9)

(24) *The Aeneid* by Virgil (19 B.C.E.).
Like Achilles and Odysseus before him, Aeneas makes sacrifices for friendship and descends into the world of the dead, but he never finds peace or a true home. Aeneas does find support and love from the Queen of Carthage, Dido, but he flees in the night, abandoning her to suicide, overthrowing comfort and home to

remain true to his quest (and the spell of the gods) to found the city of Rome.
(AB 4) (FC 5) (MD 6) (HK 9)

(23) *Blood Meridian: Or the Evening Redness in the West* by Cormac McCarthy (1985).
D. H. Lawrence famously remarked that the archetypal American hero was a stoic, a loner, and a killer. Cormac McCarthy's tale of the formation and dissolution of a band of scalp hunters in northern Mexico in the late 1840s embodies that dire maxim. Led by a soldier named Glanton and a mysterious, hairless, moral monstrosity known as the "Judge," these freebooters wipe out Indians, Mexicans, and each other amidst a landscape of such sublime desolation one feels it leaching into their very souls.
(MSB 8) (DAD 5) (BH 6) (SK 1) (GP 3)

(23) *Leaves of Grass* by Walt Whitman (1855–91).
Whitman spent half his life writing, revising, and republishing this collection, which is, at heart, a love song to the idea of America. Uneven and exuberant, Whitman acknowledges that "I celebrate myself, and sing myself," yet he celebrates all of America in his long-lined free verse. Naming himself "one of the roughs," Whitman places the natural over the artificial, native wisdom over scholarship, and praises the working man and foot soldier as fulsomely as he does President Lincoln.
(MCunn 8) (AGold 2) (AP 4) (CS 9)

(22) *Dead Souls* by Nikolai Gogol (1842).
Gogol's self-proclaimed narrative "poem" follows the comical ambitions of Chichikov, who travels around the country buying the "dead souls" of serfs not yet stricken from the tax rolls. A

stinging satire of Russian bureaucracy, social rank, and serfdom, *Dead Souls* also soars as Gogol's portrait of "all Russia," racing on "like a brisk, unbeatable troika" before which "other nations and states step aside to make way."

(MGait 2) (KK 3) (RP 3) (JSalt 4) (GS 10)

(22) *The Magic Mountain* by Thomas Mann (1924).

Hans Castorp visits his cousin at a sanatorium in the mountains of Switzerland. Soon he too becomes ill (maybe) and checks into the hospital—for seven years. In this sanctuary, Hans and the sanatorium's denizens endlessly debate questions of morality, politics, and culture, as the "real world" moves inexorably toward the horror of World War I. A meditation on time, an inquiry into how life ought to be lived, and an unflinching look at evil, Mann considered the ideas in his monumental novel so challenging that he said it must be read at least twice.

(KK 6) (RPow 1) (APat 7) (APhil 8)

(22) The stories of Eudora Welty (1909–2001).

See Louis D. Rubin, Jr.'s appreciation on page 118.

(SMK 2) (LDR 7) (LS 5) (ES 6) (BU 2)

(21) *The Master and Margarita* by Mikhail Bulgakov (1966).

Bulgakov reshaped his experience of Stalinist censorship into a surreal fable featuring three characters: an unnamed author (the Master) whose accusatory fiction is denied publication, his self-sacrificing married lover (Margarita), and the incarnation of Satan (Woland), who simultaneously orchestrates and interprets their destinies. The ambiguity of good and evil is hotly debated and amusingly dramatized in this complex satirical novel about the threats to art in an inimical material world and its paradoxical sur-

vival (symbolized by the climactic assertion that "manuscripts don't burn").
(KHarr 9) (DM 6) (AP 6)

(21) *Our Mutual Friend* by Charles Dickens (1864–65).
A miserly father dies and leaves his fortune to his estranged son—so long as he marries a woman he's never met. While returning home, John Harmon appears to be murdered. He survives and goes undercover. As John Rokesmith, he becomes secretary to the man next in line for his father's estate, Mr. Boffin. Clever coincidences and revelations follow in this novel notable for its wickedly funny treatment of middle-class society.
(JR 10) (CS 6) (RW 5)

(21) *As I Lay Dying* by William Faulkner (1930).
The Bundrens of Yoknapatawpha County have a simple task—to transport their mother's body by wagon to her birthplace for burial. Faulkner confronts them with challenges of near biblical proportions in this modernist epic that uses fifteen different psychologically complex first-person narrators (including the dead mother) through its fifty-nine chapters. Soaring language contrasts with the gritty sense of doom in this novel that includes the most famous short chapter in literature: "My mother is a fish."
(MCunn 3) (CE 4) (BH 9) (DM 5)

(21) *The Hamlet* by William Faulkner (1940).
The first novel in Faulkner's Snopes trilogy—which was followed by *The Town* (1957) and *The Mansion* (1959)—*The Hamlet* is a series of linked stories centering on the family's rise after the Civil War. Clever, ambitious, coarse, and unscrupulous, they embody Faulkner's ambivalence for the New South, which he saw as a land of greater

opportunity and diminished culture. Mixing humor, tragedy, violence, and pathos, *The Hamlet* is considered Faulkner's last great novel. (KH 7) (RP 5) (ES 9)

(21) *The Sun Also Rises* by Ernest Hemingway (1926).
Hemingway's first novel recounts the revels and misadventures of the expatriate community—including the introspective writer Jake Barnes and the tantalizingly elusive divorcée Lady Brett Ashley—in Paris and in Spain's bullfighting centers. For all their wit, wealth, or social clout and despite their rounds of drunkenness and debauchery as repetitious as the sun's daily rising, Hemingway's jaded, morally bankrupt characters can't get no satisfaction.
(BH 3) (BAM 5) (GP 9) (RPri 4)

(21) *The Iliad* by Homer (ninth century B.C.E.?).
The glory and horror of war pulse through this epic poem about the thousand ships launched in battle after the Trojan prince Paris abducts the beautiful Helen from her husband Menelaus, the King of Sparta. Through exquisite language Homer tells of capricious Greek gods and goddesses, fealty and honor between friends, and the terror of war. While crafting mythical tales, he creates an array of legendary heroes, especially Achilles, whose pride is as vulnerable as his heel.
(FC 10) (LM 8) (AW 3)

(20) *The Decameron* by Giovanni Boccaccio (1351–53).
The Big Chill meets the Black Death when a group of seven women and three men leave Florence to escape the plague of 1348. To entertain themselves, they tell stories according to topics selected by that day's appointed "king" or "queen." Like the plague, the hundred tales, mostly of love and deceit, leave no strata of society unscathed, and many of them are delightfully bawdy and irrever-

ent. Have you heard the one about the monk who seduced a woman by claiming to be the angel Gabriel?

(HJ 8) (LM 7) (VV 5)

(20) *The Possessed* by Fyodor Dostoevsky (1872).
Dostoevsky's signature theme—the future of morality and the human soul in a Godless world—takes flight in this harrowing portrait of revolutionary terrorists who have surrendered their humanity to their ideals. The political satire throbs with urgency, but Dostoevsky raises this work to the level of art through rich characterizations of his combative principals: the well-meaning, ineffectual philosophical theorist Stepan Verkhovensky; his true-believing, monomaniacal son Peter; the conflicted, "educated" serf Shatov; and two vivid embodiments of good and evil— saintly Bishop Tikhon and urbane, satanic Nicolas Stavrogin.

(PCap 5) (JH 10) (CM 5)

(20) *The Man Who Loved Children* by Christina Stead (1940).
Stead said that writing this novel "was like escaping jail," and one feels that great cathartic sweep as the dark side of family life unreels through astonishing scenes pitting Sam Pollit, the egotistical father "who loves children," against his wife Henny, a household hetaera subject to rages, or his fourteen-year-old daughter Louisa, a precocious, hulking girl whose break for freedom crowns the book. Though this novel is semiautobiographical, Stead transforms personal revenge against her own outsized father into revelation.

(RFD 10) (JF 2) (JL 8)

(20) *The Charterhouse of Parma* by Stendhal (1839).
See Francine Prose's appreciation on page 113.

(SCraw 7) (JF 4) (FP 9)

(19) The stories of Ernest Hemingway (1899–1961).

Love and war, childhood and adolescence, and initiation and experience are recurring themes in these journalistically spare, often autobiographical stories. Some, including "A Very Short Story," are merely snapshots, barely a page long. Others, such as "The Snows of Kilimanjaro" are multi-layered stories within a story. Among the best are those featuring Hemingway's doppelganger Nick Adams, whose youthful innocence in an Edenic Michigan becomes an almost jaded stoicism through combat and failed romance.

(MB 8) (CE 2) (KH 6) (SM 3)

(19) *Independent People* by Halldór Laxness (1934).

The Icelandic Nobel laureate's best novel is a chronicle of endurance and survival, whose stubborn protagonist Bjartür "of Summerhouses" is a sheepherder at odds with inclement weather, poverty, society in particular and authority in general, and his own estranged family. Laxness unflinchingly dramatizes Bjartür's unloving, combative relationships with his step-daughter Asta and frail son Nonni (a possible authorial surrogate)—yet finds the perverse heroism in this bad shepherd's compulsive pursuit of freedom (from even the Irish sorcerer who had cursed his land). This is an antihero for whom readers will find themselves cheering.

(JF 1) (JH 5) (AHas 4) (DMe 9)

(18) *The Arabian Nights: Tales from a Thousand and One Nights* (c. 1450).

Scheherazade receives the grim honor of marrying her King, who executes his wives on the day after the wedding night. Scheherazade delays her death by at least one thousand nights by telling tales that grow out of each other like the designs in a

Turkish rug. Those childhood familiars, Sindbad, Ali Babba, and Aladdin, are all here.

(HJ 10) (JSalt 8)

(18) *Notes from Underground* by Fyodor Dostoevsky (1864).
Aloof, unhappy, and tortured by his own "hyperconsciousness," Dostoevsky's narrator prefers to remain underground, away from normal life, because at least there he can be free. When he forces himself to dine with three schoolfellows, their carefree laughter and drinking sends him "into a fury." Afterward, he is seemingly moved by the plight of a young prostitute. But neither pity nor love is redeeming in this story whose narrator asks: "Which is better—cheap happiness or exalted suffering?" Dostoevsky's preference is clear.

(JB 9) (EC 9)

(18) *Their Eyes Were Watching God*
by Zora Neale Hurston (1937).
Beautiful and high-spirited Janie Crawford wants love and adventure. But, as Hurston shows in her finest novel, living in an all-black town is no shield against the sexism that dictates her young life. Forced to marry one controlling old geezer, she deserts him only to end up with another. When she marries Tea Cake, Janie finally enjoys the essence of a true relationship. Her happiness is short-lived when disaster strikes, but it becomes the catalyst for ultimate self-discovery.

(PCle 8) (ED 10)

(18) *The Stand* by Stephen King (1978).
This vivid apocalyptic tale with dozens of finely drawn characters begins with the military's mistaken release of a deadly superflu that wipes out almost everyone on earth. The few survivors, spread out

across the barren United States, are visited in their dreams by a kindly old woman in Nebraska and a sinister man in the West. They begin making their way toward these separate camps for what will prove to be a last stand between the forces of good and evil.
(DFW 9) (JW 9)

(18) *The Tempest* by William Shakespeare (1610).

The happy peace that Prospero, a powerful magician and former Duke of Milan, and his daughter Miranda share on an enchanted island is broken when a group of Prospero's former enemies and friends is shipwrecked there. Through the services of his two servants, the base Caliban, to whom the island had originally belonged, and the sprite Ariel, Prospero exacts revenge upon his stranded enemies while engineering the marriage of his daughter to a young nobleman. Anticipating themes that would inform colonial and postcolonial literature—usurpation, bondage, rebellion—this was Shakespeare's last play without a collaborator.
(KJF 9) (MG 4) (SO'N 5)

(17) *Winesburg, Ohio* by Sherwood Anderson (1919).

A collection of short stories about the inhabitants of a town whose physical isolation mirrors their psychological distance. With compassion and sadness, Anderson evokes small-town life and thought through a wide range of characters who are not visited by any tragedies save their own inability to forge a bit of happiness in their lives of quiet desperation.
(EC 8) (DC 6) (SO'N 3)

(17) *Don Juan* by Lord Byron (1819).

Byron was a gentleman, a womanizer, a cad, and a liberator. He poured a lifetime of observations into this seventeen canto poem.

Ostensibly about a Spanish boy sent abroad by his mother after an unfortunate love affair, it has the spontaneous gaiety of a man who is courteously maintaining the fiction that the reader's experience of women, politics, poetry, and the world is as extensive as his own. Thus Byron transformed his greatest masterpiece—his life—into art. (JBarn 9) (JR 8)

(17) *Robinson Crusoe* by Daniel Defoe (1719).

This rollicking yet existential adventure with deep religious undertones begins with fatherly advice: pursue a stable career. But the wastrel son denies his father because he is tempted by the sea. This salty path gets young Robinson kidnapped by Moorish pirates, sold into slavery, and shipwrecked on a remote island filled with cannibals. Yet this island seems an Eden to Crusoe, whose ingenuity enables him to tame the land, conquer the natives, and save the life of an islander, whom he makes his servant and christens Man Friday, as he comes to recognize and accept God's will. (JC 7) (AG 10)

(17) *Tom Jones* by Henry Fielding (1749).

Squire Allworthy provides a loving home to his bad nephew Blifil and the bastard orphan Tom. Lusty Tom is sent away after an affair with a local girl whom Blifil desires, and he begins his picaresque adventures on the way to London, including love affairs, duels, and imprisonment. Comic, ribald, and highly entertaining, *Tom Jones* reminds us just how rowdy the eighteenth century got before the nineteenth came and stopped the fun. (FC 1) (AHud 5) (WL 7) (DM 4)

(17) *A Passage to India* by E. M. Forster (1924).

A handful of English people searching for the "real" India get far more than they bargained for—up to and including a terrifying transcendental experience in a very dark cave. Forster's novel of the Raj is infused with a generous, liberal humanism; the author writes like a man determined that Indians should populate a novel of India, and he succeeds in this beautifully imagined portrait of both colonizer and colonized.

(JC 4) (RPri 5) (MW 8)

(17) *Clarissa* by Samuel Richardson (1747–48).

This long epistolary novel—full of sexual tension, violence, and psychic conflict—tells the tale of the virtuous Clarissa Harlowe and her rakish suitor, Robert Lovelace. Disowned by her family, confined in a brothel and raped, Clarissa pays a high price for her morality. Yet she accepts her fate with a moving acceptance in this landmark of English realistic fiction.

(EDon 10) (VV 7)

(17) *Candide* by Voltaire (1759).

In this withering satire of eighteenth-century optimism, Candide wanders the world testing his tutor Pangloss's belief that we live in the "best of all possible worlds." When Candide loses his true love, gets flogged in the army, injured in an earthquake, and robbed in the New World, he finally muses, "If this is the best of all possible worlds, what are the others?" In response to life's mysteries, he concludes, the best we can do is patiently cultivate our own gardens.

(JBarn 6) (CE 1) (GDG 10)

(16) *Labyrinths* by Jorge Luis Borges (1964).

Simultaneously philosophical and nightmarish, this collection of short stories, parables, and essays popularized both Latin American magic realism as well as metafiction. Borges, a blind Argentine librarian and polymath, here provides almost mathematically concise miniatures—of a man who remembers literally everything, for instance—that read like episodes of *The Twilight Zone* as written by a metaphysician.

(MC 10) (NM 1) (DM 3) (IP 2)

(16) *The Long Goodbye* by Raymond Chandler (1953).
Chandler's sardonic and chivalric gumshoe Philip Marlowe winds up in jail when he refuses to betray a client to the Los Angeles police investigating the murder of a wealthy woman. Marlowe's incorruptibility and concentration on the case are challenged even more when the obsessively independent private eye falls in love, apparently for the first time, with a different rich and sexy woman. She proposes marriage, but he puts her off, claiming he feels "like a pearl onion on a banana split" among her set.

(MC 1) (MCon 4) (GP 5) (RW 6)

(16) *Mrs. Bridge* (1959) and *Mr. Bridge* (1969) by Evan S. Connell.
This his and hers pairing, like twinned guest towels, reveals dirty fingerprints on the underside of a tidy looking 1930s Midwestern, middle-class marriage. Through fragments of conversations, overheard remarks, and wry observations, Connell slices into the Bridges' relationship, first revealing Mrs. Bridge's evaporation into suburban ennui, then exposing Mr. Bridge's increasing distance and disdain. The novels, set a decade apart, reveal two dimensions of the troubled family, which includes three children.

(EC 1) (DG 8) (MW 7)

(16) *Tess of the D'Urbervilles* by Thomas Hardy (1891).
When Tess's mother learns that her humble family has lofty

bloodlines, she sends her daughter out to cadge funds and land a rich husband. Instead Tess suffers cruel mistreatment and becomes pregnant. The baby's death unleashes torrents of grief, guilt, and religious doubt. However, Hardy's grim tale is lightened by his loving descriptions of the English landscape and his humorous rendering of local talk.

(JI 9) (RPri 7)

(16) The stories of Franz Kafka (1883–1924).

Kafka's fictions express existential alienation, but without the self-pity or blame; there's great humor amidst the angst. Despite his radical modernism, echoes of Talmudic and European folk traditions and Kafka's own formal High German prose style lend his fables all the timelessness of nightmare. His stories range from the slightest fragments, parables, and epigrams to the novella-length classic, *The Metamorphosis*. Featuring anthropomorphic beasts as well as magisterial paradoxes of "the Law," Kafka's inventive tales are a treasure-house of the neurotic and prophetic.

(JCO 6) (APhil 10)

(16) *1984* by George Orwell (1948).

Orwell's reputation as an antiauthoritarian arises in large part from this novel set in a totalitarian future in which citizens are constantly reminded "Big Brother is watching" as they are spied upon by the Thought Police and one another. In this landscape, Winston Smith is a man in danger simply because his memory works. He understands that the Party's total control of its citizens is based on its ability to control its message and its citizens' memories, and he is slowly drawn into a dangerous love affair and then an alliance, called the Brotherhood, of men and women united to fight Big Brother. Some of the vocabulary Orwell created for *1984—newspeak, doublethink, Big Brother*—have become part of today's vocabulary.

(SK 4) (DM 9) (IR 3)

(16) *Gulliver's Travels* by Jonathan Swift (1726, 1735).

Lemuel Gulliver, a ship's doctor, embarks on four wondrous voyages from England to remote nations. Gulliver towers over six-inch Lilliputians and cowers under the giants in Brobdingnag. He witnesses a flying island and a country where horses are civilized and people are brutes. Fanciful and humorous, Swift's fictional travelogue is a colorfully veiled but bitter indictment of eighteenth-century politics and culture.

(JB 2) (SCraw 10) (AHud 4)

(16) *The Fountain Overflows* by Rebecca West (1956).

See Margot Livesey's appreciation on page 92.

(ML 7) (DMcF 9)

(15) *A Death in the Family* by James Agee (1957).

A Pulitzer Prize–winning work of autobiographical fiction tells the story of a Knoxville, Tennessee, family torn asunder by the father's accidental death in 1915. In stunningly gorgeous prose, Agee chronicles the family's life before and after the tragedy (as well as the larger community they live in), to depict the fragility of happiness, of family, and of life itself.

(AG 6) (DH 9)

(15) *Invisible Cities* by Italo Calvino (1972).

Fearing that his empire's vastness has made it "an endless, formless ruin," Kublai Khan asks the traveler Marco Polo to describe it to him so he might understand and thereby control it. What Polo offers are accounts of surreal places—"hidden cities," "trading cities," and "thin cities" (whose buildings have no walls, floors or ceilings)—inhabited by people whose actions seem inexplicable in this novel of ideas concerned with memory and time, language and community, and the landscapes of the physical world and the imagination. (JC 9) (ML 6)

(15) The poems of Emily Dickinson (1830–86).

Quirkily punctuated and rhymed, thoughtful and unsentimental, these brief, aphoristic lyrics meditate upon God, nature, and the internal weather of the emotions—"The soul unto itself / Is an Imperial friend— / Or the most agonizing spy / An enemy could send." A spinster who published only two of her nearly two thousand poems, Dickinson saw her work as a vehicle for spiritual exploration and as messages to a world "that never wrote to me." (SA 8) (JCO 7)

(15) *Howards End* by E. M. Forster (1921).

This novel begins with literature's most famous epigraph: "Only connect." That search for human understanding—and the implied rarity of such knowledge— informs this saga of Margaret and Helen Schlegel, two bohemian sisters who become mixed up with the pragmatic, wealthy Wilcox family. In the confines of that family's estate, Howards End, Forster sets a sprawling fable of class, money, love, psychology, and a changing England. (DMcF 8) (TP 7)

(15) *The Power and the Glory* by Graham Greene (1940).

In all of Greene's prolific career, he never surpassed the stark beauty of this tale of a priest who is virtuous despite himself. Set in Mexico

during the revolution, when Catholicism was illegal, the novel follows the movements of a character known only as "the whisky priest"—he drinks, he bilks the faithful, he has fathered a child. But as his world narrows and he must make life or death choices, his life becomes a complicated display of salvation.
(GG 5) (EM 5) (SS 5)

(15) The stories of Alice Munro (1931–).

A master of the small epiphany, the moment of clarity, Alice Munro writes of men and women who struggle to reconcile the lives they have made with their sometimes confused longings. Largely set in urban and rural Canada, Munro's stories feature characters whose inner lives gradually peel away to reveal themselves in all their richness and complexity. Munro's plots do not forge ahead in a linear fashion, but loop and meander and take their time getting where they need to go, slowly revealing their characters and revealing what lies behind the choices they have made.
(EC 7) (EH 4) (LM 1) (CS 3)

(15) *A Dance to the Music of Time* by Anthony Powell (1951–75).

Powell's panoramic series of twelve freestanding novels, grouped in four "movements," charts the careers of four public-school friends from 1921 to 1971 against the backdrop of rapidly changing London. Built mosaic-like from many intimate, seemingly inconsequential encounters and scenes, the narrative moves with the pace, prismatic glitter, and cumulative force of a glacier, sweeping along sex, art, business, politics, and values in its wake. Devotees, who consider Powell to be England's answer to Proust, praise the elegant style, intricate plotting, and above all the masterly characterizations, in a work that encompasses comedy, tragedy, and realism.
(AF 9) (JL 6)

(15) *The Prime of Miss Jean Brodie* by Muriel Spark (1961).
The Miss Brodie in question is a wildly popular teacher in a 1930s Edinburgh middle school. She cultivates a group of chosen girls—the "crème de la crème," as she calls them—and in return they must give her their absolute loyalty. Massive privileges accrue to the Brodie set, but Spark is most interested in what the girls sacrifice to be included among the elite in this tense yet charming novel.
(ALK 7) (AMS 8)

(14) *Stones for Ibarra* by Harriet Doerr (1984).
Seeking renewal, Richard and Sara Everton leave San Francisco for a remote village in Mexico. There they hope to reopen Richard's grandfather's old mine, to "patch the present on to the past. To find out if there was still copper underground and how much the rest of it was true, the width of the sky, the depth of the stars, the air like new wine, the harsh noons and long, slow dusks." In lovely, spare prose, this National Book Award–winning novel describes the Evertons' flowering relationships with the vividly drawn people of Ibarra and the deadly illness that hovers over their happiness.
(SC 8) (KHarr 6)

(14) *The Tin Drum* by Günter Grass (1959).
This picaresque novel depicts the rise of Nazism in Germany and its terrible consequences through the adventures of Oskar Matzerath, "the eternal three-year-old" who stunts his growth at three feet and uses his tin drum and piercing screams as weapons against a mad world. Chilling and absurd, teeming with black comedy and dark insights into the human soul, *The Tin Drum* is both an artistic triumph and an act of reclamation. As the Swedish

Academy observed while presenting Grass with the Nobel Prize for Literature in 1999, the novel "comes to grips with the enormous task of reviewing contemporary history by recalling the disavowed and the forgotten: the victims, losers, and lies that people wanted to forget because they had once believed in them."
(JC 3) (MGri 5) (AG 1) (JI 4) (TK 1)

(14) *Romeo and Juliet* by William Shakespeare (1595).
The story of star-crossed Veronese lovers, this early romantic tragedy painfully depicts the fatal course of young lovers ruined by circumstances beyond their control, belonging as they do to two families who hate each other for long forgotten reasons. The intense violence at the heart of the play is matched only by the intense passion of Romeo and Juliet, who pay the ultimate price for the brief, intense, and pure love they shared.
(EDon 9) (LM 5)

(13) *David Copperfield* by Charles Dickens (1849–50).
Dickens's most autobiographical novel chronicles his hero's ever-changing fortunes, beginning with his famous opening line, "I am born." As a boy, David is swept between school and the workhouse; later, between the law and literature; and then between his vapid wife Dora and his true love Agnes. Ingratiating Uriah Heep, talented Mr. Micawber, devoted nurse Peggoty, and willing Barkis are some of the most memorable characters in the entire Dickens canon.
(KHarr 7) (JI 6)

(13) *Sister Carrie* by Theodore Dreiser (1900).
Ambitious farm girl Carrie Meeber comes to Chicago, gaining the favor of a wealthy bar manager named Hurstwood to avoid the sweatshops. The smitten man ditches his family, absconds with

company funds, and moves to New York with Carrie. When he can't find work his star falls as Carrie's rises in the theater. Filled with the tensions between rural America and its bustling urban future, and between propriety and ambition, *Sister Carrie* is a haunting portrait of a nation's contradictory impulses.
(WL 5) (TP 4) (TW 4)

(13) *The Bear* by William Faulkner (1942).
A highly atmospheric paean to the vanishing wilderness, this novella crisscrosses time and memory to chronicle Ike McCaslin's coming-of-age through annual hunting parties in the Mississippi woods. Beginning with his first trip at age ten, we watch him master the art of hunting, learning the ways of men and the woods. The ultimate prize is the legendary bear, Old Ben, a symbol of the untamed world "which the little puny humans swarmed and hacked at in a fury of abhorrence and fear." When sixteen-year-old Ike gets Old Ben in his sights, history, maturity, and ecological consciousness collide in a powerful rite of passage.
(RBP 10) (ST 3)

(13) *For Whom the Bell Tolls* by Ernest Hemingway (1940).
Hemingway's ambivalence toward war—its nobility and its pointlessness—are delineated in this account of Robert Jordan, an idealistic American professor who enlists with the antifascist forces in the Spanish Civil War. Jordan's idealism is quickly tested by the bloody reality of combat and the cynical pragmatism of his comrades.
(JLB 8) (MCon 5)

(13) *Jesus' Son* by Denis Johnson (1992).
Although the title comes from Lou Reed's song "Heroin," it

assumes another meaning in this collection of eleven linked short stories about a character who endures drug addiction, car crashes, and violence to learn who he is and achieve some grace. The characters sometimes seem futile as they score drugs and scrounge for money and love, but the real story is the narrator's fumbling process toward self-discovery.
(JBud 9) (WK 4)

(13) *The Leopard* by Giuseppe Tomasi di Lampedusa (1958).
While liberal rebels roam the hills of Sicily, and rumors spread that Garibaldi's army is poised for invasion, the old prince Don Fabrizio struggles to manage his vast and now threatened estates. "I belong to an unfortunate generation," he says, "swung between the old world and the new, and I find myself ill at ease in both." While charting what he sees as nineteenth-century Sicily's necessary movement toward science and liberal politics, Lampedusa uses the admirable prince to suggest the traditions and values lost in the process.
(JBarn 3) (RR 4) (JS 6)

(13) *Ship of Fools* by Katherine Anne Porter (1962).
The celebrated miniaturist's only long fiction, which was thirty years in the making, is a bitter satire depicting a 1931 ocean voyage from Mexico (Veracruz) to Germany (Bremen). Inspired by Sebastian Brant's fifteenth-century allegory of the same title, it is a portrayal of marital, class, and ethnic conflicts among passengers aboard the ship *Vera* ("Truth"). These include an ailing doctor, a drug-addicted "Contessa," various uprooted Americans, gypsy dancers, and twin malevolent children. Praised for its artistry, condemned for its vitriolic anti-German sentiment, Porter's *Odyssey* remains a fascinating, infuriating novel.
(PM 6) (AP 7)

(13) The Oedipus trilogy by Sophocles (496–406 B.C.E.).
Like an existential sadist, Sophocles explores the tragic complexities of fate by hurling his characters into situations in which they are simultaneously guilty and innocent, forced to choose between right and right or wrong and wrong—or some painfully imprecise combination of the two. In *Oedipus the King*, Oedipus is desperate to escape his fate—that he will murder his father and marry his mother—yet inexorably fulfills it with devastating effect. In *Oedipus at Colonus*, the blind, self-exiled ruler moves toward faith and goodness as his sons battle for his throne. In the third play, *Antigone*, his loving and upright daughter is forced to choose with climactic consequence between equally worthy goals as Sophocles depicts our struggles to explain a world we can scarcely comprehend.
(SMK 4) (AW 9)

(13) *East of Eden* by John Steinbeck (1952).
A retelling of Cain and Abel set in California's Salinas Valley between the Civil War and World War I, this novel takes off when Adam Trask realizes that maybe he shouldn't have married the lovely yet soulless prostitute Cathy Ames: on their wedding night she betrays him with his brother. Still, they produce twin boys, but Cathy, driven by undeniable demons, forsakes the newborns for her old life. Adam tells his rivalrous sons—Caleb, the bad penny, and sweet Aron—their mother is dead. But when Caleb learns the truth, the family's uneasy peace gives way to mayhem and a searing battle between good and evil as characters grapple with their destiny.
(MB 7) (GDG 6)

**(13) *The Strange Case of Dr. Jekyll and Mr. Hyde*
by Robert Louis Stevenson (1886).**
This novel might easily have become a victim of its own surpass-

ing fame, which has removed all suspense from its central riddle: What is the relationship between Dr. Jekyll and Mr. Hyde? Yet as our narrator plumbs Dr. Jekyll's descent into drug-addled, alter-ego madness, we are riveted by Stevenson's portrait of the good and evil that lurks in one man's heart. "This, too, was myself," Jekyll says of Hyde. Somehow we suspect it's us, too.

(ALK 9) (IR 4)

(12) *Daniel Deronda* by George Eliot (1874–76).

Daniel Deronda first sees Gwendolyn Harleth gambling at a fashionable resort and asks himself whether "the good or evil genius is dominant" in her. He is a man of ideas; she is an egotistical, spoiled girl. Can Daniel redeem her? Another character who needs saving is Mirah Cohen, yet through her, Daniel finds a form of salvation by discovering his hidden Jewish heritage in this novel that exposes the deeply rooted anti-Semitism of Victorian England.

(PF 3) (HJ 9)

(12) *Love in the Time of Cholera* by Gabriel García Márquez (1985).

Márquez takes the love triangle to the limit in this story of an ever hopeful romantic who waits more than fifty years for his first love. When his beloved's husband dies after a long, happy marriage, Florentino Ariza immediately redeclares his passion. After the enraged widow rejects him, he redoubles his efforts. Set on the Caribbean coast of Colombia, this wise, steamy, and playful novel jumps between past and present, encompassing decades of unrest and war, recurring cholera epidemics, and the environmental ravages of development.

(PC 3) (MC 2) (GDG 1) (DH 4) (RW 2)

(12) *The Transit of Venus* by Shirley Hazzard (1980).
Like planets moving across the sky—always the same yet always changing—this sumptuously written novel follows the lives of two orphaned sisters who leave Australia in the 1950s to begin new lives in England. While Grace turns to marriage for a safe transit through life, Caro charts a riskier course, one that brings her love and betrayal over the decades.
(RR 2) (AS 10)

(12) *So Long, See You Tomorrow* by William Maxwell (1979).
An old man recalls a story of murder and adultery in his childhood Illinois town, and how he came to betray the friend who witnessed them. This novel by the longtime fiction editor of *The New Yorker* is an American *Remembrance of Things Past*—heartbreaking in its portrayal of a boy's loss of innocence, and savvy about memory's self-serving nature.
(LKA 7) (APat 5)

(12) *Song of Solomon* by Toni Morrison (1977).
As witty and agile as a folk tale, psychologically acute and colorfully drawn, this novel blends elements of fable and the contemporary novel to depict a young man's search for identity. In her protagonist, Macon Dead, Morrison created one of her greatest characters, and his reluctant coming of age becomes a comic, mythic, eloquent analysis of self-knowledge and community—how those things can save us, and what happens when they do not.
(BMC 8) (SS 4)

(12) *Germinal* by Émile Zola (1884).
As in old pictures of Pittsburgh, a pall of industrial smoke seems to hang over Zola's grim, stirring novel about a miners strike.

Zola uses his usual style of fine-grained graininess to describe the lives crushed (sometimes literally) by work, and the excessive poverty to which the miners' families seem condemned. His is a collective portrait in which his main character, Etienne Lantier, gets engulfed by the hugeness and dangerousness of the mines (which bear the sinister nickname Le Voreux, or "the voracious ones") and the eventual revolt against the mining company.
(ED 8) (MD 4)

(11) *Ask the Dust* by John Fante (1939).
This coming-of-age tale features Fante's alter ego, Arturo Bandini: a poor, innocent, aspiring writer from Colorado, stretching out his limbo in 1930s Los Angeles. Bandini prowls the city's dusty alleys for experience he can turn into prose, eats oranges in his hotel room, and dreams of success. Awkward with women, he falls for a troubled Mexican waitress but can't sustain the relationship. He squanders what little money he earns. All he desires is literary glory, so that even when he nearly drowns, he thinks: "This was the end of Arturo Bandini—but even then I was writing it all down."
(DC 2) (HJ 2) (GP 7)

(11) *Parade's End* by Ford Madox Ford (1928).
Christopher Tietjens, "the last English Tory," is an exemplar of the old order; his faithless wife Sylvia represents the new. Grounded in their relationship, this rueful modernist epic dissects the intricacies of Edwardian England and the forces unleashed by World War I that would, inevitably and necessarily, slay that genteel world.
(ML 8) (BAM 3)

(11) *The Remains of the Day* by Kazuo Ishiguro (1989).
During a car trip, Stevens—a career butler who has existed at once

on the fringes and within the bird's nest of the British ruling class—reflects on his lifetime of service to the late Lord Darlington. Blinded by his devotion to "duty," he cannot admit that his late master was a fascist sympathizer and cannot see that he has forfeited the possibility of leading his own life. Now in old age, Stevens faces a sense of loss without the emotional acuity to comprehend it.
(MB 2) (TCB 9)

(11) *The Ambassadors* by Henry James (1903).
Middle-aged Lambert Strethers is sent to Paris to retrieve a young American whose wealthy parents fear he has taken up with an inappropriate woman, but Strethers sees that the young man is truly happy. Gradually, Strethers finds his flinty provincialism chipped away by Europe's ease and freedom in this novel whose signature line reads, "Live all you can; it's a mistake not to."
(DMcF 10) (RBP 1)

(11) *Nine Stories* by J. D. Salinger (1953).
Salinger gave his story collection the title *Nine Stories*, and that simple, enumerative title is just right, for the stories can be counted off like beads on a string: "For Esme with Love and Squalor," "A Perfect Day for Bananafish," and "Uncle Wiggly in Connecticut," whose last line, "I was a good girl, wasn't I?" never fails to break the reader's heart. The pitch-perfect voices Salinger provides his characters make their dead-serious search for meaning taste like candy.
(LKA 8) (MB 1) (SM 2)

(11) *Vanity Fair* by William Makepeace Thackeray (1847–48).
The subtitle is "A Novel Without a Hero," and never was a hero more unnecessary. In Becky Sharp, we find one of the most delicious heroines of all time. Sexy, resourceful, and duplicitous, Becky

schemes her way through society, always with an eye toward catching a richer man. Cynical Thackeray, whose cutting portraits of society are hilarious, resists the usual punishments doled out to bad Victorian women and allows that the vain may find as much happiness in their success as the good do in their virtue.

(JB 1) (TM 10)

(11) *Native Son* by Richard Wright (1945).

Set in Chicago in the 1930s, this novel tells the story of Bigger Thomas, an African American twisted and trapped by penury and racism. Bigger is on his way out of poverty when he accidently murders his employer's daughter, a white woman. In this highly charged, deeply influential novel, Wright portrays a black man squeezed by crushing circumstances who comes to understand his own identity.

(BMC 9) (KK 2)

(10) *Bhagavadgita* (fifth century B.C.E.).

An eighteen-chapter section of the *Mahabharata*, this "Song of God" is a dialogue between Prince Arjuna, a warrior on the battle-field, and the Supreme Lord Krishna, who appears as a charioteer. The two discuss the true self that is not destroyed in death and states of release from the human realm of suffering. As a corner-stone of Hindu faith and yogic philosophy, the *Bhagavadgita* has had a profound impact on philosophical and religious traditions in both the East and West.

(CD 10)

(10) *The Woman in the Dunes* by Kobo Abe (1962).

See Kathryn Harrison's appreciation on page 73.

(KHarr 10)

(10) *Things Fall Apart* by Chinua Achebe (1958).

Two years before Nigeria won its independence from Britain, Achebe published this clear-eyed novel set in the years leading up to colonial rule. Through the rise and fall of the admirable yet flawed tribal leader, Okonkwo, Achebe reveals the strengths and weaknesses of his nation's traditional culture: its violence and superstitions, and its compassion, honor, and pride.
(JC 10)

(10) *The Untouchable* by John Banville (1997).

Loosely based on the life of Cambridge spy Anthony F. Blunt, the novel opens in 1979, when seventy-two-year-old Vic Maskell's crimes have been publicly exposed. As the world recognizes that this art curator was not who he seemed, Vic probes his past— vividly bringing to life his co-conspirators and the city of Cambridge—to determine his accuser's identity. This suspenseful, philosophical journey reveals the fractured state of Vic's identity: Irishman and Englishman, lover of women and men, betrayer and betrayed.
(AS 6) (RW 4)

(10) *Ill Seen, Ill Said* by Samuel Beckett (1981).

In terse, haunting prose, Beckett's novella meditates on the absurdities of life and death, our grim longing for happiness, and "that old tandem" of reality and its unnamable "contrary." The narrative itself, boiled down to poetic reflections, focuses on an old woman enduring her last days in a remote cabin. In the end, though all is blackness and void, Beckett wishes on us "grace to breathe that void," even momentarily.
(JB 10)

(10) *The Book of Leviathan* by Peter Blegvad (2001).
Snappy puns, clever palindromes, stream of consciousness insights, and brilliant non sequiturs fill the dialogue bubbles of this surreal collection of comic strips that chronicle the epistemological adventures of a faceless baby named Leviathan, his wise pet Cat, and his favorite toy Bunny. Sigmund Freud, Emily Dickinson, and St. Augustine are among the luminaries whose words inform these tales that explore the world's mysteries and absurdities through a child's eyes.
(MSB 10)

(10) *The Outward Room* by Millen Brand (1937).
Also a poet, Brand wrote sensitively about mental illness when the topic was still taboo. This novel tells the story of a woman who escapes from a mental institution and tries to adjust to "normal" life on the "outside."
(PCam 10)

(10) *Casa Guidi Windows* by Elizabeth Barrett Browning (1851).
The first part of this two-thousand-line poem, composed in 1847, reveals Browning's excitement at the independence she and husband Robert found in Florence. The second part, written after Austria's reoccupation of Tuscany, is a more reflective, yet still hopeful, meditation on the streets outside the Browning home, Casa Guidi: "This world has no perdition, if some loss." *Casa Guidi* and its companion poems argue strongly for the right of women to speak on matters of politics and state, not just the moral affairs of the home.
(AT 10)

(10) *Answered Prayers* by Truman Capote (1987).
Unfinished and perhaps unfinishable at the time of Capote's

death in 1984, this roman à clef was his savage chomp at the hands that fed him—the manicured, diamond-freighted hands of Upper East Side socialites and assorted New York celebrities. Bitchiness, bile, and sexual braggadocio vie in this gossipy, literary vivisection of high society.

(DC 10)

(10) *The Golden Argosy* **edited by Van H. Cartmell and Charles Grayson (1947).**

See Stephen King's appreciation on page 86.

(SK 10)

(10) *The Professor's House* **by Willa Cather (1925).**

The professor's house was "almost as ugly as it is possible for a house to be." Now it has been dismantled. Yet the house, a symbol of the past, keeps beckoning Godfrey St. Peter, a professor in his mid-fifties whose outward success at work and home mask a passionless heart. "Theoretically he knew that life is possible, maybe even pleasant, without joy. . . . But it had never occurred to him that he might have to live like that."

(PCam 9) (ES 1)

(10) *The Awakening* **by Kate Chopin (1899).**

A terribly shocking book in its day, *The Awakening* tells the story of an artistic, twenty-eight-year-old New Orleans woman who finds life with her husband and two children unfulfilling. On summer holiday, she has an affair with a younger man. Revived, she leaves her family. But her happiness is short lived as she is punished by a society that has little tolerance for such independent women.

(SMK 10)

(10) *Disgrace* by J. M. Coetzee (1999).
Fifty-two years old and twice divorced, Professor David Lurie thought the affair with his student might bring passion back to his life. Instead, it costs him his job and his friends when he refuses to repent his sin. He retreats to his daughter's farm, hoping to build on their relationship and write about Byron. But his tranquil oasis is shattered by racial violence in this uncompromising novel by the South African Nobel laureate.
(SCraw 1) (EH 6) (VM 2) (RR 1)

(10) *Waiting for the Barbarians* by J. M. Coetzee (1980).
A magistrate for an unspecified empire finds himself thrust into a growing conflict on the frontier. Fearing an invasion, the empire sends an army to eliminate the threat of neighboring "barbarians," and the magistrate, accused of plotting with the enemy, is beaten and jailed. As he suffers these trials, the magistrate reflects on civilization and nature, suffering and oppression, and man's barbarous tendency toward violence.
(JC 8) (JS 2)

(10) *Geek Love* by Katherine Dunn (1989).
In this wild, oddball novel, Lily and Art Binewski purposely create a family of freaks and geeks by procreating under the influence of experimental drugs. This genetically altered "family" travels as a circus. Dunn's carnival of misfits is a memorable, darkly funny, and emotionally trenchant portrait of love and family on the fringe.
(JW 10)

(10) *Love Medicine* by Louise Erdrich (1984).
The form of this novel, about two Native American families, reenacts that of a traditional Chippewa Indian story cycle—

fourteen stories told by seven characters, forming a collage that forces the reader to sift through and weigh voice against voice, truth against truth. The book's main story—a long-standing love triangle among a husband and wife and the promiscuous Lulu Lamartine—is often upstaged by Erdrich's antimythic portrayal of Native Americans cut off from their traditional land, culture, and gods.

(TCB 10)

(10) *JR* by William Gaddis (1975).

This formally unique, dense, National Book Award–winning novel is composed almost entirely of dialogue and reads like a stream of conversation. This satire of high finance features an eleven-year-old named JR who uses a pay phone and mail order scheme to build a vast business empire on paper with the help of a partner, a struggling composer named Bast who serves as the company's public face.

(LMill 10)

(10) *I, Claudius* by Robert Graves (1934).

Here is everything you could want in a novel about ancient Rome: warfare and spectacle, scandal and intrigue (and still more intrigue). The Claudius of Graves's imagination—a disarmingly charming pedant and reluctant tyrant—confides his beginnings as a crippled, unwanted child and the internecine dynastic struggles that left him the last man standing. It is soap opera on an epic scale, dramatizing the fall of Roman republican ideals.

(AGold 10)

(10) *The Golden Bowl* by Henry James (1904).

Great chess players used to test their skills by playing several

matches at once. A similar sense of multiple levels and strategies animates James's final completed novel. An impoverished Italian prince marries the daughter of a fabulously wealthy American art collector, who in turn marries the daughter's best friend, who was once (unbeknownst to father and daughter) the prince's lover. James examines one of his signature themes—the terrible vulnerability of love to betrayal—in this vertiginous, psychologically acute work.
(TM 4) (RPri 6)

(10) *The Seven Pillars of Wisdom* by T. E. Lawrence (1925).
Lawrence feared that his account of the Arab revolt he helped lead against the Ottoman Empire during World War I was "too human a document." His form of warfare, composed of Bedouin raids, heartened a generation sickened by the mechanized slaughter of Flanders Fields. This sexually ambiguous, daring archaeologist fascinates us for the same reason we still read *The Iliad*: our need for stirring examples of grace under pressure.
(AF 10)

(10) *The Screwtape Letters* by C. S. Lewis (1942).
An amusing reversal of *The Divine Comedy*, this novel consists of letters from a senior devil (Screwtape) to his young nephew Wormword, teaching him how to tempt his first human "patient" to perdition. Lewis nicely balances theology and psychology, depicting hell as a bureaucracy with murderous office politics, and the loss of one's soul as an imperceptible poisoning through chains of seemingly inconsequential sins.
(DFW 10)

(10) *Embers* by Sándor Márai (1942).
Henrik, a nobleman of the Austro-Hungarian Empire, and Konrad,

a humble man with ambition, became best friends in military school. They remained inseparable, even after Henrik married Konrad's friend. Then, one night, their relationship ruptured. Forty-one years pass until they meet again before the embers of a fading fire, where they probe their relationship and their lives. (RW 10)

(10) *The Confidence-Man: His Masquerade* by Herman Melville (1857).

Truth, trust, and hope serve as plot and protagonist in this often comic, philosophical novel that anticipated postmodernism by a century. As the good ship *Fidèle* heads down the Mississippi, a long string of passengers—some modeled on Emerson, Thoreau, and Captain Ahab himself—encounter a shape-shifting confidence man who tells them exactly what they want to hear in order to get what *he* wants, in a work that raised doubt to an art form. (ALK 10)

(10) *The Birthday Party* (1958) and *The Homecoming* (1965) by Harold Pinter.

The Nobel Prize—winning master of menacing understatement subtly links exfoliating, abstract power struggles with banal domestic situations in two of his finest plays. The interrogation and abduction of a helpless (and perhaps guiltless) tenant makes *The Birthday Party* simultaneously celebrated as an ironic mockery of the phenomena of survival and continuity. In *The Homecoming*, a philosophy professor's return to the domicile he and his wife share with his male relatives becomes a struggle for sexual dominance from which the lone woman emerges triumphant. The result is opaque, disturbing, enthralling drama. (AMH 10)

(10) *The Time of the Doves* by Mercè Rodoreda (1962).
The author uses a stream of consciousness technique to describe the fraught experiences and often choked-off feelings of a Spanish shopkeeper during the 1930s and 1940s as her nation becomes gripped by civil war and fascism.
(SC 10)

(10) *Antony and Cleopatra* by William Shakespeare (1606).
One of Shakespeare's late Roman plays, *Antony and Cleopatra* has a sense of fading grandeur about it, as the great warrior Antony succumbs to the exotic luxuries of Egypt and the heady sexual powers of her queen Cleopatra, thus neglecting his duties to Rome. The play has a kind of baroque richness to both plot and language as Antony and Cleopatra delight in seclusion while the Roman forces opposing them, led by the sober and ambitious Octavius Caesar, close in on the lovers. Cornered, the emperor and queen bring the play to a suicidal climax that exquisitely fuses sexual pleasure and death.
(MD 10)

(10) *The Makioka Sisters* by Junichiro Tanizaki (1943–48).
Serialized during wartime, this epic novel chronicles the decline of the Osaka family and the transformation of traditional Japanese society. As their fortunes wither, elder sisters Tsuruko and Sachiko try to preserve the family name and marry off the talented, sensitive Yukiko. All the while the youngest sister, Taeko, aches for freedom from her sisters' conservatism. Tanizaki uses detailed descriptions of Japanese traditions, such as the tea ceremony, to underscore their fleetingness in an era of rapid modernization.
(VM 7) (DM 1) (CS 2)

(10) *L'Assommoir (The Dram Shop)* by Émile Zola (1877).

Like *Uncle Tom's Cabin*, this story—of the downfall of a Parisian laundress—turned a burning social issue into a sensational best-seller. The desperate alcoholism of Gervaise Lantier and her husband held a mirror to the shocking moral condition of the urban poor. But it is saved from mere didacticism by Zola's eye and ear. The unbuttoned urban dialogue prefigures Celine and Henry Miller; the cinematic structuring of the novel's great scenes suggests that Zola would have made a great film director.

(TW 10)

(10) *Nana* by Émile Zola (1880).

Nana is a low-born courtesan who succeeds among the French elite. Zola meant his heroine to represent the corruption of the Second Empire under the twin stresses of hedonism and capitalism. But like some uncontrollable genie uncorked from a bottle, she becomes the greatest femme fatale since Helen of Troy. The most explicit of the classic nineteenth-century novels, *Nana* exists in the vital midpoint between *Anna Karenina* and *Valley of the Dolls*.

(TW 10)

(9) *Aesop's Fables* (c. sixth century B.C.E.).

Though their origins are vague—Aesop may have been born a slave in Asia Minor in 620 B.C.E.—these tales use talking animals to personify human virtues and vices. Fables such as "The Hare and the Tortoise," "The Lion and the Mouse" and "The Fox Who Lost His Tail" show that "slow and steady wins the race," "appearances can be deceiving," and "misery loves company."

(JSalt 9)

(9) *Mahabharata* (fifth century B.C.E.).

Said to be the second-longest epic poem in the world (behind Tibet's *Epic of King Gesar*), the *Mahabarata* is also, along with the *Ramayana*, one of the two defining books of Hindu culture. Its core narrative relates the clashes between two groups of royal Indian cousins—one descended from gods, the other from demons. War, disguises, asceticism, drunken brawls, and the god Dharma as a dog swirl through this magical panorama of ancient India, which also includes the famous sermon *Bhagavadgita*, the Hindu equivalent to the New Testament.

(CD 9)

(9) *The Zoo Story* (1958), *The American Dream* (1961), and *Who's Afraid of Virginia Woolf?* (1962), three plays by Edward Albee.

Albee is American dramaturgy's master of black comedy and social satire. In *The American Dream* he lambasts that concept in a one-act farce featuring an over-the-top dysfunctional family and a murder. In *The Zoo Story*, a psychotic loner cannily provokes a complacent bourgeois into killing him. In the Pulitzer Prize–winning *Who's Afraid of Virginia Woolf?*, an older couple savage each other and their unsuspecting guests at the dinner party from hell, until the climactic revelation of the secret that binds them together. Albee's plays are less performances than ritual flayings, stripping away all pretense and artificiality in family and social life to lay bare the bleeding vitals.

(AMH 9)

(9) *Cousin Bette* by Honoré de Balzac (1847).

Lisbeth (Bette) Fischer, a seamstress for the demimonde of actresses and courtesans and the poor relation of Baron Hulot, has

a secret: she is helping to support a poor but noble Polish sculptor. Baron Hulot's daughter Hortense discovers the secret and helps herself to the handsome sculptor. Bette then unleashes an underhanded stratagem dictated by her implacably vengeful heart: using Baron Hulot's insatiable lust as a lever, Bette organizes her courtesan connections to ruin him, both morally and financially. Scary and psychologically acute.
(TW 9)

(9) *The Diary of a Country Priest* by Georges Bernanos (1937).
A profound story of Christian faith constructed of the thoughts, half-thoughts, jottings, and observations, the joys and disappointments, of a priest in provincial France. The protagonist suffers through the novel—he is a martyr to a dark, often wicked world. But as he declines, the grace he receives builds.
(MG 9)

(9) *The Way of All Flesh* by Samuel Butler (1903).
One of the great critiques of Victorian society and morality, this autobiographical novel charts the Pontifex family over several generations. Through the rise and fall of the main character's piety, Butler rebukes a religious tradition that has grown oppressive and hypocritical. Though he completed the novel in 1884, Butler, a clergyman's son, refused to publish this, his greatest work, during his lifetime.
(PE 9)

(9) *The Fall* by Albert Camus (1956).
In conversations with a chance acquaintance, a once-successful Paris lawyer recounts his fall into psychological self-destruction after ignoring a woman drowning in the Seine. Ultimately, this

existential antihero persuades himself that all good works are moti-
vated by self-interest, all virtue merely a ploy for success or popularity. With no hope of redemption, he descends into debauchery
and profligacy, impatient for the relative simplicity of death.
(IP 9)

(9) *Death Comes for the Archbishop* **by Willa Cather (1927).**
Two French missionaries come to the vast and untamed deserts of
New Mexico in 1851. Through a series of often symbolic stories
about their shared and personal experiences over forty years,
Cather depicts both vanished landscapes and timeless themes of
faith, loneliness, and our relationships with one another and the
natural world.
(PE 4) (PF 5)

(9) *The Ten Thousand Things* **by Maria Dermout (1955).**
Dermout was sixty-seven years old when she debuted with this
semiautobiographical novel about a Dutch woman named Felicia
raising her son in the Spice Islands of Indonesia. Felicia has a keen
appreciation for the beauty and mystery of this lush and exotic
world where spirits hover; she describes pearls as "tears of the sea"
while telling her boy the ten thousand things that make the
island. Her love of life and nature is challenged by violence and
murder that bring sadness and summon the courage of resilience.
(SC 9)

(9) The stories of Andre Dubus (1936–99).
The meditative leanness and working-class focus of Dubus's stories often garners comparison to Raymond Carver, although
Dubus is much more interested in religion (Catholicism) and
place (the redneck towns northwest of Boston). His stories are

shot through with brutal violence and alcohol, characters who alternate between sanctity and transgression, and tough moral choices. In Dubus's fiction, such as the novella *We Don't Live Here Anymore* from his 1979 collection *Separate Flights*, lives change slowly; marriages crumble or move on, bruised and shaken; and his characters survive, to carry on after paying a price.
(LKA 4) (JLB 5)

(9) *The Mill on the Floss* by George Eliot (1860).
Familial duty has seldom been so sadly rendered, and Eliot drew much from her own childhood in creating Maggie Tulliver and her self-righteous brother Tom. Passionate Maggie gives up her lover out of propriety and deference to Tom, but the character was thought so wicked that many nineteenth-century girls were forbidden to read this book. Despite having lived with a married man herself, Eliot dealt Maggie a harsh fate.
(BU 9)

(9) *Medea* by Euripides (431 B.C.E.).
What would you do if the man who promised you love, children, and a throne, after convincing you to slay your brother and exile yourself from your home, decided to marry a richer woman instead? This play gives a whole new meaning to "hell hath no fury like a woman scorned." Medea takes rejection to horrifying levels, killing her children as revenge on Jason for his faithlessness and his manipulation of her. That she is not punished for this deed is a stunning conclusion to this riveting play.
(PCap 9)

(9) *Sunset Song* by Lewis Grassic Gibbon (1932).
In this first and best volume of his famed trilogy, *A Scots Quair*,

Gibbon chronicles the growth to womanhood of Chris Guthrie, an intellectually ambitious Scottish girl at odds with her "backward" village and her dour Calvinist father. Succeeding volumes take Chris to Aberdeen and explore the aftermath of world war and burgeoning labor unrest, but lack the concentrated intensity of *Sunset Song's* rich renderings of individual, familial, and communal experience and destiny.
(ML 9)

(9) *Howl* by Allen Ginsberg (1956).

The title poem is considered the signature poem of the Beat generation. In language that blesses, curses, sorrows, and comforts, Ginsberg laments "the best minds of my generation . . . destroyed by madness." Begun in isolation and anger, the poem reaches a kind of saintliness and communion. What can be seen as a manifesto against the conformist society of America in the 1950s can also be read as a love poem for the promising idea of America.
(SA 9)

(9) *1982, Janine* by Alasdair Gray (1984).

In a fleabag Scottish motel, divorced and depressed, Jock McLeish once again seeks consolation and strength through massive doses of alcohol and sadomasochistic sexual fantasies (some starring a woman named Janine). Through frank, complex language Gray takes us inside the addled mind of a powerless man seeking to impose some control over his life.
(MSB 9)

(9) *The Mayor of Casterbridge* by Thomas Hardy (1886).

In the first chapter Michael Henchard sells his wife and child at a country fair. When he meets his forsaken wife Susan and daughter

Elizabeth-Jane years later, he is no longer a drunken hay-trusser but mayor of his town. Henchard has improved his position in life but not his disposition, and this tragedy of misplaced pride, torturous guilt, and immense bitterness is vintage Hardy.
(PF 4) (JI 5)

(9) *The Line of Beauty* by Alan Hollinghurst (2004).

Nick Guest is a young gay man desperate for love, the son of a modest antiques dealer who wants to climb the social ladder. In gorgeous, closely observed prose reminiscent of Henry James, much of this Booker Prize–winning novel chronicles Nick's amorous and social ascents in the drug- and sex-fueled world of 1980s England. Then comes AIDS and the cold, hard punch of Margaret Thatcher's policies, which leave everyone on their own, including Nick.
(AS 9)

(9) *A Doll's House* by Henrik Ibsen (1879).

The original desperate housewife, pampered Nora Helmer commits forgery for the money she needs to take her sick husband on a lifesaving trip. When her husband discovers her deceit, he is appalled. He realizes that he doesn't really know his wife, whom he looks on as little more than a "doll." His confusion only grows when Nora boldly moves to forge an independent identity—apart from men, motherhood, and social convention.
(SMK 9)

(9) *Buddenbrooks* by Thomas Mann (1900).

Subtitled "The Decline of a Family," Mann's first novel chronicles the shifting fortunes of four generations of German merchants. A brilliant literary colorist, adept with rich jewel tones, earthy pigments, and deep chiaroscuro alike, Mann recalls the Dutch Masters

in his painterly command of bourgeois interiors and intimate domestic scenes. In equally lucid detail, often with tongue in cheek, he probes the psychological depths of his characters as they follow the arc from Enlightenment vigor to Romantic decadence in this sprawling family saga bristling with comedy and pathos.
(NM 2) (RR 7)

(9) *Doctor Faustus* by Thomas Mann (1947).
Mann retells the Faust legend as the story of wunderkind composer Adrian Leverkühn, who trades his human feeling for a brilliant career and demonic inspiration: Leverkühn's biography, narrated by a faithful childhood friend from the vantage point of 1943 Germany, serves as a symbolic commentary on a nation's cultural hubris and downfall. Mann probes the complex tensions between aesthetics and morality, culture and politics, in his trademark dense, precise, endlessly qualified prose. Given his theme— the culpability of genius in the sins of his society—the narrator's almost infuriatingly overscrupulous command of language assumes a redemptive *gravitas*.
(JB 7) (RPri 2)

(9) The plays of Molière (1622–73).
Even those who generally find French literature inscrutable enjoy Molière. Tartuffe, for example, the Christian hypocrite who attempts to seduce a young virgin, inhabits the same plane of immortality as Falstaff or Don Quixote. Molière's comedy ranges from slapstick (*The Doctor in Spite of Himself* is as silly, and funny, as a Punch and Judy show) to the social satire of his greatest play, *The Misanthrope*, in which a man's vow never to lie collides with society's need for "white lies." Molière impartially mocks both sides.
(SCraw 9)

(9) *Life: A User's Manual* by Georges Perec (1978).
See Arthur Phillips's appreciation on page 109.
(APhil 9)

(9) *Wheat That Springeth Green* by J. F. Powers (1975).
Joe Hackett wanted to be a saint. While training for the priesthood he wore the hair shirt and abandoned the pleasures of "smokes, sweets, snacks, snooker, and handball." Twenty-five years later, his ideals dampened, his passions are baseball and beer. The arrival of an idealistic curate slowly snaps him back to life, "like wheat that springeth green," in this comic novel about both the tension between earthly and spiritual goals and their mutual dependence.
(AP 9)

(9) *Quartet in Autumn* by Barbara Pym (1977).
Barbara Pym's characters live in the margins of mid-twentieth-century English life, squirreled away in rooming houses, dead-end office jobs, and ever-shrinking church congregations. Her peculiar genius is to make these unpromising creatures the centerpieces of her work. With the acute, unflinching eye and dry sense of humor that invite comparison to Jane Austen, *Quartet in Autumn* follows four aging office workers in their dance with retirement, a changing society, and ultimate mortality.
(PCam 4) (CS 5)

(9) *Henry V* by William Shakespeare (1599).
The final play in the Second Henriad (with *Henry IV*, Parts I and II), *Henry V* is, ostensibly, a celebration of Henry's victory over his archenemy, the French, at Agincourt in 1415. Henry thus construed is a great national hero. But the play actually subverts, or at least compromises, such a reading. We see Henry collude with

the church to prosecute a vicious campaign for nationalistic, rather than necessary, reasons. The brave king broods on the burdens of kingship and the righteousness of his cause, but then casually orders the slaughter of French prisoners. The epilogue looks forward to the reign of Henry VI, who lost all that Henry V gained and more, as if to question the worth of all this killing. (GDG 9)

(9) Othello, The Moor of Venice by William Shakespeare (1604).
Othello centers on the black general of the Venetian army and his white wife, Desdemona, daughter of a Venetian senator. A brave and successful warrior essential to the security of Venice, Othello is extremely susceptible to jealousy, a weakness exploited by the villain Iago, whom Othello passes over for a lieutenancy in favor of another. Iago's swift and lethal revenge is as brilliant to behold as it is terrible to watch, as good and innocent people die at the hands of a demonic genius in a play that refuses to satisfy the expectation that tragedy must reward virtue and punish vice. (EM 9)

(9) Treasure Island by Robert Louis Stevenson (1881–82).
Young John Hawkins was told to beware a man with one leg. But after discovering a treasure map, he acquires a ship and hires—you guessed it—one-legged Long John Silver to cook for his ship and hire the crew, a band of villainous pirates. After writing this thrilling tale of adventure for his stepson, Stevenson remarked: "If this don't fetch the kids, why, they have gone rotten since my day." (TK 9)

(9) The Killer Inside Me by Jim Thompson (1952).
Lou Ford is the boy next door—a deputy sheriff in his Texas

hometown. But he suffers from "the sickness," which urges him to kill women and others who get in his way. Through Ford's chilling first-person narration, Thompson takes us inside the mind of a serial killer.

(WK 9)

(9) *The Master* by Colm Tóibín (2004).

In beautiful, perceptive prose suggestive of its subject, this novel brings readers inside the conflicted mind and soul of Henry James. Set between 1895 and 1899, when a mid-career James was reassessing his life, the novel flows with memories of his youth and accomplished family members. What emerges is the portrait of a man determined to avoid complications—especially those posed by homosexuality; who wrestles with his need to turn his life into art, and his desire to push away life so he can create his art.

(DMcF 4) (AS 5)

(9) *Kristin Lavransdatter* by Sigrid Undset (1920–22).

The Norwegian author's vast trilogy depicts its eponymous heroine's life: Kristin's impetuous union with a dangerously unstable suitor; her arduous marriage and motherhood, endangered by her husband's political activities; and the willed serenity of her later years, when her youthful folly yields to a commitment to spiritual growth. The energy of the Icelandic sagas blends with an immensely detailed panorama of fourteenth-century life.

(LS 9)

(9) *The Day of the Locust* by Nathanael West (1939).

Hollywood is not alluring in this savage, apocalyptic novel about fame and its perversions. Painter Tod Hackett comes to Hollywood to design sets and find success. Instead, he finds a

population of the physically and psychically maimed crouching at the edges of the film industry, desperately believing that only luck and time separate them from stardom. At the end, their disappointment explodes into violence and Tod sums up his despair with his single great painting: *The Burning of Los Angeles.*
(MCon 9)

(9) *A Streetcar Named Desire* by Tennessee Williams (1947).

Set in the once working-class French Quarter of New Orleans, Williams tells the story of Blanche DuBois, an alcoholic relic of the waning genteel South, and her brother-in-law, the sensuous working-class brute Stanley Kowalski. Their mutual attraction and repulsion drive the conflict in this sexually frank, lyrical melodrama about the boundaries between illusion and reality and the changing South.
(PCle 9)

(8) *Père Goriot* by Honoré de Balzac (1834).

When law student Eugène de Rastignac falls for the high-maintenance daughter of Père Goriot, a wheat merchant King Lear who has impoverished himself elevating his daughters in Parisian society, he needs more money than he can make honestly. That's when Vautrin, a fellow boarder at his *pension*, suggests that Rastignac might make his fortune . . . at the cost of a minor murder. The tension becomes almost unbearable as Rastignac wrestles with his conscience and readers confront Vautrin, whose contempt for conventional morality prefigures every existential hero since.
(TP 8)

(8) *Ficciones* by Jorge Luis Borges (1944).

Few twentieth-century literary works were as influential as Borges's first collection of surreal "fictions." Showcasing his deeply serious, brilliantly playful fascination with language, literature, and metaphysics, these seventeen stories—about imaginary books and labyrinthine libraries, cosmic detectives and strange lands—ask us to wonder about how we know what we know (or think we know) while helping light the fuse of postmodern pyrotechnics. (TCB 3) (KK 5)

(8) *Bullet Park* **by John Cheever (1967).**
Happily married with one child, Eliot Nailles is a chemist working to make better mouthwash. Paul Hammer is a Yale graduate and aimless drifter who moves to Nailles's leafy suburb of Bullet Park. There he plans to take revenge on the bourgeoisie—by murdering Nailles's son.
(AMH 8)

(8) *Uncle Vanya* **by Anton Chekhov (1895).**
Chekhov helped transform the theater through his pioneering use of indirect action—the gunshot fired offstage—and his ability to develop themes not just through dialogue but by creating a mood or atmosphere on stage. He was also a master of characterization. These skills are apparent in this wonderfully complex play, set on an estate in nineteenth-century Russia, which details the relationships among family members who look back on their lives with regret.
(PCam 8)

(8) *Life and Times of Michael K* **by J. M. Coetzee (1983).**
A retarded, nearly mute, harelipped man goes native in a South Africa torn by civil war, living off the land before being picked up and passed among institutions. The echo of Kafka in this contro-

versial novel's title is deliberate: Michael K is caught in a funda-
mental life trap, embodying both the yearning to be free of language and politics and the impossibility of doing so.
(KHarr 8)

(8) *Lord Jim* by Joseph Conrad (1900).
Marlowe, Conrad's narrator here (as he is in *The Heart of Darkness*),
ironically labels Jim, the disgraced first mate at the center of his
tale, "one of us," meaning the small British colonial elite. However,
Jim violates the code one life-defining night when, in a panic, he
abandons his sinking ship while the passengers sleep. The ship
stays afloat but not Jim's reputation. Later Marlowe finds the
exiled sailor on a remote Indonesian island, where the natives
give "Lord Jim" a last chance at self-respect.
(PM 8)

(8) *The Secret Agent* by Joseph Conrad (1907).
A darkly comic work (and thus rare for Conrad), this novel follows a group of anarchists and spies—including an American who
walks around with a bomb strapped to his chest—plotting to
blow up London's Greenwich Observatory. Often now misread as
a condemnation of terrorism, *The Secret Agent* is really an ironic critique of abstract ideology and careerist bureaucracy—both forces
that use and crush the individual.
(GG 8)

(8) The *Deptford* trilogy by Robertson Davies (1983).
A single question—"Who killed Boy Staunton?"—hovers over
this trilogy that begins when ten-year-old Percy "Boy" Staunton
throws a rock-filled snowball at his friend Dunstan Ramsay.
Instead he hits Mary Dempster, who soon gives birth, prema-

turely, to a boy with birth defects. The novels *Fifth Business, The Manticore*, and *World of Wonders* chronicle the lives of these characters and their families, developing themes of guilt, love, and responsibility while detailing "the consequences that can follow any single action."

(JI 2) (IP 6)

(8) *Hard Times* by Charles Dickens (1854).
"Now, what I want is, Facts," reads the opening of this entertaining melodrama animated by impassioned social protest and indignant satire. In the humorless martinet Gradgrind, who preaches and practices uncompromising logic and efficiency, Dickens lampoons the soulless utilitarianism of Victorian philosopher John Stuart Mill. Such reason has spawned the grimy, industrial city of Coketown—which Dickens contrasts with a traveling circus—and informs the subplot concerning Stephen Blackpool's inescapable, unhappy marriage (a sour fictionalization of Dickens's own domestic miseries).

(TM 5) (MW 3)

(8) *The Ice Age* by Margaret Drabble (1977).
Drabble is a quietly dogged social novelist, and her books can be read collectively as a history of contemporary England's soul. Here she uses Anthony Keating, a former BBC official turned failed real estate developer, to explore the gloomy interregnum between the go-go 1960s and the more seriously materialistic Thatcher era, when the cozy values of old England were growing increasingly shabby without any new values to replace them.

(DC 8)

(8) *The Bacchae* by Euripides (408–406 B.C.E.).
"Gods should be exempt from human passions," says Cadmus, but

such is not the case for Dionysus in one of the goriest Greek tragedies. Dionysus seeks revenge on Cadmus's grandson Pentheus, a Theban king who has tried to quash the Bacchus cult in Thebes. Dionysus seduces Pentheus into witnessing a Bacchanalian orgy, where he is torn to pieces by the revelers, including his own mother. (IP 8)

(8) *Light in August* by William Faulkner (1932).

This novel contains two of Faulkner's most telling characters, the doggedly optimistic Lena Grove, who is searching for the father of her unborn child, and the doomed Joe Christmas, an orphan of uncertain race and towering rage. Faulkner's signature concerns about birth and heritage, race, religion, and the inescapable burdens of the past power this fierce, unflinching, yet hopeful novel. (CE 6) (SK 2)

(8) *Joseph Andrews* by Henry Fielding (1742).

The comic trouble starts when a naive footman rejects the advances of his employer, Lady Booby, and her servant, Slipslop. Cast out, he and the saintly Parson Adams hit England's rough roads in search of Joseph's beloved, Fanny Goodwill. Like Don Quixote and Sancho Panza, the world rewards their goodness with violent complication. After Joseph finds Fanny—who might be his sister—Fielding amps up the sexually charged farce in this novel of friendship and virtue that satirizes Samuel Richardson's novel *Pamela*. (ES 8)

(8) *The Gate of Angels* by Penelope Fitzgerald (1990).

The year is 1912 and, it seems, reason is finally giving the heave-ho to faith. At least that's what rector's son turned Cambridge scientist Fred Fairly thinks, until a freakish bicycle accident connects

him to the beautiful and mysterious Daisy Saunders. Though he has made a pledge of celibacy, he is now in love and so must puzzle the questions of chaos and order, fate, chance, and the wonders of the soul in this funny, sharp novel of ideas.
(EH 8)

(8) *The Sheltered Life* by Ellen Glasgow (1932).

Glasgow's signature themes—the place of women and the crumbling Old South—reached a high point in three comedies of manners set in the fictional city of Queenborough—*The Romantic Comedians* (1926), *They Stooped to Folly* (1929), and *The Sheltered Life* (1932). Here, Glasgow depicts the declining fortunes of two tradition-bound Virginia families, the Archibalds and the Birdsongs. Through young Jenny Blair Archibald, she represents the possibility of feminine independence in this penetrating account of southerners being forced into the modern era.
(LS 8)

(8) *Red Dragon* by Thomas Harris (1981).

Imitation is the most annoying form of flattery for archfiend Dr. Hannibal Lecter in this terrifying predecessor to *The Silence of the Lambs*. *Red Dragon* describes the original capture of cannibalistic serial killer Lecter and his subsequent indignation on hearing that another monster is imitating his sadistic methods. Harris skillfully leaves open who is manipulating whom when Lecter agrees to help the FBI track down the copycat, who matches Lecter eye for eye—literally.
(DFW 8)

(8) *The Old Man and the Sea* by Ernest Hemingway (1952).

This poignant parable of an old Cuban fisherman's valiant solitary

struggle against a huge fish embodies Hemingway's definition of courage: grace under pressure. After months without a catch, and deserted by his young protégée, ancient Santiago finally hooks an enormous marlin, which is also prized by a marauding shark, in this study of self-reliance, implacable nature, and equanimity in the face of insurmountable odds.
(RW 8)

(8) *Almost Paradise* (1984) and *Shining Through* (1988) by Susan Isaacs.
The best-selling author's gift for creating strong heroines and crisp dialogue are on display in these engrossing tales of romance. *Almost Paradise* examines the price a married couple—he's a blue-eyed blue-blooded movie star, she's a brilliant, half-Jewish woman with a less than illustrious pedigree—pay for fame. Set before and during World War II, *Shining Through* mixes romance with espionage as a poor girl from Queens marries the most handsome lawyer on Wall Street and eventually is sent on a secret mission to wartime Berlin.
(JW 8)

(8) *Fiskadoro* by Denis Johnson (1985).
After a nuclear war devastates the planet, residents of what had been the Florida Keys try to rebuild their lives and communities in a landscape where shards from the obliterated past—religious stories, Jimi Hendrix records, parking decks—remain but are barely understood. By destroying and then rebuilding the world, including the invention of a strange dialect, Johnson's daring novel probes the nature of communication, memory, and knowledge amid the palpable specter of death.
(TCB 8)

(8) *The Book of Laughter and Forgetting*
by Milan Kundera (1978).
A pastiche that deliberately recalls the narrative games of *Tristram Shandy*, this novel uses seven thematically linked tales (as well as forays into philosophy, musicology, literary criticism, and autobiography) to explore the permeable borders between Eastern and Western Europe, eroticism and banal libertinism, and the public versus the private, which Kundera sees as the shrinking, doomed cradle of civilization.
(DAD 8)

(8) *Voyage of the 'Dawn Treader'* by C. S. Lewis (1952).
In this, the third book of *The Chronicles of Narnia*, King Caspian sets sail to the end of the world to rescue the seven lost lords of Narnia. Along with three English children—who have come to Narnia this time by stepping into a painting—and other companions such as the brave, sword-wielding mouse Reepicheep, Caspian has numerous adventures that resonate with Christian and classical mythology.
(LMill 8)

(8) *Man's Fate* by André Malraux (1933).
Chronicling the communist uprising against Chiang Kai-shek's nationalists in Shanghai in 1927, this novel is a revolutionary's cookbook. It shows the planning and politics of the insurrection, the street battles that accompanied it, and the successful, remorselessly cruel nationalist counterattack (the nationalist general throws captured communists in the furnaces of a train). When the book was published in 1933, the Chinese revolution looked kaput. When the communists triumphed in 1948, it seemed prophetic.
(AF 8)

(8) *Bel-Ami* by Guy de Maupassant (1885).

Like a late nineteenth-century Tom Wolfe, Maupassant reveals the codes and rivalries of social success by chronicling the rise of Georges Duroy, a handsome, down on his heels ex-soldier. Duroy's chance comes when an old army buddy hires him at his newspaper, *La Vie Parisienne*. Georges rewards his friend by coveting his wife, Madeleine, a smart, energetic free spirit who seems like Madame Bovary—after successful therapy. When her husband dies, Georges proposes literally over his corpse. But soon he is looking even higher . . .

(TW 8)

(8) *The Third Policeman* by Flann O'Brien (1967).

See A. L. Kennedy's appreciation on page 83.

(ALK 8)

(8) *Norwood* by Charles Portis (1966).

The comic conversation and surreal adventure that distinguish Portis's fiction shine in this first novel about Norwood Pratt, a war hero with country music dreams who's stuck in a small Texas town. Seeking escape, Norwood decides to find an old Marine buddy who owes him seventy dollars. His trip to Manhattan and then Memphis is filled with quirky characters (a midget, an educated chicken), strange situations, and homespun wisdom: "Don't let your mouth write a check that you're ass can't cash."

(WK 8)

(8) *The Satanic Verses* by Salman Rushdie (1988).

After terrorists blow up their plane, two Indian actors fall from the sky. When they land, one has a halo, the other horns. This lush, lyric, sensual, and surreal novel then follows two main inter-related plots that skate along the blurry lines between good and evil, love and betrayal, knowledge and ignorance. The first plot line details these men's tangled lives and strange transformations in London and Bombay; the second reimagines the life of Mohammed so critically that Iran's Ayatollah Khomeni issued a death sentence against Rushdie.

(SK 8)

(8) *Scaramouche* by Rafael Sabatini (1921).

Swashbuckling swordsman, inspiring orator, actor, lawyer, revolu-tionary politician, Andre-Louis Moreau "was born with the gift of laughter and a sense that the world was mad." He must employ all his skills in seeking revenge against the wicked aristocrat who murdered his friend, a young clergyman, for expressing demo-cratic ideas. The tension mounts when Moreau learns his adver-sary hopes to wed his beloved. A master of action-adventure (his other works include *Captain Blood*), Sabatini paints Moreau's story against the surging French Revolution, coloring his high drama with history and politics.

(MC8)

(8) *The Raj Quartet* by Paul Scott (1966–75).

Made famous by a popular television series, this rich quartet of novels dramatizes the final years of British rule ("the Raj") in India through explorations of several intersecting lives. Indian Hari Kumar's interracial relationship with Englishwoman Daphne Manners, the career and sexual opportunism of Police Super-intendent Ronald Merrick, the encroaching madness and despair of idealistic missionary Barbie Batchelor, and the failure of well-

intentioned diplomat Guy Perron to decipher the riddle India poses for its would-be conquerors are painstakingly woven into an engrossing, unforgettable extended narrative.
(SK 3) (RR 5)

(8) *Austerlitz* by W. G. Sebald (2001).

During decades of travels through Europe, a nameless architectural historian accidentally keeps meeting Austerlitz, a neurasthenic architect who is incrementally confronting his buried connection to the Holocaust. Incantatory and almost vertiginous in its repetitiveness, this one-paragraph novel depicts the struggle of a personal narrative to melt the frozen memory of collective trauma.
(JB 4) (PC 4)

(8) *The Giving Tree* by Shel Silverstein (1964).

This parable about the parent–child bond features an apple tree that gives and gives and a boy who takes and takes. As the boy matures, his needs become harder to meet. But the tree never fails, ultimately sacrificing life and limb. Silverstein, who also illustrated this children's book, casts no moral judgments in this open-ended tale that concludes with the boy, now an old man, sitting on all that's left of the tree, a stump: "And the tree was happy."
(AT 8)

(8) *Sophie's Choice* by William Styron (1979).

This novel is at once the story of a young writer's coming of age and his slow uncovering of the story of Sophie, his neighbor in a Brooklyn boarding house and a Polish survivor of the Holocaust who has had to make a biblical choice between her children. Comic and tragic, the story moves with symphonic grace toward its final denouement. Looking back across the span of years, an older, somewhat wiser Stingo recreates in lush detail post–World War II Brooklyn and one man's slow awakening to the horrors people are capable of.

(DH 8)

(8) *Galpo Guccho* by Rabindranath Tagore (1912).

These beautifully structured stories are vast in range, moving from supernatural tales to historical stories of love. Tagore, who won the Nobel Prize for literature in 1913, is especially good at portraying the little moments of daily life and creating vivid characters—often the poor and dispossessed in his native India—that continue to haunt us.

(CD 8)

(8) *A Sportsman's Notebook* by Ivan Turgenev (1852).

Set in the Russian countryside, this series of linked, introspective story-essays describes the rambles of a young nobleman shooting game on the vast estates of Russia's aristocracy. As Turgenev depicts the beauteous intricacies of the natural world, he captures the suffering of Russian serfs, helping to convince his country's leaders to abolish the feudal system.

(DMe 8)

(8) *The Adventures of Tom Sawyer* by Mark Twain (1876).

Twain's charming fictionalization of his Hannibal, Missouri, boyhood marks the passages, large and small, of youth: Tom plays hooky from school, courts Becky Thatcher, gets lost with her in the Bat Cave, and runs afoul of Injun Joe. Tom even manages to eavesdrop on his own funeral. The way he convinces his friends

to pay him for the privilege of whitewashing his fence proves that he is a trickster for the ages.
(AP 8)

(8) *The Importance of Being Earnest* **by Oscar Wilde (1895).**
"The truth is rarely pure and never simple," one character remarks in Wilde's clever comedy about double identities. And white lies are even more complicated, as two young Englishmen of leisure learn when they try to avoid undesirable social obligations by claiming their noble services are required by needy (and imaginary) friends. When the worlds of their "friends" and fiancées collide, their confabulations turn to witty farce.
(AG 4) (DL 4)

(7) The legends of King Arthur and the Knights of the Round Table.
These tales of medieval chivalry, romance, and high adventure composed primarily from the twelfth through fifteenth centuries feature a host of iconic characters: Sir Galahad, Lancelot, Mordred, Guinevere, Merlin, and the Lady of the Lake. These are stories that gave us Camelot, the Round Table, and the search for the Holy Grail. Versions abound but the best place to start is with Sir Thomas Malory's *Le Morte D'Arthur*.
(JSalt 7)

(7) *Little Women* **by Louisa May Alcott (1868).**
Meg, Jo, Beth, and Amy: for girls who grew up reading about these four sisters, the names run together as readily as John, Paul, George, and Ringo. Maybe the magic of foursomes explains this novel's enduring appeal. Readers get their pick of heroines: motherly Meg, harum-scarum Jo, goodness-personified Beth, or naughty

Amy. Cared for by their saintly mother, Marmee, while their father is away fighting in the Civil War, the sisters get into scrapes, go on larks, find love, and suffer loss. It's the ultimate *bildungsroman* for girls.
(RFD 7)

(7) *Sense and Sensibility* by Jane Austen (1811).

Austen doubled her heroines here, giving us the down-on-their-luck Dashwood sisters. Elinor, the cool-headed elder, seems to embody common sense, while Marianne is "eager in everything." The novel's joy comes from watching the girls shape-shift their way through their love troubles, trading back and forth between their roles and natures. As each girl is by turns hardheaded and hot-hearted, Austen's novel reveals the fluid nature of identity.
(DM 7)

(7) *Nightwood* by Djuna Barnes (1936).

Following the painful end of an eight-year lesbian relationship, Barnes crafted this avant-garde novel that explores love, desire, and obsession in rich lyric prose. Set mostly in Paris during the years between the world wars, *Nightwood* revolves around the mysterious Robin Vote and the two lovers she abandoned: her German husband, Baron Felix Volkbein, and an American woman, Nora Flood. Heartbroken and confused, the spurned lovers seek advice from a most unlikely source, an alcoholic transvestite named Dr. Matthew Dante O'Connor, whose solipsistic stream of consciousness ramblings suggest the mysteries and miseries of romantic love.
(AF 7)

(7) *Herzog* by Saul Bellow (1964).

Moses Herzog has two problems: his book on imagination and

the intellect has stalled and his second wife has run away with his best friend. In response to his loneliness and alienation he writes letters—funny, scathing, ruminant, intensely self-aware—to people living and dead (including Friedrich Nietzsche and Willie Sutton) about his Jewish upbringing, old friends and lovers, and the world's mad hypocrisy. Through Bellow's prose, philosophically rich yet sprightly antic, the novel takes on this quest: "The dream of man's heart, however much we may distrust or resent it, is that life may complete itself in significant pattern."
(ST 7)

(7) *My Ántonia* by Willa Cather (1918).

Featuring a beleaguered central heroine who endures her father's suicide, is driven to work in the fields, and is seduced, abandoned, and left pregnant, this ought to be a tale of tragic inevitability. Instead, this beautifully elegiac novel offers an unsentimental paean to the prairie, to domesticity, and to memory itself. As remembered by her friend Jim, Ántonia is as mythic and down-to-earth as the Nebraska she inhabits.
(TP 5) (RPow 1) (MW 1)

(7) *The Big Sleep* by Raymond Chandler (1939).

This is the first novel featuring hard-boiled Los Angeles private eye Philip Marlowe, a tough guy with a fast gun and a quick wit. Noting that he "was neat, clean, shaved and sober, and I didn't care who knew it," Marlowe goes to work for a dying L.A. oil tycoon whose two lusty daughters have fallen prey to an array of drug dealers, pornographers, and bootleggers intent on separating the old man from his money.
(CH 4) (RBP 3)

(7) *The Three Sisters* by Anton Chekhov (1901).

In this gloomy Russian drama, the youthful hopes of siblings Olga, Masha, and Irina Prozorov curdle with time into the desperate sins and bitter resentments of later life. Often called a play in which nothing happens, *The Three Sisters*—one of four major dramas written by Chekhov at the end of his life—is actually a masterly study in dramatic texture, its voices and themes counterpointing each other as if they were notes in an orchestral piece. (MD 7)

(7) *The Beans of Egypt, Maine* (1985), *Letourneau's Used Auto Parts* (1988), *Merry Men* (1994), a trilogy by Carolyn Chute.

These grimly naturalistic novels, set in an inland "world" of house trailers and logging camps, depict the harsh lives and quiet dignity of the rural poor in Maine. The trilogy moves outward: The first novel creates a series of characters that are *real* grotesques, offering vignettes of adultery, drunkenness, and destroyed dreams. Life gets no easier in the second novel, but Big Lucien Letourneau, who runs an automobile junkyard, displays a rare and generous compassion. The third novel, which has the most political overtones, echoes the legend of Robin Hood to suggest how Egypt, Maine, and her people have been exploited. (MSB 7)

(7) *The Hours* by Michael Cunningham (1998).

This Pulitzer Prize–winning novel describes three women whose lives resonate with Virginia Woolf's novel *Mrs. Dalloway*. There is Woolf herself, contemplating suicide even as she imagines her great novel; an American housewife in 1949 who can't quite fathom her discontent; and a contemporary woman, a lesbian in a

long-term relationship, whose great love, a man, is dying of AIDS. Melancholy, hope, and endurance suffuse this intimate novel that suggests, "There's just this for consolation: an hour here or there when our lives seem, against all odds and expectations, to burst open and give us everything we've ever imagined. . . . [Still] we hope, more than anything, for more."
(AS 7)

(7) The *U.S.A.* trilogy by John Dos Passos (1938).

Infused with the radical politics of the 1920s and 1930s and littered with newspaper excerpts, stream of consciousness prose, and biography, this triptych weaves an epic American narrative tapestry. Comprised of the novels *The 42nd Parallel, 1919,* and *The Big Money, U.S.A.* follows a host of divergent Americans from childhood on up in their unique attempts to find a place in a nation teetering on the verge of social unrest. Mixing newspaper reportage with fiction long before the word *postmodern* gave academics something to write about, *U.S.A.* reads like a newsreel and a dream.
(NM 5) (RBP 2)

(7) *The Radiant Way* by Margaret Drabble (1987).

While the title suggests a rational universe, this novel focuses on the jarring dislocations of three women who meet at Cambridge in the 1950s. The psychiatrist and mother Liz Headland—who ties together the trilogy *The Realms of Gold, The Radiant Way,* and *A Natural Curiosity*—is joined by her friends Alix Bowen, a do-gooding teacher, and Esther Breuer, an art scholar. Their experiences run the gamut, from comfortable wealth to family problems to labor unrest to a grisly murder, as they reflect Drabble's interest in characters trying to reach beyond their bourgeois lives.
(DC 7)

(7) The stories of Mavis Gallant (1922–).
Expatriate experience and cultural contrasts energize the knowing, roomy fiction of the native Canadian, sometime Parisian, master. Praised for her story sequences (such as the semiautobiographical Linnet Muir tales and those focused on aging French author Henri Grippes), Gallant also excels in generously detailed depictions of an unwanted arranged marriage ("Across the Bridge"), a German POW's survival skills ("Ernst in Civilian Clothes"), and numerous other vivid dramatizations of displacement and rootlessness (such as "The Ice Wagon Going Down the Street," "The Four Seasons").
(ML 2) (FP 5)

(7) *The Comedians* by Graham Greene (1966).
The poverty and desperation of Papa Doc Duvalier's Haitian dictatorship inform this cynical tale of failed individuals trying to hustle something from a failed state. The comedians—who hide their true identities behind masks—include Mr. Brown, a failed art swindler and now inheritor of a waning imperial hotel, Mr. Jones, a con man, and the oblivious Mr. Smith, who dreams of establishing a vegetarian center on the troubled island. As Greene contrasts these schemers with men combating Duvalier, he delivers a gripping geopolitical novel that packs a moral punch.
(CH 7)

(7) *The Evening of the Holiday* by Shirley Hazzard (1966).
Over the course of a festive summer in the Italian countryside, Sophie, who is half English and half Italian, has an affair with Tancredi, an Italian who is separated from his wife and family. Hazzard's first novel displays the talents and interests that mark

her career: luminous prose, the tension between desire and morality, the necessity of choice, and the inevitability of endings.
(PCam 7)

(7) *Hedda Gabler* by Henrik Ibsen (1890).
Like Anna Karenina and Emma Bovary, Hedda Gabler is trapped in a loveless marriage, which she entered into for security and cannot leave for fear of scandal. Though she is "crowing for life," societal norms constrict her, making Hedda a manipulative and frustrated woman. The appearance of her former lover—a brilliant, debaucherous writer—unspools a string of betrayals that end in death in this feminist play that showcases Ibsen's ability to dramatize the burning social issues of his day.
(PCle 3) (VV 4)

(7) *The Thin Red Line* by James Jones (1962).
Green recruits become hardened soldiers, their eyes reflecting the "thousand yard stare" of those who have seen too much, in this novel set during World War II's battle for Guadalcanal. Narrated from the perspective of various soldiers assigned to Charlie Company, the novel reflects the complexity of war—the horror and heroism of its licensed murder—while navigating the "thin red line between the sane and the mad."
(DFW 7)

(7) *One Flew Over the Cuckoo's Nest* by Ken Kesey (1962).
In Ken Kesey's first novel, the insane asylum becomes an allegory for the larger world as the patients are roused from their lethargy by the arrival of Randall Patrick McMurphy, a genial, larger than life con man who fakes insanity to get out of a ninety-day prison sentence. By the time McMurphy learns that he is now under the

cruel control of Nurse Ratched and the asylum, he has already set the wheels of rebellion in motion. Narrated by Chief Broom Bromden, an Indian who has not spoken in so long he is believed to be deaf and mute, McMurphy's rebellion is a spectacular fore-telling of what the 1960s were to bring.

(MCon 7)

(7) *Tinker, Tailor, Soldier, Spy* by John Le Carré (1974).
This is the first novel in Le Carré's Karla trilogy featuring aging, meticulous, self-effacing British spy George Smiley. Smiley is called out of forced retirement to root out a traitorous "mole" placed in the London headquarters of British intelligence by Soviet spymaster Karla. Working alone and without his agency's resources for fear of alerting the mole, Smiley methodically sets about unmasking his quarry in this quintessential Cold War cloak-and-dagger yarn.

(IP 7)

(7) *Under the Volcano* by Malcolm Lowry (1947).
It's the Day of the Dead in Mexico, and Geoffrey Firmin, a British ex-diplomat and professional alcoholic, is eager to oblige, embarking on a self-destructive bender like no other in literature. Lowry, who left hospitalization for his own drinking problem on the day the novel was published, recounts it all with a searing stream of consciousness that nods to Faulkner and Joyce and which Martin Amis called "drunkenness recol-lected in sobriety."

(WK 7)

(7) *The Heart Is a Lonely Hunter* by Carson McCullers (1940).
After his roommate of ten years becomes mentally ill, the deaf-

mute John Singer moves to a boarding house, where he serves as an emotional buffer for a host of isolated "grotesques" who project their own longing onto him. This inspiringly sad story of misfits in a working-class Georgia town is attuned to the racial and social dynamics of the Depression-era South. Yet, McCullers also conveys a pervasive loneliness and desperation broader than any given historical moment.
(GDG 7)

(7) *Death of a Salesman* by Arthur Miller (1949).
A broken Everyman, Willy Loman is about to be fired from his job as a traveling shoe salesman. In response he clings to fantasies—that he is "well liked" and that his troubled sons, Hap and Biff, are bound for greatness. A withering assault on the American Dream, the play is an affecting portrait of a man unable to understand the forces that have shaped his life.
(CE 3) (AT 4)

(7) *The Tale of Genji* by Shikibu Murasaki (c. 1001–1010 C.E.).
Reputedly the world's oldest novel, this immense epic romance chronicles the (mostly amorous) adventures of Japanese Prince Genji, a lowborn youth who is adopted by an emperor and grows into a handsome prodigy both irresistible to women and obsessively preoccupied with them. Genji's peregrinations outside the hermetic world of the imperial court stimulate an elaborate panorama of the life of the period; the author's depictions of Genji's various and ingenious sexual conquests still dazzle.
(KJF 7)

(7) *Speak, Memory* by Vladimir Nabokov (1951).
The son of a Russian aristocrat who was assassinated for his belief

in democracy, Nabokov had a preposterously privileged child-hood, including teams of governesses and servants and sojourns along the Riviera. When the Bolsheviks arrived, the family was forced to flee amid a hail of bullets. Later, as a student at Cambridge, Nabokov confronted those who romanticized the politics that exiled him. Ricocheting through time, space, and subject matter as it delves whimsically into the author's literary influences and the minutiae of family history, this is a masterpiece of literary memoir.

(AG 7)

(7) McTeague by Frank Norris (1899).

Gritty realism, social conscience, and American dreams power this tale of an oafish mineworker who becomes an unlicensed dentist in San Francisco. He marries a young woman and together they share a happy life, until she wins a small fortune in the lot-tery. This luck enflames their greed and the envy of their friends, leading to ruin for all and to one of the most memorable climaxes in literature: two men—one alive, one dead—handcuffed to one another in Death Valley.

(SK 7)

(7) The Things They Carried by Tim O'Brien (1990).

A Vietnam vet, O'Brien established himself as a chronicler of the war in nonfiction works such as *If I Die in a Combat Zone* (1973) and his National Book Award–winning novel *Going After Cacciato* (1978). In this, his crowning work, a character named "Tim" narrates a series of stories about himself and other young soldiers in his platoon who wrestle with the decision to go to war, walk through booby-trapped jungles, miss their loved ones, and grieve for their fallen comrades. Using simple, emotionally charged language, O'Brien explores the moral consequences and conundrums of the war through daily details, such as the things soldiers carry in their backpacks, and timeless issues, especially the scars they will always bear.

(SA 7)

(7) *Metamorphoses* by Ovid (8 C.E.).
Shining through Ovid's poetic encyclopedia of myths involving the transformations of gods and humans is this Heraclitean truth: existence is change. His versions of Orpheus, Narcissus, Pygmalion, and Hercules have been etched in our collective memory. Yet he was, as a critic once said, "counter-classical"—fun rather than imperial, personal rather than grave. Of all the Latin authors, Ovid, who also wrote a sex manual, is the one who never once reminds you of a marble bust.

(AB 7)

(7) *The Messiah of Stockholm* by Cynthia Ozick (1987).
In this novel from Ozick's mystical period, Lars Andemening, a mousy, fortyish book reviewer for a Swedish daily, has a grandiose fantasy: that he is the son of Bruno Schulz, a Polish writer murdered during World War II by a Nazi officer. But when a woman turns up in Stockholm also claiming to be Schulz's child and with a copy of Schulz's long-lost novel *The Messiah*, Lars's quest to learn about Schulz turns Oedipal.

(TCB 7)

(7) *Gargantua and Pantagruel* by François Rabelais (four books published between 1532 and 1552).
See Fred Chappell's appreciation on page 47.

(FC 7)

(7) *The Burning Plain and Other Stories* by Juan Rulfo (1953).
Like Ernest Hemingway, Rulfo found men who are shaped by violence too fascinating to judge or condemn. Set in the period around the Mexican Revolution, his short stories use pared down prose to portray peasants who are seized sometimes by historical forces and given the opportunity to create and destroy on a mass scale. More usually, they decimate or are decimated in miserable increments.
(SC 7)

(7) *The Rings of Saturn* by W. G. Sebald (1995).
An idiosyncratic chronicle of a walk along England's eastern coast, this novel moves between physical encounters and prolonged meditations on history and memory. As the narrator visits derelict estates and slumbering villages, he ponders among other things Thomas Browne's skull, Rembrandt's *Anatomy Lesson*, Conrad's journey into the heart of the Congo, the battle of Waterloo, and a villager's model of Herod's temple. Seemingly unrelated, the sketches weave a strange tapestry of grief, tranquility, nostalgia, and despair.
(EH 7)

(7) *The Lorax* by Dr. Seuss (1971).
This picture book is a poignant environmental fable about a beautiful forest of Truffula trees destroyed for the sake of the mass production of curious garments called Thneeds. Long after the forest has been destroyed, the Once-ler who destroyed it comes out of his "Lerkim on top of his store" to tell this cautionary tale to children.
(LMill 7)

(7) *A Tree Grows in Brooklyn* by Betty Smith (1943).
Despite its hopeful title, this coming-of-age story set in 1912 offers an unflinching look at poverty, cruelty, sex, and death. As we watch eleven-year-old Francie Nolan vie with her favored brother for their mother's love and deal resourcefully with privations and prejudice, Smith offers frank depictions of tenement squalor through the eyes of her resilient heroine.
(JW 7)

(7) *Kidnapped* by Robert Louis Stevenson (1886).
A coming-of-age story filled with high adventure and Scottish history, this is the story of David Balfour, an orphan sent in 1751 to live with his greedy uncle. To steal David's inheritance, his uncle has him kidnapped and taken aboard a ship to America to be sold into slavery. David and another captive escape the ship. Then, while fending off a charge of murder, David heads back to the Highlands where he hatches a clever plan to expose his uncle's wrongdoings.
(AMS 7)

(7) *The Lord of the Rings* by J. R. R. Tolkien (1954–56).
An Oxford medievalist, Tolkien drew on his vast knowledge of mythology, theology, and linguistics to imagine this epic trilogy. The books chronicle the hobbit Frodo's attempt to destroy the magical ring of Sauron, Lord of Darkness. *The Fellowship of the Ring* introduces the men, dwarves, and elves summoned by the wizard Gandalf to protect Frodo. In *The Two Towers* Frodo and his companion Sam continue their quest toward Mount Doom, while the rest of the fellowship are brought into the battle detailed in *The Return of the King*.
(CD 6) (RPow 1)

(7) *A Confederacy of Duces* by John Kennedy Toole (1980).
"The funniest novel of the twentieth century," says Donald Harington of this sprawling picaresque, which was awarded a Pulitzer Prize after Toole's suicide. Its blustering, bumfuzzled anti-hero is Ignatius J. Reilly, an unintentionally hilarious, altogether deluded, and oddly endearing student of man who lives with his mother in New Orleans. Forced by a series of misadventures to finally find work, he endures stints as a pirate-clad hot dog vendor and a file clerk. As he meets strippers, lotharios, and other sharply drawn comic characters, Ignatius rants against the world's stupidity and ponders his magnum opus, *The Journal of a Working Boy*.
(DH 7)

(7) *Phineas Finn: The Irish Member*
by Anthony Trollope (1869).
A handsome, romantically profligate young Irishman, Phineas Finn leaves his sleepy home and secret fiancée for the political world of London. As he charts the rise and fall of his calculating yet endearing hero, Trollope plunges us into the machinations of the day (especially "the Irish question") and, for good measure, introduces not one, not two, but four fascinating love interests. The novel—the second in the Palliser series—is long. But Trollope reminds us that sometimes more is more.
(CS 7)

(7) *The Color Purple* by Alice Walker (1982).
As if being black weren't hard enough, Walker's Pulitzer Prize–winning novel shows how bad life can get if you're also a woman. Wondrously, Walker gives voice to the unlikeliest of heroes—a barely literate teenager named Celie who writes letters to God as an escape from life with her monstrous stepfather. After raping and

impregnating her, he forces her to marry Mr., a cruel older man. Hope comes in the form of Shug, Mr.'s lover, and together the two women begin to loosen the shackles of race and gender.
(BMC 3) (ED 3) (SMK 1)

(7) *Charlotte's Web* by E. B. White (1952).

If cats have nine lives, pigs have two—at least Wilbur did. First he is saved by eight-year-old Fern, who can talk to animals; then he is rescued by a wise spider named Charlotte, who spins a web that convinces people Wilbur is "Some Pig." This clever, gentle, and funny children's book offers much wisdom on life, death, and friendship before ending on a five-hankie note.
(AT 7)

(7) *The Story of the Stone* by Cao Xueqin (c. 1760).

This bawdy, funny, surreal, and encyclopedic Chinese classic stretches across 120 chapters. Reality and illusion shift constantly in the world of Jia Baoyu, scion of the wealthy but declining Jia family. He is a master at the arts of poetry, philosophy, and love but meets his match in his frail, beautiful cousin Lin Daiyu, one of the twelve beauties of Jinling.
(AGold 7)

(7) *Disturbing the Peace* by Richard Yates (1975).

A meticulous, relentless account of failure and depression, this mordant novel examines the American pursuit of success in accents that echo Fitzgerald and O'Hara. Its protagonist, John Wilder, is a prototypical Yates underachiever: an advertising salesman misled by delusions of an artistic career (as a movie producer) and hampered by inherited weaknesses, a hopeful yet doomed marriage made during

the glamorous Kennedy era, and a series of breakdowns that reveal his irreversible ordinariness. Not quite tragedy, but memorable indeed for its uncompromising, compassionate bleakness.
(AMH 7)

(6) The *Regeneration* trilogy by Pat Barker (1995).

These three novels—*Regeneration* (1991), *The Eye in the Door* (1993), and *The Ghost Road* (1995)—offer an unflinching look at World War I. Starting with the real-life psychiatric treatment of poet and British officer Sigfried Sassoon for shellshock, Barker shows how the war ruined but failed to replace nineteenth-century norms of gender, class, sexuality, and honor.
(DMcF 6)

(6) *Waiting for Godot* by Samuel Beckett (1953).

Two vagabonds, Vladimir and Estragon, "blathering about nothing in particular," provoke, challenge, and defend each other while they wait for the appearance of the mysterious Godot. Twice the tramps ponder hanging themselves from the branches of a nearby willow tree; twice they try to make sense of a stranger named Pozzo and his leashed servant Lucky. All the characters abide in a world peculiar for its absences: of meaning, rationality, consolation, and of course the slyly named Godot.
(KH 3) (VM 1) (GS 2)

(6) *Woodcutters* by Thomas Bernhard (1984).

In this darkly humorous, hypnotically repetitious, stream of consciousness novel, an embittered and idealistic Austrian writer attends an "artistic" dinner party soon after the suicide of an old friend. With sharp psychological and emotional insight, Bernhard

takes readers inside the mind of his narrator as he ruminates angrily on his hosts and their other guests, picking over his memories of his relationship with them and the dead woman.
(LMill 6)

(6) *The Sheltering Sky* by Paul Bowles (1949).
This signature exploration of dislocation follows three young Americans—a married couple and their friend—journeying across the North African desert in search of deeper truths. As their surroundings become more foreign and forbidding, they become unmoored as their connection to the world, each other, and themselves unravels in this work of deep psychological acuity.
(DG 6)

(6) *Manchild in the Promised Land* by Claude Brown (1965).
Fierce, unsparing language and plenty of street jive power this autobiographical novel recounting Brown's early life as a drug dealer, hustler, and thief amid the numbers runners, prostitutes, cops, and hardworking parents of Harlem in the 1940s and 1950s. His portrait of inner-city blight rises to high tragedy as Brown paints it against the hopes of Southern blacks who came north for the promise of a better life.
(AMH 6)

(6) The stories of Raymond Carver (1938–88).
Culled from his own hard-drinking, working-class upbringing in the Pacific Northwest, Carver's stories depict relationships in various states of decay, the unsung losses of unsung people, and the prolonged misery of ordinary people delivered in a sly understated tone sometimes called dirty realism. A master of the short story, Carver's name was only beginning to be mentioned in the

same breath as Hemingway and O'Connor when lung cancer brought him down at the age of fifty.

(MB 5) (TP 1)

(6) *The Horse's Mouth* by Joyce Cary (1944).

Just out of jail, sixty-seven-year-old Gulley Jimson, a fast-talking, derelict painter obsessed with William Blake, works to complete his depiction of the Fall of Man in this wicked comic novel. Jimson is brilliant, irredeemable, and obnoxious. It is impossible not to cheer him on as he refuses to be defeated by the repeated setbacks he brings on himself through his selfish obsessiveness, insults, and thievery in this culmination of Cary's London trilogy.

(MSB 6)

(6) *Troilus and Criseyde* by Geoffrey Chaucer (1381).

The first great love story in English, this epic poem tells the story of what befell two lovers, Criseyde and Troilus, during the Trojan war. Criseyde is a stunner: "So aungellyk was hir natyf beautee / That lyk a thing immortal semed she." Troilus is a Trojan prince. Alas, Criseyde can't dally in Troy—she is forced to leave to go to the Greeks, for whom her father, a soothsayer, is working. Her pledge of eternal fidelity to Troilus is broken when she is seduced by the Greek warrior Diomedes. Is she a tramp or a victim of circumstances? Chaucer overturns the tiresome clichés of medieval misogyny in his humanistic treatment of this story.

(LM 6)

(6) *The Rime of the Ancient Mariner* by Samuel Taylor Coleridge (1798).

Intermingling the fantastic with the real, this long poem begins when a mariner with "long grey beard and glittering eye" asks a trio

of wedding guests to hear his tale. One guest stays to learn how the mariner shot the albatross, considered an omen of good luck, and doomed his ship. Though saved from death, the mariner is condemned to walk the earth and tell his story, which may be read as a Christian allegory or as a warning against defiling nature.
(BAM 6)

(6) *The Idiot* by Fyodor Dostoevsky (1868).

Prince Myshkin—epileptic, unworldly, sensitive—is the "idiot" of the title, but his gentle, generous nature forces readers to question that assumption. Myshkin (a scarcely disguised self-portrait of the author) tries again and again to help the people he encounters, only to have his efforts mocked or misunderstood. On the surface a love story, the novel is a contemplation of goodness in the world, and while its conclusions are dark, the portrait of this simple, good man endures.
(BU 6)

(6) *A Fan's Notes* by Frederick Exley (1968).

A cross between Charles Bukowski and John Kennedy Toole, this harrowing, hilarious autobiographical novel portrays a raw and likable barstool dreamer. He is a slovenly, all-American misfit headed for the psychiatric institution, who fills his head with all-American fantasies of fame, wealth, and beautiful women. He doesn't live life but watches it; his great passion is California golden boy Frank Gifford of the New York Giants, who symbolizes his hopes and whose injury triggers his self-reckoning.
(GP 6)

(6) *A Room with a View* by E. M. Forster (1908).

While the Brits might be repressed at home, they seem to lose

their heads (and sometimes their clothes) in hot, hot Italy. This eagle-eyed satire of the Italian effect stars the wealthy and young Lucy Honeychurch, who switches hotel rooms in Florence with a lower-class British father and son and then fights her mounting attraction to the son as well as her building rebelliousness against the corset of Victorian manners.
(RR 6)

(6) *Lord of the Flies* by William Golding (1955).
Usually the most disturbing book on the ninth-grade reading list—who can forget the pig's head?—the Nobel laureate's most famous novel depicts a group of boys stranded on an island after a plane crash. Some, like the intellectual Piggy, try to develop rules and society, but savagery takes hold and the boys revert to an order based on violence, tribalism, and eerie rites.
(SK 6)

(6) *The Maltese Falcon* by Dashiell Hammett (1930).
Shortly after San Francisco private eye Sam Spade accepts a case from a beautiful and mysterious young woman, his partner, Miles Archer, is killed. Though Spade despised him, his code of honor compels him to solve Archer's murder. As the two cases intersect, Spade finds himself involved with an eccentric assortment of thugs and con men, all in search of the titular black statue of a falcon said to be worth millions.
(RBP 6)

(6) *A Raisin in the Sun* by Lorraine Hansberry (1959).
Hansberry's award-winning play was the first by a black woman to be produced on Broadway. It focuses on the Youngers, a struggling African American family in 1950s Chicago, who must

decide how to spend the $10,000 insurance money Mama collects from her deceased husband. Mama wants a home, her daughter Beneatha an education, and her son Walter a business. What ensues is a generational debate over values and whether or not African Americans can realize the American Dream.
(PCle 6)

(6) *Jude the Obscure* by Thomas Hardy (1895).
Hardy's protagonists are souls ahead of their time, who dare to aspire and love in defiance of Victorian class structure and social mores. In this bleak but moving novel, class barriers stymie Jude, a self-educated stonemason and would-be scholar, while convention damns his lover Sue, a pagan protofeminist. The flawed hero and heroine win modern hearts, while the author's ferocious outcry against legal marriage, established religion, and nature itself, still challenges us today.
(TM 6)

(6) *Washington Square* by Henry James (1880).
James deeply admired Balzac. Here he pays homage to the Frenchman by recasting the novel *Eugénie Grandet*. The setting now is New York but the dynamic is the same: despite her father's best, often cruel, efforts, an unexceptional, though wealthy young woman falls in love with a dashing fortune hunter. James leaves the reader to wonder which man hurt her worse: the father who told the truth or the lover who deceived her?
(MB 3) (LM 3)

(6) *Fear of Flying* by Erica Jong (1973).
This iconic feminist novel of fantasy, liberation, and "the zipless

fuck" kicked up plenty of dust in the early 1970s. The unpublished writer and unhappily married Isadora Wing yearns to fly free and receives her epiphany through an affair and the discovery of her own sexuality and power. Many critics dismissed Jong as a pornographer in literary clothing; her protagonist, they claimed, was as self-absorbed as the baby boomers themselves. But the book sold millions and became a touchstone for a much greater social movement.

(DFW 6)

(6) *Lucy* by Jamaica Kincaid (1990).

Nineteen-year-old Lucy happily leaves her West Indian home and domineering mother to work as an au pair for a well-off and well-meaning American family. But as she develops a new sense of self and independence, she is forced to grapple with life as an outsider, a servant, and a woman of color in a country obsessed with race yet blind to history. Conveyed in Kincaid's stinging yet poetic prose, Lucy's awakening illuminates the divides between power and powerlessness, complacency and outrage, comfort and justice.

(TCB 6)

(6) *The Poisonwood Bible* by Barbara Kingsolver (1998).

Set in the Belgian Congo in 1959, it details Baptist preacher Nathan Price's one-man campaign to convert African natives to Christianity in an unforgiving land. Kingsolver juxtaposes Nathan's monomania with his wife Orleanna's stoical solidarity with their four daughters, who react variously to their father's missionary zeal and the culture it never manages to reach (much less transform), in this rich portrayal of American innocence and arrogance run amok.

(EDon 6)

(6) *Bertha* (1959) and *George Washington Crosses the Delaware* (1962), two plays by Kenneth Koch.

These two plays about the exuberance of war are from the renowned New York School poet who said his dramatic influences included Shakespeare's chronicle plays, Alfred Jarry's parody of *Macbeth*, *Ubi Roi*, the experimental music of John Cage, and *A Visit from Saint Nicholas* by Clement Moore. Koch's plays are brief, abrupt, language-centered, and childlike in their wonderment and humor, often undercutting heroic stances with a joke but always striving to capture what the playwright called "Dionysiac things."

(AT 6)

(6) *The Towers of Trebizond* by Rose Macaulay (1956).

In the tradition of novels satirizing encounters between eccentric British characters and foreign cultures, Macaulay follows the efforts of four travelers to improve women's rights, and spread the blessings of the Anglican church, in Turkey. The novel's first half brims with sharp comic insights. The second half is far more meditative as it focuses on the character Laurie—a church-goer conducting an adulterous affair—who suffers a crisis of faith that becomes a profound spiritual journey.

(PCam 6)

(6) *Tropic of Cancer* by Henry Miller (1934).

Banned in America for twenty-seven years because it was considered obscene, this autobiographical novel describes the author's hand-to-mouth existence in Paris during the early 1930s. A later inspiration to the Beat generation, Miller offers various philosophical interludes expressing his joy in life, hostility to social convention, and reverence for women and sex, which he describes with abandon.

(PCle 4) (JH 2)

(6) *A House for Mr. Biswas* by V. S. Naipaul (1961).

An Indian man living in Trinidad, Mr. Biswas is a tenant in some houses and an unfavored relative in others. All he wants is a home of his own. His adult son narrates this story of his monumental search for a home and all that implies. The quest becomes a metaphor for the displacements of postcolonial life in this novel that, while filled with poverty and loneliness, is also a teeming, comic epic of Hindu life in Naipaul's native West Indies.

(HJ 3) (CM 3)

(6) *Tell Me a Riddle* by Tillie Olsen (1961).

A progressive activist and single mother who toiled beside and fought for the working class, Olsen was fifty years old when this, her first book, was published. This deceptively slim volume of four short stories contains a lifetime of experience, depicting the often anguished lives of women and their children, the difficulties of aging, and the challenges faced by immigrants. The title story showcases her rich, spare language as it explores a troubled marriage: "how deep back the stubborn, gnarled roots of the quarrel reached, no one could say . . . but the roots swelled up visible, split the earth between them."

(ST 6)

(6) *Sheila Levine Is Dead and Living in New York*
by Gail Parent (1972).

Perhaps the funniest suicide note ever written, this novel is the last goodbye of a single New York woman. When Shelia Levine hits thirty she decides it's time to tie the knot. But finding a proper mate proves impossible in swinging Manhattan and her quest turns to hopeless despair in this clever, insightful, and often heartbreaking book.

(JW 6)

(6) *Cry, the Beloved Country* by Alan Paton (1948).

Written just before apartheid became law in South Africa, this novel exposes the nation's racial problems through the story of a rural black minister who travels to Johannesburg to save a friend's daughter, who has become a prostitute, and later, his son, who is accused of murder. This vivid portrait of South Africa is informed by the white author's Christian faith, which suggests that only changed hearts can reform, and redeem, his nation.

(AMS 6)

(6) *Pale Horse, Pale Rider* by Katherine Anne Porter (1939).

The title novella of Porter's celebrated collection follows her semi-autobiographical protagonist Miranda (who appears elsewhere in Porter's fiction) through the ordeals of World War I and the 1918 influenza epidemic. Detailed stream of consciousness narration depicts Miranda's remembered Texas childhood, her work as a newspaper critic, and her romance with a handsome soldier, as well as the hallucinatory visions provoked by her own illness and slow recovery, the soldier's death in combat, and an encompassing sense of personal and wider worlds threatened by encroaching catastrophe.

(MG 6)

(6) *All Quiet on the Western Front*
by Erich Maria Remarque (1929).

Remarque drew on his military experience to craft this seminal

antiwar novel. At the outset of World War I, Paul Baumer and his fellow Germans are gung-ho. As the senseless bloodbath continues, hope turns to disillusionment, and death comes to seem a welcome reprieve in this gritty and poignant tale.
(SV 6)

(6) *Good Morning, Midnight* by Jean Rhys (1939).
On hell's short bookshelf of great writing about alcohol, this novel is narrated by Sasha Jansen, a semi-writer at loose ends who is planning a permanent swan dive into the bottle. While Virginia Woolf thought women needed a room of their own for creative work, Jansen believes "a room is a place where you hide from the wolves outside." Jansen's fugue through 1930s Paris, while pursued by age, disapproving bartenders, and a stubborn gigolo, is a café blues song: stylish and haunting.
(SC 6)

(6) *Impressions of Africa* by Raymond Roussel (1910).
The masterpiece of one of France's leading experimental writers, this novel begins with the shipwreck of a band of Europeans held for ransom in a mythical African kingdom. As they await their release, each displays a theatrical or technical skill to be showcased at a gala ball. In the novel's second half, Roussel describes how the characters developed these surprising skills in pun-filled, allusion-fueled prose.
(BM 6)

(6) *The Emigrants* by W. G. Sebald (1992).
The German writer's works are melancholy compressions of life stories lined with large, historical themes. *The Emigrants* presents four portraits of exile: a doctor who flees to England, a persecuted teacher who takes his own life, a relative of Sebald's who receives

shock treatment in an American sanatorium, and a painter who moves to Manchester to escape the gathering Holocaust. Sebald's haunted, almost hypnotic prose is juxtaposed with numerous photographs, which give the stories the feel of powerful documentaries. "And so they are ever returning to us," he writes, "the dead." Sebald is their archivist.

(DL 6)

(6) *Henry IV*, Parts I and II by William Shakespeare (1596–98). These plays follow the rise of Prince Hal, son of Henry IV, from wastrel cavalier to powerful King Henry V, who would lead the English army to victory over the French at Agincourt in 1415, as dramatized in *Henry V*. Hal's maturation from rioting prince to deadly serious king is not without complications, however, as he renounces a festive underworld of great verbal richness, unparalleled wit, and creative energy for a ruthless, sinister, and murderous world of Machiavellian politics where might equals right. The most famous casualty of this transformation is Shakespeare's greatest comic creation, Sir John Falstaff, Hal's boon companion in Part I, whom the prince summarily rejects in Part II.

(JSalt 6)

(6) *A Midsummer Night's Dream* by William Shakespeare (1595). The summit of Shakespeare's early romantic comedies, this play explores the troubled course of love leading to the marriages of King Theseus of Athens and Hippolyta, Queen of the Amazons, and two young aristocratic Athenian couples. The trouble begins when the king of fairies interferes with the Athenian couples via his agent Puck, who administers love potions to the wrong characters. The ensuing confusion is finally resolved in the fifth act as

the royal marriage is celebrated by the performance of a hilarious piece of nonsense staged by simple guildsmen led by Bottom the weaver, whose dream gives the play its name.
(KJF 6)

(6) *The Pillow-Book of Sei Shōnagon* (1592).
This groundbreaking nonfiction work by a tenth-century lady of the Chinese court uses the list as the structure for personal essays that are bold, funny, unapologetic, and cantankerous. With titles such as "Embarrassing Things," "Hateful Things," and "Depressing Things," Shōnagon reflects on her society, its mores in particular, and on humanity in general.
(HJ 6)

(6) *The Old Forest and Other Stories* by Peter Taylor (1985).
Set in the South of the 1920s and 1930s, the genteel surfaces of Taylor's stories cloak the unspoken tensions and the rigors of class and economics. Taylor creates stories that are novelistic in their pacing as he digresses and speculates on alternative possibilities to the narrative at hand. Often told by men reflecting on the past, these stories suggest that time does not slay mores and ideas but reinvents them.
(EC 6)

(6) *Resurrection* by Leo Tolstoy (1899).
As a juror on a Moscow murder trial, the middle-aged dandy Prince Nekhlyudov recognizes the defendant as a girl from his family's country estate whom he had once seduced and abandoned. Blaming himself for her fate, he follows her into exile in Siberia to atone for his actions and the loss of his youthful idealism. Part social exposé, part religious tract expounding Tolstoy's

unorthodox Christianity, the book lambastes Russia's social divisions and inept justice system.
(VM 6)

(6) *Cane* by Jean Toomer (1923).
A hybrid of literary forms—poetry, prose, and drama—and a groundbreaking work of black literature, this book is a collage of portraits of African Americans from the urban North to the rural South. "Kabnis," the third part of the book, unites the work's themes in a story of Ralph Kabnis, an educated northerner who has come to Georgia to teach and is transformed as an artist by the beauty and violence of life there.
(PE 6)

(6) *The Last Chronicle of Barset* by Anthony Trollope (1867).
Trollope's inimitable gift for combining the chatty and the epic found its greatest flowering in this, the sixth and final volume of his Barsetshire series. From a simple premise—a proud but poor clergyman, Josiah Crawley, is accused of stealing twenty pounds—Trollope creates a web of vivid characters and intrigues while completing a monumental set of works about mid-nineteenth-century England that rival the classics of George Eliot and Charles Dickens.
(JR 6)

(6) *The Green House* by Mario Vargas Llosa (1965).
See David Anthony Durham's appreciation on page 59.
(DAD 6)

(6) *The Ponder Heart* by Eudora Welty (1954).
In this comic monologue filled with witty Southern colloqui-

alisms and vivid images, Miss Edna Earle Ponder, who manages a hotel in a small Mississippi town, describes her family's wonderfully peculiar history. Her story focuses on her uncle, the eccentric and irrepressible Daniel Ponder, whose poor marriages created as many problems as his generous heart.
(LKA 6)

(6) *Miss Lonelyhearts* by Nathanael West (1933).
In this short novel on the soul-sickness of mass society, a New York advice columnist with a Christ complex is laid low by his taste for married women and his belief in his own redemptive powers. The letters in *Miss Lonelyhearts* were based on actual missives to residents of two hotels the novelist managed in the 1920s—letters West steamed open to read.
(WK 3) (APat 3)

(6) *Black Lamb and Grey Falcon: A Journey Through Yugoslavia* by Rebecca West (1941).
While England slept, West clearly saw the danger of Hitler, who embodied for her the "genius of murder which has shaped our recent history." Her account of a trip from Dalmatia to Kosovo reads like the cry of a modern Cassandra. As she details the stirrings of blind ethnic hatred among the Serbs and Croats, she offers a preview of nightmares to come.
(AF 6)

(6) *The Age of Innocence* by Edith Wharton (1920).
Martin Scorsese called his 1993 movie of this novel the most violent film he had made—quite a statement from the director of *Raging Bull*. The innocence here is not in the setting of 1870s upper-crust New York, whose starch-stiff social code hides a viper's nest of

jealousies and conspiracy, but in hero Newland Archer, a newlywed socialite who fancies himself simply an observer of his class. His infatuation with a European divorcée leads to a most unsentimental education on his true position.

(SM 6)

(6) *Revolutionary Road* by Richard Yates (1961).

Trying to avoid the conformity of their suburban neighbors on Revolutionary Road, Frank and April Wheeler talk of moving to France where Frank might write the great book or think the great thoughts April believes he is capable of. However, infidelity and alcohol abuse dissolve their dreams as Frank and April lose faith in each other and themselves in this exquisitely painful novel.

(KA 3) (JBud 3)

(6) *Memoirs of Hadrian* by Marguerite Yourcenar (1951).

The French author started her novel at age twenty-one; she rediscovered it at forty-six, ending a mammoth bout of writer's block. Two years later she completed this intimate first-person narrative of the second-century emperor. Through Yourcenar's magisterial prose, Hadrian—a thoughtful, sensual man aware of both the fleeting nature of time and eternal verities—details his rise and his liberal policies, especially his belief that it is wiser to embrace your neighbors than to go to war against them. Ever the pragmatist, he notes, "Catastrophe and ruin will come; disorder will triumph, but order will too, from time to time."

(ML 5) (JS 1)

(5) *Gorilla, My Love* by Toni Cade Bambara (1972).

A feminist and civil rights activist, Bambara strove to create litera-

ture that reflected the experiences of black women, the strength of black communities from the urban North to the rural South, and the challenges they faced. Showcasing Bambara's talent for transforming her social concerns into art, the fifteen stories in this collection feature sharp-tongued first-person narrators who draw on their charm, resolve, and compassion to triumph over—or at least make peace with—life's obstacles.
(PCle 5)

(5) *The Sot-Weed Factor* by John Barth (1960).
Digressions, asides, and stories within stories fill this bawdy, raucous parody of eighteenth-century fiction that reimagines the life of Ebenezer Cooke, who wrote a satirical poem titled *The Sot-Weed Factor* in 1708. Overseeing his father's Maryland tobacco plantation, Cooke tries to defend his prized virginity against women and men, while extricating himself from intrigues and counterintrigues. Language sizzles in this Rabelasian tale that includes one of the longest lists of insults ever committed to paper.
(DH 5)

(5) *A Legacy* by Sybille Bedford (1956).
See David Leavitt's appreciation on page 89.
(DL 5)

(5) *Henderson the Rain King* by Saul Bellow (1956).
Bellow's characters often stumble along comic paths toward equilibrium, and none of the Nobel laureate's creations is more rollicking than Eugene Henderson. A multimillionaire cut loose in Africa, Henderson is a portrait of human striving, with his battle cry: "I want, I want, I want." We follow him off the beaten tourist path, watching him blow up a cistern filled with frogs, make

friends with a lioness, and be crowned the Rain King after he seems to end a long drought. As always with Bellow, comedy is the handmaiden of an ultimate optimism. "I am a true adorer of life," Henderson says, "and if I can't reach as high as the face of it, I plant my kiss somewhere lower down."
(EC 5)

(5) *A Clockwork Orange* by Anthony Burgess (1962).
The linguistic virtuosity of this futuristic tale—told in *nadsat*, a russified English—lures us into an unwilling complicity in the drug-fueled bouts of ultraviolence committed by Alex and his *droogs* (comrades). While the book's first part portrays these alienated sociopaths, the second part is an old-fashioned allegory: to win release from prison, Alex submits to behavior modification, trading his free will for freedom in this Cold War–era novel that protests against the intimate threat of totalitarian power.
(PE 5)

(5) *Mildred Pierce* by James M. Cain (1941).
After shedding her philandering, unemployed husband, Mildred Pierce works menial jobs to support her two children before discovering a gift for making and selling pies in Depression-era California. She's a strong woman with two fatal flaws—an attraction to weak men and blind devotion to her monstrously selfish daughter Veda. These weaknesses join to form a perfect storm of betrayal and murder in this hard-boiled tale.
(JLB 4) (MCon 1)

(5) *The Postman Always Rings Twice* by James M. Cain (1934).
When a drifter enters her roadside diner, a sexy young woman

imagines a new life. Together they plot the murder of her boorish husband in this noir classic, in which spare prose and desperate characters raise dime-store pulp to an art form.
(WK 5)

(5) *The War with the Newts* by Karel Čapek (1936).
This prescient and humorous Czech novel—part allegory, part satire, part science fiction romp—begins with the discovery of a new species of giant newt by a sea captain in an obscure tropical bay. Initially exploited for their pearl-harvesting abilities, the newts become the objects of scientific experimentation and then a massive global slave trade before they rise up and revolt, bringing humanity to its knees.
(LMill 5)

(5) *Blithe Spirit* by Noël Coward (1941).
As the Nazis bore down on Britain, Coward filled London theaters with this gay and witty farce about death. The sublime silliness begins when a writer holds a séance to research his novel on a murderous fake psychic. Who should appear but his first wife, dead these six years and none too happy about wife number two.
(AT 5)

(5) *White Noise* by Don DeLillo (1985).
Professor Jack Gladney teaches Hitler studies at the local college and trawls through the tabloid mall of American culture with his pill-popping fourth wife and their four preternaturally knowing children. Then an accident near their town generates a huge poisonous cloud—"an airborne toxic event"—and disrupts their uneasy idyll. This apocalyptic cult classic amusingly and then

chillingly captures how media culture has become not just our atmosphere but our food and oxygen.
(TCB 5)

(5) *Play It as It Lays* by Joan Didion (1970).
So pared to the bone is Didion's prose, so intimate her understanding of psychic pain, one pictures her writing not with a pen but a razor. In this stark novel of soulless Hollywood, Maria, once beautiful and prized, now gaunt and withdrawn, struggles to regain her footing after her mother's death, her young daughter's institutionalization, an illegal abortion, and a divorce. As Didion exposes with steely restraint the poisonous contempt accorded women, she turns Los Angeles's death-defying expressways and the lethal desert beyond into stunning metaphors for alienation.
(DC 5)

(5) *The Count of Monte Cristo* by Alexandre Dumas (1844).
The fastest fifteen hundred pages in world literature begins on the wedding day of Edmond Dantès, when he is falsely accused of treason. He is condemned to a remote prison where he finds out who framed him and about a treasure hidden on the Island of Monte Cristo. After fourteen years he escapes, finds the fortune, and returns to Paris where he dazzles the swells while seeking revenge on his enemies.
(ST 5)

(5) *The Lover* by Marguerite Duras (1984).
This Prix Goncourt–winning work might now be considered an early "fictional memoir." Drawn from Duras's life in prewar Indochina, it tells the story of the ill-fated love between a young girl and her Chinese lover. Lyrical, imagistic, and structured in

cumulative short passages, Duras combines the beautiful and the terrible in this slim, compelling novel.
(KHarr 5)

(5) *The Love Song of J. Alfred Prufrock* by T. S. Eliot (1915).
Eliot's first major poem is a dramatic monologue in the voice of a spiritually exhausted, emotionally sterile Everyman. Prufock has "measured out my life with coffee spoons." He tells himself "There will be time to murder and create," though he fears to act—"Do I dare to eat a peach?" Prufrock was only the first of Eliot's many dis-illusioned city dwellers, but with his ridiculous name and fastidious appearance, he may well have been the most poignant.
(RBP 5)

(5) *Red Shift* by Alan Garner (1973).
An ancient stone ax head connects the three young protagonists in this bleak science fiction novel set around Cheshire, England, during three time periods—the Roman Empire, the English Civil War, and the present day. Alienated from themselves and those they love, the three men—who share a similar name—feel the pull of a mystic force that they can't quite fathom. Their experi-ences echo each other in this experimental tale told almost entirely in dialogue.
(EDon 5)

(5) *Death of the Fox* (1971), *The Succession* (1983), *and Entered from the Sun* (1990), a trilogy by George Garrett.
Packed with conspiracies, intrigues, bright language, and even more colorful characters, these novels enter the mind and mores of late Elizabethan and early Stuart England through dramatic events: *Death of the Fox* hinges on the rise, fall, and execution of Sir

Walter Raleigh in 1618; *The Succession* re-creates the royal rivalries that surfaced as James I assumed the throne in 1603; *Entered from the Sun* focuses on the possible political implications of the murder of poet and playwright Christopher Marlowe in 1597.
(MSB 5)

(5) *Lanark: A Life in Four Books* by Alasdair Gray (1981).
In the maverick Scottish author's testy allegory, four (eccentrically illustrated) "books," which are presented nonsequentially, trace the lives of two protagonists who are a single frustrated artist. Grim naturalism depicts Glaswegian painter Duncan Thaw's losing battles with public indifference and chronic illness. Blakean fantasy traces the parallel sufferings of Thaw's eponymous alter ego, whose misadventures in the dystopian city of Unthank represent Thaw's continuing miseries in the hereafter he inhabits following his suicide. Accusatory, opaque, redundant—the novel is also, oddly enough, compulsively readable and perversely memorable.
(ALK 5)

(5) *Nothing* (1926), *Doting* (1950), and *Blindness* (1952)
by Henry Green.
Green was the pen name for British industrialist Henry Vincent Yorke, whose kaleidoscopic, impressionistic novels (including cryptic plots and sentences without articles or verbs) have drawn comparisons to fellow high-modernists Gertrude Stein, Picasso, and Monet. *Blindness* details the terror of a blind young man confined to a room by his wife. *Doting* (a comedy of adulterous near-misses) and *Nothing* (about two ex-lovers whose children are getting married) consist almost entirely of pitch-perfect dialogue.
(HJ 5)

(5) *The Silence of the Lambs* by Thomas Harris (1988).
Dr. Hannibal "the Cannibal" Lecter is a deranged serial killer and a brilliant psychiatrist—who better to help the FBI profile psychos like Buffalo Bill, who loves peeling the skin off his lovely young victims? So the Bureau dispatches Clarice Starling, a smart, charming, slightly vulnerable agent, to Lecter's prison cell. While playing mind games with Clarice, Lecter provides her with strange but telling clues, which she pursues against her superiors' wishes and the clock ticking out the seconds for Buffalo Bill's next victim.
(DFW 5)

(5) The stories of Nathaniel Hawthorne (1804–64).
A child of the Romantic era, Hawthorne nonetheless remained haunted by his Puritan forefathers. Tales such as "Young Goodman Brown," "My Kinsman, Major Molineux," and "The Wives of the Dead," are steeped in the subject matter and sensibility of colonial New England, and clouded by crime, sin, and persecution. He peoples them with Puritans, witches, American Indians, and revolutionaries, and narrates the fate of all with his trademark combination of lively Gothic fantasy and critical irreverence.
(HK 5)

(5) *A Farewell to Arms* by Ernest Hemingway (1929).
Based on Hemingway's experiences during World War I, this romantic tragedy recounts the story of Frederic Henry, an American volunteer in the Italian ambulance corps who meets and eventually falls in love with a maternal yet alluring English nurse, Catherine Barkley. Eventually, they abandon the war for neutral Switzerland—Frederic and Catherine have made "a separate

peace"—though other dangers await in this story of commitment, individual choice, and the narrow line separating courage and hypocrisy.
(SV 5)

(5) *The Europeans* by Henry James (1878).

After the dissolution of her marriage to a German prince, Eugenia Munster and her artist brother Felix visit their wealthy relatives in the countryside near Boston. Felix's easy sophistication and Eugenia's fierce independence contrast with the pious Yankee values of their hosts in this sparkling novel of romantic intrigues that depicts the clash between European and American cultures and values.
(AMS 5)

(5) *The Metamorphosis* by Franz Kafka (1915).

This harrowing narrative of a clerk, Gregor Samsa, who wakes from "uneasy dreams" to find himself transformed into a giant insect, is the quintessential Kafkaesque tale. Gregor is not dreaming; he really has become a bug who hides under the sofa to keep from horrifying his mother, and who is pummeled with apples and cursed by his father. The strange magic of the story is the way Kafka sustains our empathy with this creature, such that the bizarre and claustrophobic scenes intensify, and even haunt, our awareness of human vulnerability.
(CH 5)

(5) *Pearl* by Tabitha King (1988).

A small inheritance brings Pearl Dickenson—a smart, resourceful, and independent African American woman—to rural Maine. She stays for the peace and security it seems to offer. She takes over a

local diner and takes on two lovers, both of whom have troubled pasts. These liaisons turn to trouble, threatening Pearl and her community.
(JW 5)

(5) *Darkness at Noon* by Arthur Koestler (1940).
An old Party member is arrested for treason in Stalin's Russia. As his interrogators try to pry a false confession out of Rubashov, the state's twisted logic—that Rubashov's innocence, and his identity itself, are bourgeois luxuries compared to the task of preserving the revolution from exterior threats—is exposed in this novel, which deeply influenced how intellectuals in the West and dissidents in the East interpreted the Cold War experience.
(AF 5)

(5) *Hombre* by Elmore Leonard (1961).
Displaying his trademark ability to turn pulp into art, Leonard elevates the classic Western through the story of John Russell, a white man raised partly by Apache Indians who taught him how to fight and survive. The action begins when Russell boards a stagecoach and is rejected by passengers because of his roots. When outlaws pounce, the others turn to him for protection. Will he or won't he? Leonard answers that question in this action-filled tale while probing Western myths, issues of race, and our responsibilities to our unlikable fellow man.
(GDG 5)

(5) *The Betrothed* by Alessandro Manzoni (1827).
Romeo and Juliet had nothing on Renzo and Lucia, whose union is threatened by famine, plagues, riots, and the Thirty Years' War.

A vibrant portrait of seventeenth-century Lombardy, this novel combines a Dickensian cast of characters with Sir Walter Scott's flair for romance. It is also a deeply religious work whose tragedies raise profound questions about God's will and whose ultimate message is one of faith.
(BU 5)

(5) *The Chateau* by William Maxwell (1961).

Plus ça change: Harold and Barbara Rhodes, a young American couple, expect smiles and bouquets from their liberated hosts as they vacation in France soon after the end of World War II. Instead, they find—surprise!—European chilliness and inscrutability. While this novel's situation comes straight from Henry James, its language and sensibility—deep empathy and a sense of lost worlds that is not the least bit nostalgic—is pure Maxwell.
(PCam 5)

(5) *A Severed Head* by Iris Murdoch (1961).

Infused with Freudian theories—especially about male sexuality—and Jungian archetypes, this novel centers on a man who must search his soul and his mind after his wife leaves him for her psychoanalyst. With often dark, deadpan humor, Murdoch uses deception, adultery, and sex to address morality and responsibility, the nature of reality, and the power of the unconscious.
(AMH 5)

(5) *Appointment in Samarra* (1934) and *BUtterfield 8* (1935) by John O'Hara.

The man Brendan Gill credited with inventing *The New Yorker* short story also wrote nicely observed novels of cynical slumming and sexual frankness. *Appointment in Samarra* relates the long weekend in

which a Cadillac dealer gleefully destroys his life; *BUtterfield 8* follows a cheap-date actress through the ferocious demimonde of speakeasy New York.
(TW 5)

(5) *The Bell Jar* by Sylvia Plath (1963).
This autobiographical novel, a raw, eloquent articulation of a young woman's nervous breakdown after a summer working at a New York fashion magazine, is especially unsettling because it was published after Plath's suicide. Her alter ego, Esther Greenwood, is a girl's Holden Caulfield, ripping away the phoniness of the suburbs, the city, and the doctors who would shock her back into submission. Ultimately, Esther rallies against a sterile world and finds a way to live. Plath did not.
(SMK 5)

(5) *Tales of Mystery and Imagination*
by Edgar Allan Poe (1836–47).
These pieces influenced almost every contemporary genre, from adventure stories ("The Narrative of A. Gordon Pym") to amateur detective mysteries ("The Purloined Letter") to lurid horror tales ("The Cask of Amontillado"). Poe's fascination with psychology and the dark sides of human behavior jump-started the first great age of American fiction and, through his influence on French symbolists such as Baudelaire, helped to transform literature in the nineteenth century.
(MC 5)

(5) *La Flor de Lis* by Elena Poniatowska (1988).
See Sandra Cisneros's appreciation on page 49.
(SC 5)

(5) *His Dark Materials* by Philip Pullman (1995–2000).

This epic trilogy, comprised of *Northern Lights* (a.k.a., *The Golden Compass*), *The Subtle Knife,* and *The Amber Spyglass,* reconceives *Paradise Lost* as an adventure/fantasy from an atheist, humanist perspective. Like Adam and Eve, Lyra and Will embrace knowledge. But for them it is the path to liberation, not damnation. In thrilling quests across magic universes filled with demons, angels, and talking animals, they battle "the Authority" that demands faith while repressing freedom.

(CD 5)

(5) *Frankenstein* by Mary Shelley (1818).

Readers should be grateful that Dr. Phil was not around in 1818. If he had been, Mary Shelley may have chosen to discuss her traumatic life with him. Instead, she turned trauma into art and wrote *Frankenstein,* in which the outcast Dr. Victor Frankenstein usurps God's and woman's life-giving power to create a monster who for all his desire cannot be loved. This novel about unwanted things is gripping, frightening, inspiring, and very different from the movies based on it.

(AB 5)

(5) *Ceremony* by Leslie Marmon Silko (1977).

Like many returning soliders, Tayo, who is half white and half Laguna Indian, has a hard time readjusting to civilian life after World War II, when he was held prisoner by the Japanese. Instead of venting his rage or turning to drink, he connects with a medicine man who helps him find solace through traditional ceremonies that reveal life as a process of change and growth.

(SA 5)

(5) *On the Eve* **by Ivan Turgenev (1860).**
Turgenev's ur-themes of authenticity and humanism are highlighted in this tragic love story in which Elena Stahov, the novel's passionate and do-gooding heroine, falls in love not with the suitor her father has picked for her, but with Dimitry Insarov, a Bulgarian revolutionary who blazes like a flame against the feckless upper-middle-class Russians that make up Elena's other suitors.
(ES 5)

(5) *Brideshead Revisited* **by Evelyn Waugh (1945).**
Waugh was one of the twentieth century's great satirists, yet this novel, widely considered his best, is not satiric. It is, instead, an examination of Roman Catholic faith as it is used, abused, embraced, and rejected by the Flytes, an aristocratic English family visited by alcoholism, adultery, and homoeroticism.
(PM 5)

(5) *The Custom of the Country* **by Edith Wharton (1913).**
A sharp critique of the limits society placed on women and the empty dreams it manufactured for them, this novel tells the story of Undine Spragg, a relentless social climber who will attach herself to any man to raise her station. Her ambition and her unquenchable need for prestige and flattery blinds her to the strengths of these men, whom she injures, and to her own humanity, which she surrenders.
(JBarn 5)

(5) *Right Ho, Jeeves* **by P. G. Wodehouse (1934).**
Including perhaps the funniest scene in the Wodehouse canon—Gussie Fink-Nottle's drunken speech at the Market Snodsbury

Grammar School—this madcap farce once again finds Bertie Wooster and his brilliant manservant Jeeves working to point Cupid's arrows toward other hearts. Truth be told, newt-loving Gussie Fink-Nottle and droopy Madeline Basset belong together just as surely as Angela was made from Tuppy Glossop's rib. After a series of gentle misunderstandings, Bertie and Jeeves may lift the scales from everyone's eyes. Right ho!
(AGold 5)

(5) *The Waves* by Virgina Woolf (1931).

This grand experiment in narrative depicts six characters—from nursery school to the brink of old age—through a series of interior soliloquies. Stages in their lives are framed by bits of description of a day on a deserted beach; the book's finale, their reunion at a London restaurant, is a tour de force. "The light of civilization is burnt out," one character thinks while gazing at London's night sky in this haunting, poetic meditation on time's passage.
(BM 5)

(4) *How German Is It* by Walter Abish (1980).

Abish wields not pen, but scalpel, vivisecting Germany's cult of appearances and culture of denial. His protagonist is Ulrich, whose father was executed for plotting against Hitler. Ulrich—a cipher who married, conspired with, and has now informed on a left-wing terrorist—has returned to his fatherland after a long absence to seek his estranged wife and his own true paternity and patrimony. With the discovery of a mass grave and the descent of his model citizen brother into debauchery and thuggery, Ulrich sees the residue of prewar Germany in the postwar world.
(HJ 4)

(4) *Borderlands/La Frontera* **by Gloria Anzaldúa (1999).**
The author uses poetry and prose—mythology, history, memoir—in this passionate account of two types of borders. The first is the physical one between Texas and Mexico. The second is psychological, mapping borderlands defined by sex, race, class, culture, and religion. She is particularly interested in intersections, "where the space between two individuals shrinks with intimacy."
(SC 4)

(4) *The Handmaid's Tale* **by Margaret Atwood (1986).**
Atwood offers another piercing fiction about humankind's place in nature and women's place in society in this chilling futuristic novel in which widespread sterility has led to totalitarian control of procreation. Offred has been forced into service as a Handmaid and will become a surrogate mother if the Commander manages to impregnate her before his embittered wife harms her. Garbed in a red habit and living like a slave, Offred covertly records her harrowing story, finding freedom in preserving her observations and in expressing her mordant wit and unnerving wisdom.
(CD 3) (JW 1)

(4) *Oryx and Crake* **by Margaret Atwood (2003).**
In this richly imagined speculative novel spiked with doomsday humor, Atwood envisions a world where our hubris, obsessions with technology and profit, and environmental abuse result in hell on earth. As her rueful narrator, Snowman, struggles to survive in a harsh postapocalyptic world, he becomes a reluctant guru for a bioengineered tribe of innocents (created by the mad

genius, Crake), recalls his ruthlessly competitive lost world, and asks: What does it mean to be human?
(GDG 4)

(4) *Mansfield Park* by Jane Austen (1814).

Fanny Price is the least loved of Austen's heroines: "prig" is a common complaint of her critics. It's true that reticent, unsure Fanny Price, sent to live with her cold, wealthy relatives, lacks the Austen spunk. She doesn't offer witticisms but recoils in horror at her cousins' display of vices, including amorous behavior, sexual jealousy, and unbridled snobbery. Her passivity can grow wearing. But Fanny enables Austen to craft her darkest work, which asks: What happens when a good soul finds itself trapped in an immoral world?
(SM 4)

(4) *Splendeurs et misères des courtisanes (A Harlot High and Low)* by Honoré de Balzac (1847).

Balzac claimed a crime lay behind every great fortune. Here his master criminal from *Père Goriot,* Vautrin, tests that hypothesis by orchestrating the rise of the poet, dandy, and social parasite Lucien de Rubempré. Vautrin is in love with him. So is Esther, a reformed prostitute. Vautrin counts on Esther's feelings as the linchpin of his complex scheme. But love turns out to be one of life's incalculables in this central novel in Balzac's series, *The Human Comedy*.
(IP 4)

(4) *Continental Drift* by Russell Banks (1985).

Working-class New Hampshirite Bob Dubois flees his existence as an oil burner repairman for what he assumes will be a warmer future in Florida. Not far from his new home, but in another social

universe, Vanise Dorsinvilles undergoes a much more brutal journey to the sunshine state from her native Haiti. How their fates intertwine is at the heart of this story of the tenuousness of class, fate, and opportunity in a harsh country.
(MSB 4)

(4) *The Book of Evidence* by John Banville (1989).
Frederick Charles St. John Venderveld Montgomery is an Irishman who has traveled the world. Back in his dull hometown, he becomes obsessed with a three hundred-year-old painting. He murders an old woman to secure it. Upon his capture for that crime, he offers a confession that reveals his savage heart and soulless existence.
(ALK 4)

(4) *Correction* by Thomas Bernhard (1975).
This dense philosophic novel consisting of two long paragraphs begins with the suicide of an Austrian scientist named Roithamer. As his childhood friend (and our nameless narrator) remembers him and sorts through his papers, we learn about an unhappy man who built a protective Cone in a local forest to provide his sister "supreme happiness." Instead it leads to her death. Roithamer's papers are defined by incessant revisions; his "corrections" deny all that came before; his last act emerges as his final correction.
(BM 4)

(4) *The Death of the Heart* by Elizabeth Bowen (1938).
When orphaned teenager Portia Quayne comes to London to live with her effete, older half-brother Thomas and his cynical, sophisticated wife Anna, she finds warmth only in a crusty family servant—and in the inappropriate attentions of family friend

Eddie, who toys heartlessly with the girl's emotional adoration. Bowen brings Jamesian subtlety to bear on Portia's revivifying loss of illusions and steady growth toward maturity. The result is a triumph of analytical precision in this tragedy of innocence endangered by unfeeling adults.
(GG 4)

(4) *Auto-da-Fé* by Elias Canetti (1935).
Peter Kien, an obsessive collector who only feels comfortable in his world of books, is tricked into marriage by his conniving and much older housekeeper. Soon she forces him out of his own home and into the streets, where Kien spirals into madness, plotting how to save his books from his wife and employing a desperate chess-playing dwarf to help him "carry" his invisible library around with him.
(LMill 4)

(4) *The Amazing Adventures of Kavalier & Clay*
by Michael Chabon (2000).
The golden age of comics and the Holocaust power this Pulitzer Prize–winning saga about two Jewish cousins in Brooklyn who create the Nazi-bashing superhero, the Escapist. Through the tragic, comic, often superhuman adventures of Joe Kavalier—a refugee determined to rescue the relatives he left behind in Nazi-controlled Czechoslovakia—and Sammy Clay, Chabon weaves a lyrical and magical tale about war and mysticism; the connections between love, fear, hope, and art; and the nature of escape.
(DAD 4)

(4) *Pricksongs & Descants* by Robert Coover (1969).
The story lies in the telling in this groundbreaking collection of

metafictions. Through rich, playful language, Coover reimagines traditional tales, including *Hansel and Gretel*, *Little Red Riding Hood*, and the Virgin birth. In stories such as "The Elevator" and "The Babysitter," he makes the familiar surprising, suggesting that there is always another (and another and another) way of looking at things. (KA 4)

(4) *Silence* by Shusaku Endo (1969).
Set during the early seventeenth century, when Japanese Christians and the European priests serving them were persecuted and forced to renounce their faith, this novel focuses on a Portuguese priest whose travails force him to ponder "the silence of God . . . the feeling that while men raise their voices in anguish God remains with folded arms, silent."
(HaJ 4)

(4) *Where Angels Fear to Tread* by E. M. Forster (1905).
"For fools rush in where angels fear to tread," wrote Alexander Pope. That quote informs this biting tale that begins when a rich young widow, Lilia Herriton, travels to Italy. There she meets and marries a penniless Italian and dies in childbirth. Her relatives rush to retrieve the infant and give him a "proper" English upbringing. But his father objects in this first novel that signals Forster's lifelong interest in cultural collisions and British hubris.
(ES 4)

(4) *Don't Let's Go to the Dogs Tonight*
by Alexandra Fuller (2001).
When Fuller was a toddler in 1972, her loving, resilient, no-nonsense parents moved their family from England to Rhodesia (now Zimbabwe) just as the indigenous peoples were rising up

against their colonial rulers. This affectionate but unflinching memoir recounts the hardships and violence her family endured while farming in this poor land—three of her four siblings perished there—as well as the racism that infected her family and the segregation that strangled her community.
(AS 4)

**(4) Chronicle of a Death Foretold
by Gabriel García Márquez (1983).**
Everyone knows that Santiago Nasar will be murdered by Pedro and Pablo Vicario when the bishop comes to bless their sister's marriage. The story of Nasar's last hours is recounted by his cousin, a reporter who returns to the small South American town twenty-seven years later to find out what happened. This quick but densely packed novella looks at how honor and ritual contribute to an entire community's culpability in a single crime.
(TCB 4)

(4) *The House of Breath* by William Goyen (1950).
Poetic, serpentine prose becomes cascades of memory and emotions in this story of a man who returns to his tiny hometown of Charity, Texas. As he lovingly depicts the town—its landscape, folk, speech, superstitions, and fables—Goyen provides what the novelist Katherine Anne Porter described as "a sustained evocation of the past, a long search for place and identity, and the meaning of an intense personal experience; an attempt to cleanse the heart of its mysterious burden of guilt."
(JBud 4)

(4) *She Had Some Horses* by Joy Harjo (1983).
Harjo is a celebrated Native American writer whose poetry often

explores the connection between ancient traditions and the modern world. This collection of rhythmic, free-form poems searches for meaning in a mythic, mysterious world and for survival strategies in an often harsh landscape.

(SA 4)

(4) *Stranger in a Strange Land* **by Robert A. Heinlein (1961).**
A counterculture favorite during the 1960s, this novel tells the story of Valentine Michael Smith, who was born during the first flight to Mars. Reared by Martians, the orphan returns to Earth as a young man, where he questions the customs and values taken for granted there. Michael also learns he inherited a large fortune and the deed to Mars. As the world government tries to seize his assets, Michael forms a church preaching free love. His followers think he is the Messiah—and that spells trouble.

(DFW 4)

(4) *Finnegans Wake* **by James Joyce (1939).**
In H. C. Earwicker's dream, he is seen exposing himself in Dublin's Phoenix Park and thrown in jail. This dream is Joyce's famously impenetrable book, whose first sentence is a continuation of the last (making it, technically, impossible to begin or end). Joyce chronicles Earwicker's dream—which is at once his sexual fantasy, a universal history, and a history of Ireland—in a punning variant of English that must be read out loud to be appreciated (or understood). This novel is surely the mad orphan of literature.

(FC 4)

(4) *Les Liaisons Dangereuses*
by Pierre Choderlos de Laclos (1782).
A candidate for "most cynical fiction ever penned," the story fea-

tures two charming but depraved aristocrats, the Marquise de Merteuil and the Vicomte de Valmont, who try to relieve their boredom by plotting the seduction of a young virgin and a virtuous wife. Glittering like Milton's Satan against the pallid ranks of the virtuous, they skillfully seduce the reader through the urbanely immoral philosophy they detail in letters to each other in this wicked satire of the Age of Reason.

(EDon 4)

(4) *The Rainbow* by D. H. Lawrence (1915).
Declared obscene and banned by British authorities, Lawrence's novel about three generations of an English family boldly challenged conventional mores by openly depicting emotional and sexual needs. His protagonist, Ursula Brangwen, breaks from family tradition by going off to college and becoming a teacher. Free-spirited Ursula also experiments with her sexuality, having an affair with a Polish exile, Anton Skrebensky, and developing an intense attraction for an older woman. Her search for love is alternately disillusioning and liberating.

(JCO 4)

(4) *Dom Casmurro* by Joaquim Maria Machado de Assis (1899).
See Michael Griffith's appreciation on page 69.

(MGri 4)

(4) *A Heart So White* by Javier Marías (1994).
Juan knows only this about his shady, twice-widowed father: before marrying Juan's mother, he had wed her older sister, who committed suicide shortly after the ceremony. As Juan's new wife becomes his father's confessor, eliciting troubling truths, his own experiences begin to mirror those of his father in this Spanish

novel that recalls the work of Henry James, Marcel Proust, and Thomas Bernhard.

(VV 1) (RW 3)

(4) _Lonesome Dove_ by Larry McMurtry (1985).
Memorable characters (including prostitutes, outlaws, heroes, and Indians) grace this Pulitzer Prize–winning novel that examines the myths and reality of the American West through the story of two men driving cattle from Texas to Montana. As Augustus McCrae and W. F. Call undertake their adventure-filled journey, McMurtry debunks innumerable legends while suffusing his complex protagonists with the rugged dignity and loyalty of cowboy lore.

(AGold 4)

(4) _The Black Prince_ by Iris Murdoch (1973).
Bradley Pearson is a fifty-eight-year-old tax inspector who has written three books. Convinced he has a masterpiece within him, he quits his job and rents a tranquil cottage. His plan is thwarted at every turn, however, by the needs of his ex-wife, quarreling friends, his sister's suicide, writer's block, and his sudden passion for his friends' twenty-year-old daughter. A murder caps off this philosophical thriller about marriage, love, and art.

(JL 4)

(4) _The Enigma of Arrival_ by V. S. Naipaul (1988).
This chilly yet hypnotic antinovel—devoid of plot or conventional psychologizing—shuttles among the narrator's childhood memories of his native Trinidad, fictionalized accounts of that island's colonization, and elegiac descriptions of his present life in Wiltshire, England, where the charms of rural English life are

eroding under the pressures of modernization. With an immigrant's attentiveness, Naipaul details the minutiae of bleak exile, revealing a writer at home only in language.
(AW 4)

(4) *Fight Club* by Chuck Palahniuk (1996).
An aimless insomniac, who makes his living helping an insurance company avoid paying valid claims, relieves his boredom by attending therapy groups for people suffering from deadly illnesses. His life takes a deadly turn when he and a friend start a fight club, where men gather to beat one another senseless. Soon anarchy is loosed upon the world, including a terrorist attack on the world's tallest building, in this testosterone-fueled novel rippling with nihilistic irony and dark humor.
(DC 4)

(4) The stories of Grace Paley (1922–).
Paley's political beliefs inform her stories, but she never writes cant. Her Greenwich Village surroundings infuse her work, making New York City seem like a small town. Her stories of what she calls "everyday life, kitchen life"—of frustrated wives, knife-wielding children, and cold men—are written in the freshest, loosest, most modern language imaginable.
(AH 3) (DL 1)

(4) *True Grit* by Charles Portis (1968).
In this epic and often comic tale of retribution, greed, and ambition, sixty-nine-year-old spinster Mattie Ross recalls her youthful struggle to hunt down her father's killer in the wild Indian territory of the 1870s. While Ross studies her scripture, she breaks bread with the foul-mouthed, seldom-sober Marshall who is help-

ing her. Both a woman's coming-of-age saga and an adventure rid-
dled with biblical allegory, the novel reveals the depth of grit in
characters plagued by contradictions.
(GP 4)

(4) *American Pastoral* by Philip Roth (1997).

Seymour "Swede" Levov embodies the American success story: a
Jewish boy who became a football hero, a conscientious businessman, a good citizen. Then his alienated daughter commits an atro-
cious political crime and his idyllic world is blown apart by the same
radical energies assaulting American innocence during the 1960s.
Conflicting perspectives on its protagonist's vulnerable combination
of decency, righteousness, and naiveté make this Pulitzer Prize–
winning novel both sweetly nostalgic and extremely angry.
(EC 4)

(4) The works of William Shakespeare (1564–1616).

In a writing career of only two decades, from 1590 to 1610,
Shakespeare produced the most influential canon of dramatic literature in history. His early romantic comedies (*A Midsummer Night's
Dream*), his darker mature comedies (*Measure for Measure*), his history-
shaping history plays (*Henry IV*, Parts I and II, and *Henry V*), the
great core tragedies (*Hamlet, Macbeth, Othello,* and *King Lear*), the late
Roman plays (*Antony and Cleopatra*), and the final romances (*The
Tempest*) are enduring monuments to an unparalleled genius. He was
also a great poet. His 154 sonnets have shaped the efforts of every
true poet thereafter. Indeed, Shakespeare's two nondramatic
poems—the Ovidian erotic poem *Venus and Adonis* of 1593 and its
darkly brilliant sequel *The Rape of Lucrece* of 1594—were blockbusters
that launched the young writer's brilliant career.
(ST 4).

(4) *One Day in the Life of Ivan Denisovich*
by Alexander Solzhenitsyn (1962).
The author draws on the eight years he spent in Soviet prisons to
write this harrowing novel of the Soviet gulags. Inmates and prisoners are always cold, always hungry, always scheming for
crumbs, and willing to betray each other for less in this Siberian
labor camp. Though brutally dehumanized, many of Solzhenitsyn's
characters remain indomitable, making this novel an indictment
of human nature and an ode to the human spirit.
(BH 4)

(4) *Confessions of Zeno* by Italo Svevo (1923).
Hypochondriac, philanderer, dilettante, neurotic, and raconteur,
Zeno is a hyperconscious modern man. His subversive memoirs,
ostensibly undertaken as a psychoanalytic "cure," relate youth,
courtship, marriage, affairs, and business misadventures with a
disarming blend of frankness and humbug. A savagely funny work
about addiction, and fiction's juiciest raspberry at psychoanalysis,
Confessions of Zeno embraces his sickness and vices as his irreducible
humanity.
(CM 4)

(4) The stories of William Trevor (1928–).
Trevor is less an innovator than a perfectionist of the short story
form, with each instance featuring two or three well-drawn characters, a stoutly alluring situation, and not a word out of place.
The hundreds of stories he has crafted during his long career are
nearly all set in the Irish countryside, which Trevor reveals as sur-
prisingly erotic, sinister, and altogether contemporary, its residents often bent like trees by the wind of a single event.
(ML 1) (AP 3)

(4) *Everybody Pays* **by Andrew Vachss (1999).**

A master of the amped-up, neonoir style, whose work reflects a deep concern with child abuse and a taste for raw vengeance, Vachss offers here forty-four stomach-churning stories featuring prostitutes and pederasts, neo-Nazis and savage punks, hit men and kidnappers, who inhabit a world where merciless street justice provides the only brake on evil.

(JW 4)

(4) *The Loved One* **by Evelyn Waugh (1948).**

Dennis Barlow is an English poet working at a Hollywood pet cemetery. Arranging a friend's funeral, he falls for a cosmetician at the posh Whispering Glades, a paradise for the human deceased, or Loved Ones. The funeral business and its ridiculous jargon (survivors of Loved Ones are Waiting Ones; bodies are viewed in the Slumber Room) provide lively "meat" (as employees privately refer to corpses) for Waugh to skewer.

(AMH 4)

(4) *Vile Bodies* **by Evelyn Waugh (1930).**

This careening novel follows a group of shallow, well-off Brits to motor races and antic parties. Joining in on the Bright Young Things' mad doings are a writer named Adam Fenwick-Symes and his on-again, off-again fiancée. War looms, but Waugh's style—dry and bubbly as the novel's flowing champagne—keeps us laughing, even as characters descend into madness or head for the battlefield.

(AG 3) (TW 1)

(4) *Night* **by Elie Wiesel (1958).**

In this harrowing memoir of the Holocaust, Wiesel describes his journey from a religious Jewish childhood in Hungary to the Nazi concentration camps. Subsisting on bread and soup, forced to watch prisoner executions, the fifteen-year-old narrator struggles to support his father, who eventually dies one night in the cot below his. Ultimately freed by American soldiers, he is scarred by images that "consumed my faith forever" and "turned my life into one long night." (ED 4)

(3) *Going to Meet the Man* by James Baldwin (1965).

Baldwin is best known for his political and autobiographical essays, but these eight short stories showcase his ability to capture the disparate manifestations of race in America. He vividly depicts an impotent white southerner who can only get aroused by thinking of racial violence and an African American man married to a Swedish woman. Baldwin also revisits his tried and true stomping ground of family violence in Depression-era Harlem. (DMcF 3)

(3) *Peter Pan* by J. M. Barrie (1904).

"All children, except one, grow up," reads the opening line of this swashbuckling tale of that boy, named Peter Pan, who takes the Darling children to Neverland. There they encounter a host of immortal figures, including Tinker Bell and Tiger Lily, the Lost Boys, and Captain Hook, as readers learn that the best hedge against old age is to believe in our imaginations (and fairies). Initially produced as a play, the story was published as a book in 1911 under the title *Peter and Wendy*. (MGait 3)

(3) *Molloy, Malone Dies,* and *The Unnamable,* a trilogy by Samuel Beckett (1951–54).

Like the runner's high or Zen meditation, Beckett's opus yields the transcendence that succeeds tedium and pain. The trilogy chronicles a descent into living death by three narrators: vagabond, cripple, misfit. These characters are by degrees banished from the landscape, stripped of their paltry possessions, thrown back on the scatological world of the body, and ultimately confined to the madhouse of their heads, where language alone sustains and betrays them. Beckett's trademark black humor and the stubborn, paradoxical endurance of these voices lighten a terminally bleak vision. (PA 2) (LMill 1)

(3) *Stories and Texts for Nothing* by Samuel Beckett (1955).
The Nobel Prize–winning playwright's fiction shares the elliptical, elusive qualities of his celebrated dramas *Waiting for Godot* and *Endgame*. The *Stories* are bitterly comic acknowledgments of sexual failure and mortality (such as the masterly "Assumption") that clearly foreshadow the later *Texts for Nothing*. These thirteen nonnarrative prose pieces are fatalistic outcries uttered by moribund outcasts awaiting oblivion: the resigned, the dying, and the dead—all saved from meaninglessness by the grave, eloquent music of a measured style that redeems, even as it snatches away, their humanity. (BM 3)

(3) *Flat Stanley* by Jeff Brown (1964).
If Kafka had watched a lot of children's cartoons, this is the book he might have written. Young Stanley Lambchop wakes up one morning flat as a pancake, another victim of a falling bulletin board. He enjoys his flatness at first—sliding into envelopes, slipping through metal grates, foiling a gang of art thieves—but then others begin to mock him. The book's imagination and deadpan humor is enhanced by Tomi Ungerer's charming and very 1960s-looking illustrations. (AMH 3)

(3) The *Studs Lonigan* trilogy—*Young Lonigan* (1932), *The Young Manhood of Studs Lonigan* (1934), and *Judgment Day* (1935)—by James T. Farrell.
See Tom Wolfe's appreciation on page 131.
(TW 3)

(3) *A Simple Heart* by Gustave Flaubert (1877).
Included in the volume *Three Tales*, this is the story of Félicité, an uneducated and loyal servant who never questions her lot in life. She is sustained by her unquestioning faith and her great love for her nephew and for her mistress's daughter Virginie. When she loses them both, she finds an unlikely recipient for her ardent affections—a parrot named Lulu.
(ML 3)

(3) *Cold Mountain* by Charles Frazier (1997).
Frazier won the National Book Award for Fiction for his first novel, set in North Carolina during the Civil War. In rich language that evokes his nineteenth-century landscape, Frazier tells two interconnected stories exploring the themes of love and war and the natural world. The first concerns the Confederate soldier Inman who, like Odysseus, endures a series of deadly obstacles as he crosses the state to return to his home and the woman he loves. The second story centers on that woman, Ada, a pampered Southern belle who, with the help of the mountain woman Ruby, learns to fend for herself in a war ravaged landscape.
(ES 3)

(3) *The Book of Embraces* by Eduardo Galeano (1989).
"Why does one write, if not to put one's pieces together?" the Uruguayan author asks in this work of "literary collage." Through

scores of brief pieces both whimsical and earnest, Galeano recalls his personal life—including years of political exile and his heart attack—and topics large and small, ranging from his wife's dreams to the art of graffiti to repression in Latin America. Together with his imaginative drawings, they render a vivid portrait of this compassionate and visionary author's life and mind.
(SC 3)

(3) *New Grub Street* by George Gissing (1891).
One of the earliest examples of English naturalism, this grim chronicle of literary life in late-Victorian London bitterly portrays its author's own struggles to live from his writing. In contrasting dedicated artist Edwin Reardon's commercial failure with superficial romancer Jasper Milvain's popular success, Gissing pointedly skewers the distorted values of the marketplace, while tirelessly enumerating the many forces working against artistic purity and sincerity. The novel *is* a diatribe, yet lucid characterizations (particularly that of Reardon's depressed, demanding wife) and raw accusatory intensity give it a claustrophobic, nagging power.
(JL 3)

(3) *Oldest Living Confederate Widow Tells All*
by Allan Gurganus (1989).
Smart, funny, sharp-tongued Lucy Marsden was seventeen when she married a fifty-year-old veteran of the Civil War, Captain William Marsden. Now ninety-nine, she recalls her historic life—especially her husband's military service and the psychological trauma it inflicted, a slave's journey from Africa, and Sherman's march through the South—in vivid, colorful language.
(EDon 3)

(3) *The Big Sky* by A. B. Guthrie, Jr. (1947).
Set in the 1830s and 1840s this epic tale of adventure captures the American West when it truly was wild, primitive, and free. Its central character is Boone Caudill, a Kentucky mountain man whose desire for virgin earth and clear skies pushes him across rough and glorious landscapes, where he encounters other intrepid searchers, while winning the love of an Indian chief's daughter.
(JLB 3)

(3) *A Prayer for Owen Meany* by John Irving (1989).
Set in a vividly drawn New Hampshire town in the 1950s and 1960s, this novel's title character is a tiny boy with a "wrecked voice" and no talent for baseball. In fact, the only ball he hits kills the mother of his best friend, narrator Johnny Wheelwright. Owen's disabilities make him the butt of jokes, yet he believes he is an "instrument of God." Familiar Irving hijinks and humor abound in this story, which delivers a stirring meditation on history, hypocrisy, social justice, and faith.
(JW 3)

(3) *The Castle* by Franz Kafka (1926).
K. has been summoned to work as a land surveyor at a giant castle, which he is never allowed to enter. As his confusion grows, he breaks a series of laws he cannot understand. Such is the stuff of dreams—and of Kafka's final novel, which uses K.'s strange plight to portray the absurd, nightmare logic of the bureaucratic state.
(PA 3)

(3) *Women in Love* by D. H. Lawrence (1920).
An angry young man before there were angry young men, Lawrence explores politics, art, economics, and sexuality through

sisters Gudrun and Ursula Brangwen and their respective lovers. A sequel to his 1915 novel *The Rainbow*, this sprawling transcontinental saga challenges the limitations of traditional marriage, while detailing the potency of human sexuality, the quest for bohemia, and the destructiveness of World War I.
(JCO 3)

(3) *The Golden Notebook* by Doris Lessing (1962).
In her epic fusion of structural experiment and exhaustive realism, Lessing lays bare the splintered state of modern womanhood. In four separate notebooks, Anna Wulf records different aspects of her life: her consecutive and unfulfilling love affairs, her memories of Africa, her struggles with motherhood, and above all, her growing disenchantment with communism. Lessing's novel foreshadowed the concerns of the women's movement, becoming a major feminist text.
(MD 3)

(3) *Death in Venice* by Thomas Mann (1912).
With a skillful use of classical allusion, Mann's vaguely homoerotic novella describes an aging writer's platonic infatuation with a beautiful young boy in Venice. Gustav von Aschenbach is a tragic idealist who has dedicated his life to the study and pursuit of high art and beauty. In young Tadzio he recognizes both the embodiment and inevitable transience of perfection in this story of heartrending poignancy.
(PM 3)

(3) *At Play in the Fields of the Lord* by Peter Matthiessen (1965).
Two Americans try to expand white culture in the jungles of Peru: a Christian missionary hopes to "civilize" the local tribes, and a

mercenary plans to remove the locals through terror. In alternating chapters, Mathiessen chronicles their exploits, motives, and changing sense of self (the mercenary eventually goes native, with deadly results) in this complex story of good and evil and missionary zeal, of the quest for personal identity, and of the danger of imposing one culture on another.
(EC 3)

(3) *Fuzz* by Ed McBain (1968).

Fueled by clever plots, sharp dialogue, and vivid characters, McBain's series of novels set in New York City's 87th Precinct is a gold standard of the police procedural. This novel features one of the genre's great villains, the murderous Deaf Man, who taunts and ridicules his blue-clad adversaries.
(DFW 3)

(3) *Ninety-two in the Shade* by Thomas McGuane (1973).

McGuane has always been fascinated by people who seek a truer life by living on the edge. Here he tells the story of a refugee from America's consumer society who returns to Key West, where he lives in an old airplane fuselage and tries to realize his dream of becoming a skiff guide in the tropical waters. But that hope makes him seem threatening to a rival guide, who will kill to protect his turf.
(CH 3)

(3) *Lies of Silence* by Brian Moore (1990).

A failed Irish poet who loathes his country decides to run away with his mistress to London. But then IRA terrorists snatch his shrewish wife, threatening to kill her unless he parks an explosive-laden car outside a hotel where a Protestant minister will be

speaking. That is only the first moral vise that squeezes him in this fast-paced, philosophical thriller.
(AS 3)

(3) *Pnin* by Vladimir Nabokov (1953).
This episodic novel details the often comic, unexceptional life of Timofey Pnin, a Russian teaching at an American college who has never mastered English or learned how to drive a car (like Nabokov himself). It is the telling of the tale that matters here, as Nabokov shifts time, mood, and perspective, eventually introducing a character, Mr. N., who makes us wonder about all we've seen and heard.
(HaJ 3)

(3) *Ahab's Wife* by Sena Jeter Naslund (1999).
"Captain Ahab was neither my first husband nor my last" reads the opening line of this novel, which imagines the life of the woman married to the obsessive captain from *Moby-Dick*. And what a life it was—running away from home, posing as a boy to get aboard a whaling ship, tragedy at sea, cannibalism, and then domestic life in New Bedford, Massachusetts. Naslund captures all in rich detail as she deepens her portrait of this lively, intellectually and spiritually curious heroine.
(SV 3)

(3) *The Famished Road* by Ben Okri (1991).
Azaro, the hero of Nigerian-born Okri's spellbinding and hallucinatory novel, is a spirit child, or *abiku*, born to mortals. Though other spirits insist that he return to their comfy land, he chooses to stand by his suffering mother and bombastic, foolhardy father amid the poverty, violence, and instability of modern Africa. "It is

more difficult to love than to die," Azaro's father says in this Booker Prize–winning novel that is equal parts dark mythology and political satire.
(DAD 3)

(3) *Homage to Catalonia* by George Orwell (1940).
Orwell's memoir of going to fight on the republican side in the Spanish Civil War combines early Hemingway's disabused attitude toward war with Leon Trotsky's talent for political analysis. Through vivid accounts of battle and political machinations, he defines the true meaning of the term Orwellian: "If you had asked me why I had joined the militia I should have answered: 'To fight against Fascism,' and if you had asked me what I was fighting for, I should have answered: 'Common decency.'"
(AF 3)

(3) *The Radetzky March* by Joseph Roth (1932).
At the Battle of Solferino, a young peasant soldier saves the Austrian emperor's life, and from that moment forward the fortunes of the von Trotta family are linked with the "Old Man," Franz Joseph. Roth tracks the decline of the Austro-Hungarian Empire, and the era of honor and order it represents, through the dissolution of the von Trottas, especially the timid, exhausted Carl Joseph, who almost ruins his family through carelessness and risks his life in battle trying to imitate his grandfather's lost heroism.
(AB 1) (AF 2)

(3) *Light Years* by James Salter (1975).
This compact novel offers achingly perceptive scenes from a marriage during a twenty-year period. As Viri and Nedra Berland host

dinner parties, shop in New York City, summer on Long Island, and take on lovers, they experience happiness, bereavement, isolation, and divorce. Through this portrait, Salter suggests that each person's life is "mysterious, it is like a forest; from far off it . . . can be comprehended, described, but closer it begins to separate, to break into light and shadow, the density blinds one."
(PCam 3)

(3) *Dirty Snow* by Georges Simenon (1950).
As this darkest of noirs opens, nineteen-year-old Frank Friedmaier, already a pimp, thug, and petty thief, has just become a murderer. What follows are searing portraits of the cruel and alienated young man who sees violence as a form of self-definition and the corrupt grim world that made him.
(JB 3)

(3) The Maigret series of detective novels
by Georges Simenon (1903–89).
See Iain Pears's appreciation on page 107.
(IP 3)

(3) *The Lost Father* by Mona Simpson (1992).
Featuring the heroine from *Anywhere but Here*, the novel tracks Mayan Atassi's search across two continents and to the point of madness for the man who has become her God—the father who abandoned her.
(ALK 3)

(3) *Enemies, A Love Story* by Isaac Bashevis Singer (1972).
Herman Broder, who survived World War II by hiding in a hayloft for three years, marries the woman who hid him, and he

now lives a life of duplicity in 1949 Brooklyn—having an affair, pretending to be a traveling book salesman while really ghost-writing for a rabbi. To top it off, his first wife—a concentration camp survivor who Broder thought was dead—shows up. *Enemies* is a classic Holocaust survivor tale, filled with guilt, paranoia, a little humor, and raw desperation.

(SS 3)

(3) *Red the Fiend* by Gilbert Sorrentino (1995).
See Lydia Millet's appreciation on page 101.

(LMill 3)

(3) *A Far Cry from Kensington* by Muriel Spark (1988).
Like all of Spark's work, this novel is hard to define. Metaphysical farce? Literary mystery? At bottom it is a dark, elegant, hilarious tale centered on the zaftig widow Mrs. Hawkins. She spends her days and evenings giving advice to her eccentric rooming house mates and her coworkers in book publishing. Blackmail, suicide, and a crash diet power this story, but it is Spark's all-too evident disgust with the business end of literature that gives the story its special kick.

(DL 3)

(3) *Angle of Repose* by Wallace Stegner (1971).
"It's perfectly clear that if every writer is born to write one story, that's my story," Stegner said of this Pulitzer Prize–winning novel. The narrator is a divorced, wheelchair-bound professor recalling the life of his pioneer grandparents. He was crude and adventurous, she sophisticated and self-possessed. Together they crossed the country during the nineteenth century; the vivid landscape

becomes a character in this story of marriage, American mythology, and the flow of time and memory.
(PE 3)

(3) *River of Earth* by James Still (1940).

Hailed upon its publication, then forgotten until it was reissued in 1978, this classic of Appalachian literature is narrated by a young boy whose Kentucky family is at a crossroads: Do they continue to lead their poor but independent life on the farm or go to work at the mining company? In portraying a changing world, Still evokes the constants of life: love, dignity, land.
(LS 3)

(3) *The Confessions of Nat Turner* by William Styron (1967).

Based on an 1831 uprising, this Pulitzer Prize–winning novel is narrated by Nat, a slave who feels commanded by God to lead a rebellion. Yet even as he plots the murders of white slave-owners, Nat recognizes that all men are slaves to their own passions and greed. Poetically narrated, the book probes the essence of subjugation and freedom, the peculiar bonds that complicated the relationships of slaves and masters, and the meaning of history itself.
(BU 3)

(3) *Street of Lost Footsteps* by Lyonel Trouillot (1998).

Although set during a single night of horrific violence in Port-au-Prince, this fierce, surreal novel resonates with Haiti's long history of blood and broken dreams. With irony and black humor, three narrators—a madam, a taxi driver, and a postal employee—witness chaotic clashes between forces of the Prophet and the vicious dictator Deceased Forever-Immortal, while reflecting on a

society where "you can count yourself lucky . . . whenever you find you're still alive."
(MSB 3)

(3) *Life on the Mississippi* by Mark Twain (1883).
This isn't a book, but a two-part time machine. The first part is a work of literature, as Twain reimagines his salad days as a cub pilot learning to navigate the "fickle Mississippi." His vivid you-are-there prose transports readers to the untamed land filled with rough-hewn people. The book's second section, a travelogue begun seven years later, in 1882, is memoiristic and meditative. Having lived so long in the West and East, Twain sought to reconnect with the land of his youth and wellspring of his art, taking readers on a journey of discovery and rediscovery down a still fickle river.
(PCap 3)

(3) *Montana 1948* by Larry Watson (1993).
In language that is as direct and spare as the title, twelve-year-old David Hayden tells of the summer when his father, the sheriff of Mercer County, Montana, is forced to choose between justice and family. Watson evokes the Montana landscape and mindset masterfully, but his true accomplishment is the unadorned but subtle portrayal of a flawed man seeking to do the right thing in the face of terrible pressure.
(GDG 3)

(3) *Decline and Fall* by Evelyn Waugh (1928).
This hilarious send-up of the English code of honor begins with Paul Pennyfeather's "sending down" (expulsion) from Oxford. Reduced to teaching at a fourth-rate school, he encounters wonderfully named characters, including Lady Circumference and Lord

Tangent, who prove ripe for satire. Pennyfeather also finds love with the impossibly rich and lovely Margot Beste-Chetwynde. But l'amour leads to a spell in the clink. Fortunately, Waugh says, "any one who has been to an English public school will always feel comparatively at home" in jail.

(DC 3)

(3) *Jacob's Room* by Virginia Woolf (1922).

Woolf's first novel to depart from a linear, traditional style follows Jacob Flanders as he goes through Cambridge, carries on love affairs in London, and travels in Greece. Sitting with a girlfriend, he thinks, "It's not catastrophes, murders, deaths, diseases, that age and kill us, it's the way people look and laugh, and run up the steps of omnibuses." Ultimately, it *is* catastrophe that kills Jacob, as Woolf suggests war's devastations through this novel's final description of Jacob's empty room.

(TM 3)

(3) *The Branch Will Not Break* by James Wright (1963).

A poet with finely honed social and political concerns, Wright wrote beautiful lines about outcasts and human suffering. This collection marks the poet's turn from more conventional forms toward lyrical free verse. Wright's *Collected Poems* was awarded a Pulitzer Prize in 1971.

(SA 3)

(3) *Eleven Kinds of Loneliness* by Richard Yates (1962).

Yates's debut collection set the tone for what his career would bring: quiet, well-crafted stories and novels about people whose dearest hopes were thwarted, often by their own inability to realize them. Unrelentingly realistic in setting and subject matter,

Yates repudiates any easy redemption in these stories. Like Walter Henderson, protagonist of the aptly titled "Glutton for Punishment," these are men and women who slowly, bitterly, come to understand that their one true talent is for defeat.
(AGold 3)

(2) *Eugénie Grandet* by Honoré de Balzac (1833).
Part of Balzac's almost endless *La Comédie humaine*, *Eugénie Grandet* is his masterwork on the virus of greed and miserliness. Felix Grandet, a French millionaire, tyrannizes his family with his frugality, going so far as to personally measure the ingredients for each day's meals. He dashes the romance between his daughter Eugénie and her penniless cousin Charles, setting in motion a bitterly ironic plot worthy of O. Henry, rendered with Balzac's characteristic detail.
(TM 2)

(2) *Rule of the Bone* by Russell Banks (1995).
Holden Caulfield meets Dean Moriarty in this sprawling coming-of-age story narrated with crisp assurance by a fourteen-year-old runaway. A victim of parental neglect, this lost, angry boy who names himself Bone commits crimes and acts of violence. After saving a seven-year-old boy from a pedophile, he lives in an abandoned bus with a pot-dealing Rastafarian. Together they travel to Jamaica where strange and murderous events take place as this wounded boy finds and defines himself.
(JW 2)

(2) *Sixty Stories* by Donald Barthelme (1981).
Giant of postmodernism, creator of worlds both surreal and mundane whose only constants are surprise and change, master of brief, epiphanic stories called sudden fiction, Barthelme juggled

many balls, wore many hats. Though he wrote four novels, he was best known for his short stories. This compilation of stories from the 1960s and 1970s includes the tale of a giant balloon that engulfs Manhattan, "The Balloon," and the youngsters who bring death to everything they touch, in "The School."
(JBud 2)

(2) *The Loser* by Thomas Bernhard (1983).

Our narrator had studied the piano with his friend Wertheimer and the virtuoso Glenn Gould. Gould's unapproachable brilliance compelled them to give up music. While this abandonment leads to their ruin, Gould's career does not bring him happiness. The Austrian writer probed these themes—of the joy, pain, and meaning of art—in this and his next two novels, which comprise his "arts trilogy," *Cutting Timber: An Irritation* and *Old Masters: A Comedy*.
(CM 2)

(2) *Dreamtigers* by Jorge Luis Borges (1964).

Borges called this "straggling collection" of tiny prose pieces and poems his most personal book. It contains meditations on the usual Borges themes: doubles, time as a fiction, the incursion of literature on reality. Its famous piece, *Borges and I*, is the most compact confession in all literature, as the real Borges seeks to disentangle himself from the writer Borges, concluding: "I do not know which of us two is writing this page." Such abysses of Escher-like perspective mark this Argentinian's unique style.
(SC 2)

(2) *Fahrenheit 451* by Ray Bradbury (1953).

Books are dangerous. They fill heads with ideas, make people think, question, causing harmful confusion. This is the ideology that informs Bradbury's dystopia, whose citizens have traded independence for safe conformity, curiosity for the pleasures of wall-sized televisions. Fireman Guy Montag, who doesn't douse blazes but burns books, seems happy until his wife attempts suicide and he seeks answers that make him an enemy of this brave new world. (AH 2)

(2) The Public Burning by Robert Coover (1976).
It is 1953 and Russian spies are everywhere, according to Fightin' Joe McCarthy. Ethel and Julius Rosenberg are scheduled to fry in the electric chair in Times Square, and Uncle Sam has delegated Vice President Richard Nixon (who narrates much of the story) to ensure that the show goes off. Coover is a master of lingos, from Uncle Sam's Davy Crockett yawps to Nixon's resentful Rotarian tones. Oddly, Tricky Dick comes off as a rather endearing soul, a 1950s Everyman helplessly folded, spindled, and mutilated in Coover's funhouse mirrors.
(MCon 2)

(2) Seven Gothic Tales by Isak Dinesen (1934).
The pseudonymous Danish noblewoman (Baroness Karen Blixen) revived the texture and resonance of myths and folklores in this landmark debut collection. Its richly detailed stories, set in aristocratic surroundings and steeped in romantic hyperbole, explore conflicts between civilization and primitivism, notably in the magical transformation of a cloistered woman into an animal (*The Monkey*); the power a celebrated singer exerts over her admirers' imaginations (*The Dreamers*); and four interlocking tales about concealed or mistaken identities, told by flood survivors (*The Deluge at Nordeney*).
(GG 2)

(2) *An American Tragedy* by Theodore Dreiser (1925).
Clyde Griffiths wants to be more than just the son of a Midwestern preacher. Leaving home, he follows a path toward the American Dream that is littered with greed, adultery, and hypocrisy. The brass ring seems close when he wins a wealthy girl's love, but then very far away when a factory girl he impregnated demands that he marry her. In this disquieting social novel, Clyde faces a moral dilemma that reveals the corruption of his soul and the materialistic culture that seduces him.
(BMC 2)

(2) *The Three Musketeers* by Alexandre Dumas (1844).
"An almost endless chain of duels, murders, love affairs, unmaskings, ambushes, hairbreadth escapes, wild rides," is how the critic Clifton Fadiman described this swashbuckling tale. In 1625, young D'Argent travels to Paris where he joins three Musketeers who guard King Louis XIII and live by the motto "All for one, and one for all." Together they foil a plot against the king hatched by the evil Cardinal Richelieu and the gorgeous spy "Milady."
(APhil 2)

(2) *The Beginning of Spring* by Penelope Fitzgerald (1988).
"It is Jane Austen crossed with Chekhov and Turgenev," observed A. S. Byatt of this witty domestic novel set in Moscow on the eve of war and revolution. In the spring of 1913, Frank Reid's wife leaves him and their three children to return to England. Frank, who was born in Russia and runs the print shop his British father founded there, deplores change. Character, not plot, rules Fitzgerald's fictions; with subtlety and insight she reveals him navigating his new circumstances (and hoping for

his wife's return) while dealing with a host of vividly drawn, often idiosyncratic characters.
(DL 2)

(2) Grimm's Fairy Tales (1812–14).
Where Hans Christian Anderson was sweetly folklorish and gentle, the German folk tales collected by Jakob and Wilhelm Grimm are gritty and fearless. Their legendary stories—among them *Hansel and Gretel*, *Snow White*, and *Sleeping Beauty*—are as violent as they are enchanting. Though versions of the Frog Prince abound, the Grimms reject sentimental romance to tell a moral tale about keeping a promise. Their princess is a brat who throws the frog against the wall rather than kissing him to turn him into a prince. *Grimm's Fairy Tales* deliver enchantment and moxie.
(AH 1) (JSalt 1)

(2) Airships by Barry Hannah (1978).
Barry Hannah can make readers laugh about the grimmest subject while never for a second losing sight of the essential horror. In this story collection, the Mississippi writer creates a cast of scarred, hyperkinetic characters—including a Confederate soldier recalling the tragedy and glory of war to a contemporary man obsessed with his estranged wife—who are stumbling toward illumination.
(BH 2)

(2) Dune by Frank Herbert (1965).
Winner of the Hugo and Nebula awards, and one of the best-selling works in science fiction history, *Dune* is a Shakespearean drama set on a withered planet. Conflict centers on Melange, a miraculous substance that extends life, grants psychic powers, and makes space travel possible. When the emperor transfers authority

over this plant from the Harkonnen Noble House to the House Atreides, he sparks a chain of events that encompasses political intrigue, romance, war, and perhaps, the coming of the messiah. (DAD 2)

(2) *The Turn of the Screw* by Henry James (1898).
A young governess who is the sole caregiver for two charming children living in a remote country manor finds herself battling for their very souls. James's story of psychological duress and obsession has been called a ghost story, a thriller, and a horror tale. But its haunting power stems less from the supernatural than from the primal fear that we can't always protect our children. (MCunn 2)

(2) *Alligator* by Shelley Katz (1977).
He's the Moby-Dick of the Everglades—a twenty-foot-long alligator with eighty razor sharp teeth who stalks men for pleasure. Like all legendary beasts, this killer is a symbol of mankind's weakness and a challenge to those who dream of proving their mettle. When two death-hardened adventurers vow to pursue this leviathan, the hunters become the prey in this atmospheric thriller. (DFW 2)

(2) *China Men* by Maxine Hong Kingston (1980).
Kingston won the National Book Award for this richly detailed, multigenerational novel about the Chinese American experience. Drawing on ancient legends, family lore, and history, she begins in the 1840s, with the building of the transcontinental railroad, and continues through the challenges posed by the Vietnam War era. (PCle 2)

(2) *The Marquise of O— and Other Stories*
by Heinrich von Kleist (1777–1811).
See Paula Fox's appreciation on page 63.
(PF 2)

(2) *Cal* by Bernard MacLaverty (1983).
Cal is a young Catholic trapped by the violence strangling Northern
Ireland. With other members of the Irish Republican Army, he helps
murder a Protestant policeman. Life takes a turn when he falls in love,
and then offers a cruel twist when he learns that she is his victim's
daughter. Ultimately, though, love offers a glimpse of life apart from
sectarian violence and a path to redemption.
(AS 2)

(2) *The Moon and Sixpence* by W. Somerset Maugham (1919).
Loosely based on the life of Paul Gauguin, this novel portrays a
London stockbroker overcome by the need to paint. Abandoning
his family, he moves to Paris and then Tahiti, where he lives in
poverty and neglects his health, social conventions, and the
feelings of others to pursue his obsession. Charles Strickland is
selfish, but he is also a genius. And so the novel asks: What
price art?
(JLB 2)

(2) *The Member of the Wedding* by Carson McCullers (1946).
Twelve-year-old Frankie Addams's summer has been routine until
her brother, set to be sent to the battlefields of World War II,
announces he is getting married. As the family's cook Berenice
says, Frankie falls "in love with the wedding." McCuller's evocation of a 1940s Georgia town in August will make you sweat, but

Frankie's desperation to connect with somebody sticks in your head like a sad, crazy tune.
(EH 2)

(2) *The Wind-Up Bird Chronicle* **by Haruki Murakami (1994).**
A cross between Dante's *Inferno*, *Through the Looking Glass*, and *Catch-22*, this novel depicts the bizarre and often inexplicable journey of Japanese Everyman Toru Okada, whose missing cat prompts the disappearance of his wife, encounters with psychics and call girls, days huddled in meditation at the bottom of a well, and the breathtakingly graphic depiction of a man being skinned alive.
(VV 2)

(2) *A Bend in the River* **by V. S. Naipaul (1979).**
A fictionalized account of the violence and political tyranny that gripped Zaire after its independence from Belgium, the novel focuses on an African of Indian descent named Salim who opens a small store at a bend in the Congo River. Ambitious, multicultural, and interested in the West, Salim represents the hopes of the "new Africa." These hopes are dashed by a corrupt and vicious government in this grim saga of the challenges faced by postcolonial nations.
(HaJ 2)

(2) *The English Teacher* **by R. K. Narayan (1945).**
The Indian author reimagines the sudden death of his beloved wife through the life of an English teacher whose deeply satisfying marriage ends with his wife's fatal illness. His deep despair is broken by devotion to their daughter and his successful efforts to

communicate with his departed wife. Yet he does not achieve the inner peace he craves in this novel infused with Hindu spirituality, until he realizes that true happiness does not come from other people, but from within.
(AMS 2)

(2) *The Selected Poems of Pablo Neruda* (1970).
Neruda's biography is an impressive one, maybe even a heroic one: poet, ambassador, winner of the Nobel Prize for Literature. But his poetry is human-size stuff, packed with concrete images and honest emotion. The Chilean-born Neruda, who merged his leftist politics with Whitmanesque exuberance, took the objects and experiences around us and turned them into something bigger through stunningly immediate language.
(CD 2)

(2) *Long Day's Journey into Night* by Eugene O'Neill (1956).
As one family unravels over the course of an evening, O'Neill offers harrowing portraits of the emotional abuse and the descent into madness and addiction that can result when parents and children withhold love and understanding from each other. O'Neill's drama cuts close to the bone, but his artistry and dramatic timing lift this dark tale to heights of sheer beauty.
(AHas 2)

(2) *The Black Book* by Orhan Pamuk (1990).
An Istanbul lawyer searches for his wife, who seems to have disappeared with her half-brother, Jelal, a famous newspaper columnist. Chapters detailing Galip's quest through the city's twisted streets alternate with excerpts from Jelal's writings, which Galip scours for clues. Both draw on Turkish history, religion, and culture—its con-

flicted place as a nation both Eastern and Western—to tell a rich, cerebral tale about the nature of storytelling and identity.
(AP 2)

(2) *W, or The Memory of Childhood* by Georges Perec (1975).
Perec was an experimental French author fascinated by literary boundaries—one of his novels, *A Void*, does not contain the letter E. Here, autobiographical chapters recalling (and trying to recall) childhood memories, when most of his family was murdered in the Holocaust, alternate with those telling the fictional story of an Aryan island called W that becomes totalitarian. Gradually, we see that each section says what the other cannot, as the riveting stories form a meta-meditation on narrative form.
(DM 2)

(2) *Clockers* by Richard Price (1992).
When cocaine dealer Strike Dunham's hardworking brother confesses to murder, burnt-out detective Rocco Klein is convinced that Strike is behind the crime. As Klein turns the ulcer-ridden nineteen-year-old's world upside down, Price provides a street-level look at America's drug epidemic and searing portrayals of addiction—to drugs, power, status, and action.
(GP 2)

(2) *V.* by Thomas Pynchon (1963).
This sprawling postmodern spy novel spiked with Rabelasian humor is ignited by a cryptic line in the journals of Herbert Stencil's late father: "There is more behind and inside V. than any of us had suspected. Not who, but what: what is she." The son's search for the mysterious V.—involving a range of deliciously named characters, including the "schlemiel and human yo-yo"

Benny Profane—stretches across three continents and two centuries, bringing Stencil ever closer to the secret powers that have conspired to control, and thereby corrupted, the modern world. (TCB 2)

(2) *Sergeant Getulio* by João Ubaldo Ribeiro (1971).
This deeply unsettling novel features one of literature's most loathsome creations—a Brazilian policeman adept at torture, maiming, and beheadings. Yet, as he transports a political prisoner across remote and dangerous terrain, we see a man both resourceful and persistent. As he explains himself, we see a man driven by honor, loyalty, and morality. In the process this appalling figure seems almost appealing.
(ALK 2)

(2) *Goodbye, Columbus* by Philip Roth (1959).
Even if it only hinted at the depth of humorous rage Roth would later unload, this is the book that put him on the map. A novella coupled with five short stories, *Goodbye, Columbus* confronts issues of identity, class tensions within American Jewry, and a suffocating veil of conformity that exists amid so much American opportunity. By airing what many saw as his people's dirty laundry, Roth gained a reputation as a self-hating Jew that was so pervasive even his mother asked if it was true.
(MW 2)

(2) *Midnight's Children* by Salman Rushdie (1981).
Years before *The Satanic Verses*, Rushdie had already won the Booker Prize for this reverential and blasphemous novel. Two babies born at the precise moment modern India came into

existence—one Muslim, one Hindu—are then switched at birth and grow up in the other's faith. *Midnight's Children* sets a plot of comic-book proportions—people with superpowers too lazy to band together—against the backdrop of the subcontinent's conflict-ridden history, the language and idioms of Rushdie's youth careening against each other with madcap imagination and jolting fury.

(KHarr 2)

(2) *What's for Dinner?* by James Schuyler (1978).
Best known as a poet, Schuyler brings his eye for intimate details to this quirky comedy about three families in suburban Long Island. As his characters deal with rowdy children, alcoholism, and loneliness, Schuyler subtly explores the forces that tear people apart and bring them back together.

(PCam 2)

(2) *Sullivan's Travels* (1941), *The Lady Eve* (1941), and *The Palm Beach Story* (1942), three screenplays by Preston Sturges.
Sturges enjoyed one of the great comic runs in Hollywood history while the world was at war. A master of sparkling dialogue, he revealed the zany absurdity of American life in the twelve pictures he wrote and/or directed from 1940 to 1944, especially these three classics that feature, respectively, a runaway director, a brilliant female con artist, and a runaway heiress.

(AT 2)

(2) *Sacred Hunger* by Barry Unsworth (1992).
Unsworth explores the "ancient urge" to "command attention, dominate one's fellows" in this Booker Prize–winning novel that

offers a gripping, panoramic view of the slave trade during the eighteenth century. Following a mutiny aboard a slave vessel and the creation of a utopian community in Florida, Unsworth portrays the fight against greed, disease, and humanity's inhumanity. In this novel of two cousins who have opposing dreams, Unsworth faces the heights and depths of human nature.
(EC 2)

(2) *Bluebeard* by Kurt Vonnegut (1987).

On one level this is a wickedly hilarious satire of the world of art. Yet, it is also a heartfelt story of American dreams, as a minor artist, whose lack of confidence led him to put down his brush and start collecting other people's work, looks back on his life, analyzing his high points and low.
(PE 2)

(2) *Masquerade and Other Stories* by Robert Walser (1878–1956).

Beloved of other writers but not known to a broad reading public in America, Walser was a formative influence on many writers, including Franz Kafka and Robert Musil. This collection of sixty-four short, sometimes essayistic, and always piercing stories published in the early twentieth century offers the Swiss writer's take—meditatively, dreamily, truthfully, and often joyously—on subjects both microscopic and vast, from women's gloves to medieval battles.
(LMill 2)

(2) *A Handful of Dust* by Evelyn Waugh (1934).

Leading lives of empty desperation, Waugh's characters kill the days of their lives with petty concerns, silly parties, and unfulfilling affairs. A withering satire of England's declining aristocracy, the novel showcases Waugh's caustic eye and comic wit.

(JR 2)

(2) *Voss* by Patrick White (1957).
A fearless man with a titanic ego, Johann Voss decides to prove his almost divine greatness by leading a party across the untamed Australian continent in 1845. Before his trip, he meets a young spinster with whom he will carry on a spiritual courtship through telepathy and dreams. Voss suffers immensely during his arduous journey; as he is humbled, he learns the meaning of Christian spirituality in this novel by the Australian Nobel laureate.

(TK 2)

(2) *Our Town* by Thornton Wilder (1938).
This enduringly popular, Pulitzer Prize–winning play depicts small-town New England life (in fictional Grovers Corners, New Hampshire) with a unique combination of warm sentiment, wry comedy, and even a touch of surreal modernism in its moving final act. Childhood's passage to maturity, love and marriage, birth and death are memorably enacted by the closely knit families of newspaper editor Webb and Doctor Gibbs, and observed by the benign Stage Manager who sagely connects their experiences to all our lives. Irresistible Americana.

(TW 2)

(2) *Tennessee Williams: Plays 1937–1955*.
Through raw yet lyric depictions of violence, alcoholism, homosexuality, rape, loneliness, and frustrated passion, Williams helped transform and liberate the American theater. His most celebrated

dramas, including his breakthrough hit *The Glass Menagerie* (1944) and the two plays for which he won Pulitzer prizes, *A Streetcar Named Desire* (1947) and *Cat on a Hot Tin Roof* (1955), written in the Southern Gothic tradition of his native region, offer indelible portraits of fragile characters—especially lonely, frustrated Southern women—trying to hold on in a harsh world.
(DMcF 2)

(2) *The Passion* by Jeanette Winterson (1987).
Henri is Napoleon's cook. For eight years he has followed his diminutive idol. But now, in Russia—as the land turns deathly cold, soldiers starve, and Moscow burns—Henri becomes disenchanted by war. His life takes an exotic turn when he falls for Villanelle, a Venetian pickpocket and croupier who has literally lost her heart to another woman. In Venice, Henri's passion turns toward madness as he learns "the difference between inventing a lover and falling in love."
(EDon 2)

(1) *Watership Down* by Richard Adams (1972).
This imaginative epic chronicles the adventures of a band of English rabbits who possess their own language, history, and myth and who are searching for a new home after a human developer has destroyed their old one. Like the fables of Aesop, *Watership Down* is sneakily dark, full of drama and death and warnings about the fascist tendencies of the modern world, and explores moral ideas, including freedom and responsibility.
(DAD 1)

(1) *London Fields* by Martin Amis (1989).
Nicola Six, a psychic femme fatale in a soul-sick, lightly futuristic

London, has a premonition that one of two men she's just met will murder her, and then she works to make that happen. All of Amis's tropes—the coming apocalypse, the self-consciousness of authorship, and hilarious clashes of sexes and classes—get full play in this sprawling romp of a novel.

(RW 1)

(1) *Money* by Martin Amis (1984).

Subtitled "A Suicide Note," this novel follows the death spiral of hedonistic film director John Self as he wrestles with Hollywood stars, New York producers, a flauntingly unfaithful London girlfriend, an anonymous ca.ller that seems to be coming from inside his head, and the writer Martin Amis. *Money* marries Amis's comic talents and his preoccupation with the self-annihilating twilight of civilization.

(CH 1)

(1) *The Conference of the Birds* by Farid ud-Din Attar.
A lyrical tale about the desire to become one with the divine, this epic allegory by the twelfth-century Sufi mystic follows a group of birds who vow to find the legendary Simurgh bird. Their limitations and faults—the basis for rich parables—are revealed through their quest, which has long inspired readers to begin their own spiritual journeys.

(MSB 1)

(1) The haiku of Matsuo Bashō.
A spiritual seeker who practiced Zen Buddhism while wandering throughout seventeenth-century Japan, Bashō helped transform the form of light verse that would become haiku into a serious art form. "Traveling sick; / My dreams roam / On a withered moor,"

reads the last of his spare, evocative poems that recount his life and travels, while reflecting a range of moods.
(AP 1)

(1) *The Old Wives' Tale* by Arnold Bennett (1908).
This is the tale of two sisters, shy Constance, who never strays from her rural English home, and adventurous Sophia, who marries and moves to Paris. Through absorbing depictions of their ordinary lives, which includes a masterful depiction of English provincial life and mores, Bennett suggests how character shapes destiny and how every destiny is fascinating.
(MD 1)

(1) *Maud Martha* by Gwendolyn Brooks (1953).
Brooks is best known for her poetry about African American life in Chicago, winning the Pulitzer Prize for *Annie Allen* (1949). In *Maud Martha*, Brooks switches to prose fiction, recounting the stages of a young woman's life during the 1930s and 1940s. The story follows Maud as she struggles with school, work, marriage, childbirth, and motherhood against the all-pervasive backdrop of racism and sexism. Told with unflinching honesty, sensitivity, and humor, *Maud Martha* is also a work of lyrical beauty.
(SC 1)

(1) *Oscar and Lucinda* by Peter Carey (1988).
Carey explores some of his favorite themes—chance, risk, and dreams—in this Booker Prize–winning novel. Set in nineteenth-century England and Australia, it uses Dickensian details and set pieces to chronicle the lives of two protagonists who share a love of gambling: an English clergyman who has broken with his past and an Australian heiress with utopian dreams. This unconven-

tional love story climaxes with a bold yet fragile scheme: to move a crystal church across the Australian outback.
(CM 1)

(1) *Nights at the Circus* by Angela Carter (1984).
Nineteenth-century London, St. Petersburg, and Siberia are the three rings of Carter's surrealist circus starring Fevvers, a trapeze artist with wings. As the bewitching Fevvers describes her life of brothels, freak shows, mad noblemen, and flying fame in high-octane Cockney slang, Carter also gives voice to a host of other characters, including the strong man, the lion tamer, and Sybil the pig. When a journalist tries to expose Fevvers as a hoax, this comic novel with feminist overtones becomes a meditation on identity and storytelling.
(PE 1)

(1) *The Sum of All Fears* by Tom Clancy (1991).
The Cold War meets the age of terror in this pulsing techno thriller. Hoping both to derail Israeli–Palestinian peace and darken U.S.–Soviet relations, terrorists smuggle a nuclear weapon into the United States. Only one man can save the day, Clancy's series hero, Jack Ryan, a CIA agent racked by personal and professional problems. Clancy brandishes his encyclopedic knowledge of the military—including plans for building a hydrogen bomb—while capturing a hero filled with doubt.
(DFW 1)

(1) *Amours de Voyage* by Arthur Hugh Clough (1858).
A nineteenth-century figure who expressed twentieth-century skepticism about action and belief, Clough set this tragicomic

narrative poem during the unsuccessful Italian Revolution of 1848–49. Much of the poem consists of letters from an erudite Englishman named Claude to his friend Eustace, describing his inability to commit to the woman he loves or engage himself in the political turmoil swirling around him. Yet, his self-awareness is so acute that he does not offer a lament of his limitations so much as an ironic self-portrait of an oddly decisive man.
(JBarn 1)

(1) *Little, Big* by John Crowley (1981).
When Smoky Barnable marries Daily Alice Drinkwater, in a pagan ceremony attended by guests seen and not seen, he enters a strange and magical family. Through the pages of this multigenerational fantasy epic, Crowley details the Drinkwater family's connection to the world of Faerie—"the further in you go, the bigger it gets"—and the tale that shapes their fate.
(HK 1)

(1) *Break It Down* by Lydia Davis (1986).
Through crisp, propulsive sentences laced with knowing irony, Davis plunges readers into various streams of consciousness in her debut collection. Ideas rather than action animate these thirty-four stories—some no more than a paragraph long, most set in a character's racing, obsessive mind. "I'm going to break it all down," says the man in the title story, trying to calculate the cost of his last love affair. Like most Davis characters, he finds more questions than answers. And like most Davis characters, he is drawn with such empathy that he pulls the reader into his madness. Only when we take a step back can we laugh, deeply, at the absurdity of it all.
(EH 1)

(1) *The Book of Ebenezer Le Page* by G. B. Edwards (1981).
The delight of this novel, set in England's Channel Islands, is the cranky voice of its eponymous narrator. Recalling his long life on the isolated island, the farmer/fisherman Le Page describes his world on a local scale: family squabbles, romances, deaths. But history on a grander scale intrudes through the German occupation during World War II. "What a big fool this world is," Le Page declares in an account of human folly suffused with wisdom.
(RPri 1)

(1) *Rites of Passage* by William Golding (1980).
The first volume of Golding's sea trilogy, this Booker Prize–winning novel is set on an early nineteenth-century ship bound for Australia. The story, told through the journal entries of aristocrat Edmund Talbot, centers on the death of a parson on board. But the plot is secondary in this deeply observed, highly atmospheric tale that tackles three of the Nobel laureate's favorite themes— the British class system, the nature of cruelty, and the sea.
(BU 1)

(1) *When I Grow Too Old to Dream*, lyrics by Oscar Hammerstein (1935).
Hammerstein's credits are a history of the American musical, including *Oklahoma, Carousel, South Pacific, The King and I,* and *The Sound of Music.* He wrote this sweet love song, which has been recorded by everyone from Nelson Eddy to Nat King Cole to Doris Day, for the film *The Night Is Too Young.* The singer asks for a parting kiss, then adds, "And when I grow too old to dream / That kiss will live in my heart."
(AT 1)

(1) *The Thin Man* by Dashiell Hammett (1932).

Retired gumshoe Nick Charles returns to Manhattan with his new heiress wife Nora, and their schnauzer Asta. The couple is quickly drawn into an investigation of a missing inventor and his murdered mistress. Hammett's comic talents and infectious, rapid-fire dialogue take the lead in this stylish, cocktail-fueled yarn.

(ST 1)

(1) *Some Other Place. The Right Place.*
by Donald Harington (1972).

This picaresque road novel with a ghostly twist centers on a young woman, a recent college graduate, and a shy eighteen-year-old boy who might be the reincarnation of an exuberant poet. Together they light out to learn about the dead man's life and death; visits to his old haunts showcase Harington's gift for describing the natural world. As the couple's bond turns to love, the dead man's spirit comes ever closer.

(DH 1)

(1) *Closely Watched Trains* by Bohumil Hrabal (1965).

As if he doesn't have enough trouble living in German-occupied Czechoslovakia during World War II, Milos Hrma learns he is impotent during his first sexual encounter. After trying to commit suicide, he returns to his job tending German trains while imagining ways to reassert his manhood. In an alternately funny and sad, lusty and bleak novel, politics and sex merge in a tragic climax that suggests the heroism of the common man.

(ALK 1)

(1) *The Hunchback of Notre Dame* by Victor Hugo (1831).

Hugo's grand populist opera stars the cathedral and medieval

Paris itself as much as the hunchbacked bell-ringer Quasimodo, whose unrequited love for the gypsy dancer Esmeralda ends very, very badly. The book is far more nineteenth century than fifteenth, brimming with melodrama, anticlericism, and Hugo's characteristic outrage at social injustice. The novel's huge popularity in France was instrumental in a neo-Gothic revival there, as well as the preservation of Notre Dame itself.
(MGait 1)

(1) *Les Misérables* by Victor Hugo (1862).

Twenty years in the writing, this masterpiece of melodrama sweeps across unspeakable poverty, assumed identities, the sewers of Paris, and the battle of Waterloo while also making time for love, politics, architecture, history, and Hugo's burning invective against social inequities. The novel's central struggle—between good-hearted prison escapee Jean Valjean and the indefatigable, by-the-book detective Javert—is about the need to temper the law with mercy and redemption, qualities often sorely lacking in Hugo's time.
(CB 1)

(1) *Pictures from an Institution* by Randall Jarrell (1954).

What happens when a brilliant poet writes a campus comedy? You get this lacerating look at academic pretensions and jealousies. Set in a women's liberal arts college, the tale centers on Gertrude Johnson, a professor writing a novel about the "little people," who has no clue about "what it was like to be a human being." This somewhat plotless novel proves the perfect vehicle for Jarrell's acid wit; every page boasts some beautifully put put-down, as here: "People did not like Mrs. Robbins, Mrs. Robbins did not like people; and neither was sorry."
(CS 1)

(1) *Heat and Dust* by Ruth Prawer Jhabvala (1975).
In 1920s India, the wife of an English officer strangled by propriety falls for a minor prince with a taste for crime. She aborts their child and leaves her husband. Fifty years later, her ex-husband's granddaughter returns to India to investigate the scandal. Through these two women Jhabvala suggests how the past informs the present, while presenting a vivid picture of India.
(HaJ 1)

(1) *Harold and the Purple Crayon* by Crockett Johnson (1955).
"One night Harold decided to go for a walk in the moonlight." But there was no moon. So the little boy drew one with his purple crayon. Then he drew a path to walk on. Soon he was using his purple crayon to create real adventures in the forest, ocean, and the air, before drawing a bead for home and bed. Creative, resourceful, and full of surprising purpose, Harold and his trusty crayon reveal the imagination's power to remake the world.
(RPow 1)

(1) *The Known World* by Edward P. Jones (2003).
Winner of both the Pulitzer Prize and National Book Critics Circle Award for fiction, this rich, sprawling novel centers on the life and legacy of an African American man who was also a slaveholder. Through a wide cast of characters, who display a wide range of perspectives and emotions, Jones examines the concept of slavery, especially how the master–slave relationship corrupts the soul.
(GP 1)

(1) *Parables and Paradoxes* by Franz Kafka (1935).
Composed after the author's death of snippets from his novels,

stories, notebooks, and letters, this collection ranges widely—
from short pieces on Sancho Panza and Robinson Crusoe to
Poseidon and Abraham. As he retells, often with dark humor,
some of the West's central myths, Kafka entertains as he reminds
us that every story suggests another story.
(SO'N 1)

(1) *On the Road* by Jack Kerouac (1957).
The ur-novel of the Beat generation, Kerouac mythologizes an
America that is always just over the next hill or waiting in the
next bar, the next town, the next bottle, or a lover's bed, and "the
mad ones" who chase such visions. Fueled by postwar recklessness
and a desire for kicks, Sal Paradise and Dean Moriarty hitchhike
and ride trains, but mostly they drive nonstop from coast to coast,
seeking music, a tank of gas, new lovers, whatever they can find.
Composing on a scroll of butcher paper run through a typewriter,
Kerouac sought a language that would match the velocity of his
characters and their exploits.
(GS 1)

(1) *Nice Work* by David Lodge (1988).
Opposites attract in this third volume of Lodge's campus trilogy
that includes *Changing Places* (1975) and *Small World* (1984). A
British government program aimed at bridging the gap between
the academy and industry pairs a leftist feminist academic and a
hard-driving businessman. Their relationship turns from hostility
to respect in this comic novel that uses snippets from nineteenth-
century English novels to explore divisions in society and literature's power to bring people together.
(IP 1)

(1) *The Assistant* by Bernard Malamud (1957).

New York shopkeeper Morris Bober will do anything to support his family, except compromise the best values drawn from his Jewish faith. He is sad, and his family suffers, as they struggle to maintain their integrity in a grasping postwar world. The arrival of a new assistant, an Italian with a checkered past named Frank, presents complications (he falls in love with Bober's daughter) and opportunities, as Malamud develops a surprising father–son relationship that suggests people are essentially good.

(HJ 1)

(1) *Kaputt* by Curzio Malaparte (1944).

Troubled by corruption in Rome, Malaparte embraced fascism as a young man. He soon wised up, and his Italian newspaper reports on the eastern front during World War II led the fascists and Nazis to imprison him. *Kaputt*, an episodic novel drawn from his reportage, juxtaposes the decadence of fascist leaders with harrowing depictions of war, including the murder of Jews in Romania, the siege of Leningrad, and Malaparte's famous image of horses frozen on Lake Ladoga.

(AF 1)

(1) *Outer Dark* by Cormac McCarthy (1968).

Outer Dark is a dark, Gothic tale set in Appalachia around the turn of the twentieth century. A woman is impregnated by her brother, who steals the child, leaves it in the woods, and tells her it has died of natural causes. She learns of her brother's lie; separately they set out across the dangerous wilds to find the child, embarking on strange and chilling journeys informed by evil, dread, and mercy.

(MGri 1)

(1) *That Night* by Alice McDermott (1987).
Primal emotions surge beneath the veneer of 1960s suburban placidity in McDermott's searing tale of innocence lost. With her teased hair and elaborate makeup, teenage Sheryl epitomizes glamour. But after her father dies, Sheryl becomes pregnant and is sent away, precipitating a violent confrontation between the neighborhood men and Sheryl's aggrieved boyfriend. McDermott's exquisite and haunting rendering of the painful revelations of youth and the mysteries of death and sex is mythic in its resonance.
(AS 1)

(1) *Atonement* by Ian McEwan (2001).
When Briony Tallis, a precocious adolescent on an English estate, writes a play to mark her brother's homecoming in 1935, she sets in motion a real-life tragedy that marks the end of her innocence. Through the awful ramifications of her one lie, McEwan explores the mysteries of writing itself, the moral ambiguities of art, and the arc of twentieth-century English history, especially during World War II.
(GG 1)

(1) *Death in Midsummer and Other Stories*
by Yukio Mishima (1968).
The diversity of this collection's subject and form will surprise anyone who knows only Mishima's legend, which he carefully created through an ascetic life and a failed attempt to ignite a bushido (samurai) movement in Japan—a move that ended with his ritual suicide in 1970. The tales—including a Noh play, a Buddhist fable, a comedy of manners, and a love triangle among three men—all reflect Mishima's profound alienation from the drift and purposelessness of modern life.
(PF 1)

(1) *The Railway Children* by E. Nesbit (1906).

This hopeful and heartbreaking tale begins when the father of three children is taken away one night by the authorities. Their resourceful mother tells them they must leave London for the country, where they will "play at being poor for a while." Their adventures on and off the railway lines near their new home are touched with melancholy, as they long for and wonder about their missing father.

(KA 1)

(1) *A Personal Matter* by Kenzaburō Ōe (1969).

The preeminent voice of Japan's New Left from the 1960s, Ōe brings a most un-Japanese rawness and rebellion to his semiautobiographical story of a young intellectual who fathers a brain-damaged baby. This modern morality tale juxtaposes its protagonist's tortuous cerebral musings with a visceral world of blood and bile, sexual deviance, and medically sanctioned infanticide. Ōe's grotesqueries paradoxically render his characters more human and sympathetic, rather than less, while the sometimes self-conscious artifice of his language accommodates a society adrift from tradition and meaning.

(DMe 1)

(1) *The Human Stain* by Philip Roth (2000).

Mentioning two students who never come to class, seventy-one-year-old professor Coleman Silk asks, "Do they exist or are they spooks?" The students are black, and Silk is soon engulfed in a racially charged campus controversy that may expose his secret life. The imbroglio also sparks Silk's libido, and he begins an affair

with one of Roth's most finely drawn female characters, an illiterate janitor. An attack on political correctness, the novel also explores Roth's signature theme: the quest for personal identity free from society's labels and expectations.
(APat 1)

(1) *Portnoy's Complaint* by Philip Roth (1969).
"I am the son in the Jewish joke," Alexander Portnoy quips, "only it ain't no joke." Narrated as a confession to a doctor, the novel portrays Portnoy's life as a long and tentative escape from the world of his hard-working, constipated father and his overbearing mother. Outrageous and frank in its treatment of sex, family, and Jewishness, this controversial novel is also a tale of generational shift, a rare ode to masturbation, and a stage for Roth's usual nostalgia: "so piercing is my gratitude—yes, my gratitude!—so sweeping and unqualified is my love."
(WK 1)

(1) *Masters of the Dew* by Jacques Roumain (1947).
See Edwidge Danticat's appreciation on page 55.
(ED 1)

(1) *The Street of Crocodiles* by Bruno Schulz (1934).
Out of his childhood experiences in the Polish city of Drogobych, Schulz (who was also an artist and a Jew) fashioned this fantastical semiautobiographical short story collection in which his father becomes a bird, a year has thirteen months, and the very furniture is aquiver with kinesthetic metaphor and the sudden transformational power of dreams. The book is one of the few surviving works of

Schulz, who was murdered by a Nazi officer in Drogobych in 1942. (JBud 1)

(1) *Ulverton* by Adam Thorpe (1992).
The fictional town of Ulverton—and the English language itself—are the central characters of this debut novel in which a dozen different voices detail three hundred years in the life of an English village. As he moves from the time of Cromwell to the 1980s in twelve rich chapters, Thorpe deploys language drawn from the period described. He also displays a mastery of literary form, inventing diary entries, sermons, drunken conversations, and film scripts to tell his story.
(EDon 1)

(1) *The Power of Now: A Guide to Spiritual Enlightenment* by Eckhart Tolle (1997).
Beginning with his own spiritual crisis at age twenty-nine, Tolle describes how he achieved enlightenment by learning to live "present, fully, and intensely, in the Now." Drawing on a variety of traditional teachings and techniques, Tolle urges readers to shed their attachments to the past, the future, and "the myriad forms of life that are subject to birth and death argues," showing them how to tap into "consciousness in its pure state prior to identification with form."
(CD 1)

(1) *A Connecticut Yankee in King Arthur's Court* by Mark Twain (1889).
Few writers made ideas as entertaining as Twain, whose gifts are on full display when he transports an ingenious American named

Hank "The Boss" Morgan to sixth-century England. The clash of sixth- and nineteenth-century mores allows Twain to offer scorching satires of compulsory religion, aristocracy, and superstition—and smart considerations of subjects ranging from slavery, trade unions, and technology to death and taxes—within the thrilling atmosphere of the Round Table and its legendary characters, including Lancelot, Merlin, and Guenever.
(RP 1)

(1) *A Voice Through a Cloud* by Denton Welch (1950).
"Though Welch has the abilities of a novelist," John Updike wrote, "misfortune made him a kind of prophet." In this autobiographical novel, Welch describes the bicycle accident that left him partially paralyzed at age twenty, the painful treatments he suffered, and the loneliness he endured. Filled with acute observations and revealing self-analysis, this intimate novel offers a wrenching portrait of despair.
(PCam 1)

(1) *The House of Mirth* by Edith Wharton (1905).
Caught up in the web of old New York society, Lily Bart angles for a wealthy husband. Though presented with ample opportunity, the beautiful and well-connected Lily rejects one man after another as not rich enough, including her true love, Laurence Stern. When she becomes a hapless victim of her own ambition—blackmailed and wrongly accused of adultery—Lily is cast out of high society before making one final attempt to redeem herself.
(KHarr 1)

(1) *Breaking and Entering* by Joy Williams (1988).

A teenage couple breaks into empty vacation homes in Florida to live "the ordered life of someone else. . . . For they themselves were not preparing for anything, they were not building anything." This picaresque novel describes the offbeat adventures of these alienated drifters—with alcoholic aristocrats and aged female bodybuilders—in sharply observant language that evokes the sadness, loneliness, and isolation of modern life.

(DC 1)

(1) *Summer Lightning* by P. G. Wodehouse (1929).

In more than ninety comic novels graced with odd names and perfectly weighted sentences, Wodehouse imagined a daft world of British privilege. He wrote many different series of books built around specific characters, including Mr. Mulliner, Psmith, Ukridge, and his most famous creations, Bertie Wooster and Jeeves. One of the Blandings Castle novels, *Summer Lightning* is an intricate farce that displays Wodehouse's penchant for anchoring his humor in ridiculous yet common circumstance—here it is a local competition to find the best pig—while exploring his great themes: social decorum and love.

(JR 1)

(1) *The Prelude* by William Wordsworth.

Wordsworth wrote this poem three times, in 1799, 1805, and finally in 1850. The subject matter, his own life, was endlessly fascinating to him. Of greater interest today is Wordsworth's theory of "spots of time," moments or hours so illuminated by memory we revisit them throughout our lives. Wordsworth's childhood ramblings through the English countryside, his education, walking tours of England and Scotland, and his witnessing of the Paris

Rebellion are all captured here, yet this poem is less narrative than meditation by a poet determined to "have felt whate'er there is of power in sound."
(AHas 1)

(David Mitchell's wild card) *Lolly Willowes*
by Sylvia Townsend Warner (1926).
The first-ever pick of the Book of the Month Club, Warner's debut novel is a fantastical light comedy with feminist overtones. Lolly is a forty-seven-year-old spinster whose yearnings impel her to leave her London family for life in the rural village of Great Mop. With the help of a black cat, she enters "into a compact with the devil." It turns out that this sleepy village—and much of Europe—is full of witches who are less menacing than bohemian. They "know they are dynamite," she says of these women, "and long for the concussion that may justify them."

APPENDIX: LITERARY NUMBER GAMES

TOP TEN WORKS OF THE TWENTIETH CENTURY

1. *Lolita* by Vladimir Nabokov
2. *The Great Gatsby* by F. Scott Fitzgerald
3. *In Search of Lost Time* by Marcel Proust
4. *Ulysses* by James Joyce
5. *Dubliners* by James Joyce
6. *One Hundred Years of Solitude* by Gabriel García Márquez
7. *The Sound and the Fury* by William Faulkner
8. *To the Lighthouse* by Virginia Woolf
9. The stories of Flannery O'Connor
10. *Pale Fire* by Vladimir Nabokov

TOP TEN WORKS OF THE NINETEENTH CENTURY

1. *Anna Karenina* by Leo Tolstoy
2. *Madame Bovary* by Gustave Flaubert
3. *War and Peace* by Leo Tolstoy
4. *The Adventures of Huckleberry Finn* by Mark Twain
5. The stories of Anton Chekhov
6. *Middlemarch* by George Eliot
7. *Moby-Dick* by Herman Melville
8. *Great Expectations* by Charles Dickens
9. *Crime and Punishment* by Fyodor Dostoevsky
10. *Emma* by Jane Austen

TOP TEN WORKS OF THE EIGHTEENTH CENTURY

1. *Tristram Shandy* by Laurence Sterne
2. *Robinson Crusoe* by Daniel Defoe
3. *Clarissa* by Samuel Richardson
4. *Candide* by Voltaire
5. *Tom Jones* by Henry Fielding
6. *Gulliver's Travels* by Jonathan Swift
7. *Joseph Andrews* by Henry Fielding
8. *The Story of the Stone* by Cao Xueqin
9. *The Rime of the Ancient Mariner* by Samuel Taylor Coleridge
10. *Les Liaisons Dangereuses* by Pierre Choderlos de Laclos

TOP TEN WORKS OF THE SIXTEENTH AND SEVENTEENTH CENTURIES

1. *Hamlet* by William Shakespeare
2. *Don Quixote* by Miguel de Cervantes
3. *King Lear* by William Shakespeare
4. *Macbeth* by William Shakespeare
5. *Paradise Lost* by John Milton
6. *The Tempest* by William Shakespeare
7. *Romeo and Juliet* by William Shakespeare
8. *Antony and Cleopatra* by William Shakespeare
9. The plays of Molière
10. *Henry V* and *Othello, The Moor of Venice* by William Shakespeare

TOP TEN WORKS OF THE FIFTEENTH CENTURY AND EARLIER

1. *The Odyssey* by Homer
2. *The Divine Comedy* by Dante Alighieri
3. The Bible
4. *The Canterbury Tales* by Geoffrey Chaucer
5. *The Oresteia* by Aeschylus
6. *The Aeneid* by Virgil
7. *The Iliad* by Homer
8. *The Decameron* by Giovanni Boccaccio
9. *The Arabian Nights: Tales from a Thousand and One Nights*
10. *Oedipus the King* by Sophocles

TOP TEN AUTHORS BY NUMBER OF WORKS SELECTED

1. William Shakespeare—11
2. William Faulkner—6
3. Henry James—6
4. Jane Austen—5
5. Charles Dickens—5
6. Fyodor Dostoevsky—5
7. Ernest Hemingway—5
8. Franz Kafka—5

(tie) James Joyce, Thomas Mann, Vladimir Nabokov, Mark Twain, Virginia Woolf—4

TOP TEN AUTHORS BY POINTS EARNED

1. Leo Tolstoy—327
2. William Shakespeare—293
3. James Joyce—194
4. Vladimir Nabokov—190
5. Fyodor Dostoevsky—177
6. William Faulkner—173
7. Charles Dickens—168
8. Anton Chekhov—165
9. Gustave Flaubert—163
10. Jane Austen—161

TOP TEN WORKS BY AMERICAN AUTHORS

1. *The Adventures of Huckleberry Finn* by Mark Twain
2. *The Great Gatsby* by F. Scott Fitzgerald
3. *Moby-Dick* by Herman Melville
4. *The Sound and the Fury* by William Faulkner
5. The stories of Flannery O'Connor
6. *Absalom, Absalom!* by William Faulkner
7. *To Kill a Mockingbird* by Harper Lee
8. *Invisible Man* by Ralph Ellison
9. *Beloved* by Toni Morrison
10. *The Portrait of a Lady* by Henry James

TOP TEN WORKS BY BRITISH AUTHORS

1. *Hamlet* by William Shakespeare
2. *Middlemarch* by George Eliot
3. *Great Expectations* by Charles Dickens
4. *Ulysses* by James Joyce
5. *King Lear* by William Shakespeare
6. *Emma* by Jane Austen
7. *Dubliners* by James Joyce
8. *To the Lighthouse* by Virginia Woolf
9. *Tristram Shandy* by Laurence Sterne
10. *Pride and Prejudice* by Jane Austen

TOP TEN WORKS BY RUSSIAN AUTHORS

1. *Anna Karenina* by Leo Tolstoy
2. *War and Peace* by Leo Tolstoy
3. *Lolita* by Vladimir Nabokov
4. The stories of Anton Chekhov
5. *Crime and Punishment* by Fyodor Dostoevsky
6. *The Brothers Karamazov* by Fyodor Dostoevsky
7. *Pale Fire* by Vladimir Nabokov
8. *Red Cavalry* by Isaac Babel
9. *Dead Souls* by Nikolai Gogol
10. *The Master and Margarita* by Mikhail Bulgakov

TOP TEN WORKS BY FRENCH AUTHORS

1. *Madame Bovary* by Gustave Flaubert
2. *In Search of Lost Time* by Marcel Proust
3. *The Stranger* by Albert Camus
4. *Candide* by Voltaire
5. *Germinal* by Émile Zola
6. *L'Assommoir (The Dram Shop)* by Émile Zola
7. *Nana* by Émile Zola
8. *Cousin Bette* by Honoré de Balzac
9. *The Diary of a Country Priest* by Georges Bernanos
10. *The Fall* by Albert Camus

TOP TEN WORKS BY LIVING WRITERS

1. *One Hundred Years of Solitude* by Gabriel García Márquez
2. *To Kill a Mockingbird* by Harper Lee
3. *Beloved* by Toni Morrison
4. *The Catcher in the Rye* by J. D. Salinger
5. *Rabbit Angstrom* by John Updike
6. *Slaughterhouse-Five* by Kurt Vonnegut
7. *Blood Meridian* by Cormac McCarthy
8. *The Stand* by Stephen King
9. The stories of Alice Munro
10. *The Prime of Miss Jean Brodie* by Muriel Spark

TOP TEN COMIC WORKS

1. *Don Quixote* by Miguel de Cervantes
2. *Tristram Shandy* by Laurence Sterne
3. *Joseph Andrews* by Henry Fielding
4. *Norwood* by Charles Portis
5. *The Importance of Being Earnest* by Oscar Wilde
6. *A Confederacy of Dunces* by John Kennedy Toole
7. *A Midsummer Night's Dream* by William Shakespeare
8. *The Ponder Heart* by Eudora Welty
9. *Blithe Spirit* by Noël Coward
10. *Right Ho, Jeeves* by P. G. Wodehouse

TOP TEN WORKS OF FANTASY AND SCIENCE FICTION

1. *Alice's Adventures in Wonderland* by Lewis Carroll
2. *The Stand* by Stephen King
3. *Gulliver's Travels* by Jonathan Swift
4. *The Strange Case of Dr. Jekyll and Mr. Hyde* by Robert Louis Stevenson
5. *The Voyage of the 'Dawn Treader'* by C. S. Lewis
6. *Fiskadoro* by Denis Johnson
7. *The Lord of the Rings* by J. R. R. Tolkien
8. *The War with the Newts* by Karel Čapek
9. *His Dark Materials* by Philip Pullman
10. *Dune* by Frank Herbert

TOP TEN MYSTERIES AND THRILLERS

1. *The Long Goodbye* by Raymond Chandler
2. *The Killer Inside Me* by Jim Thompson
3. *Red Dragon* by Thomas Harris
4. *The Big Sleep* by Raymond Chandler
5. *Tinker, Tailor, Soldier, Spy* by John Le Carré
6. *The Postman Always Rings Twice* by James M. Cain
7. *The Maltese Falcon* by Dashiell Hammett
8. *Mildred Pierce* by James M. Cain
9. *The Silence of the Lambs* by Thomas Harris
10. *Everybody Pays* by Andrew Vachss

ONE-HIT WONDERS: TWENTY-THREE WORKS
THAT EARNED A TOP SLOT BUT NO OTHER

Answered Prayers by Truman Capote (DC)

Antony and Cleopatra by William Shakespeare (MD)

The Awakening by Kate Chopin (SMK)

Bhagavadgita (CD)

The Birthday Party and *The Homecoming* by Harold Pinter (AMH)

The Book of Leviathan by Peter Blegvad (MSB)

Casa Guidi Windows by Elizabeth Barrett Browning (AT)

The Confidence-Man: His Masquerade by Herman Melville (ALK)

Embers by Sándor Márai (RW)

Geek Love by Katherine Dunn (JW)

I, Claudius by Robert Graves (AGold)

Ill Seen, Ill Said by Samuel Beckett (JB)

JR by William Gaddis (LMill)

The Golden Argosy edited by Van H. Cartmell and Charles
  Grayson (SK)

L'Assommoir (The Dram Shop) by Émile Zola (TW)

Love Medicine by Louise Erdrich (TCB)

Nana by Émile Zola (TW)

The Screwtape Letters by C. S. Lewis (DFW)

Seven Pillars of Wisdom by T. E. Lawrence (AF)

The Outward Room by Millen Brand (PCam)

Things Fall Apart by Chinua Achebe (JC)

The Time of the Doves by Mercè Rodoreda (SC)

The Woman in the Dunes by Kobo Abe (KHarr)

INDEX OF AUTHORS
BY INITIALS

GG ... Gail Godwin
GP ... George Pelacanos
GS ... George Saunders
HaJ ... Ha Jin
HJ ... Heidi Julavits
HK ... Haven Kimmel
IP ... Iain Pears
IR ... Ian Rankin
JB ... John Banville
JBarn ... Julian Barnes
JBud ... Judy Budnitz
JC ... Jim Crace
JCO ... Joyce Carol Oates
JF ... Jonathan Franzen
JH ... Jim Harrison
JI ... John Irving
JL ... Jonathan Lethem
JLB ... James Lee Burke
JR ... Jonathan Raban
JS ... Jim Shepard
JSalt ... James Salter
JW ... Jennifer Weiner
KA ... Kate Atkinson
KH ... Kent Haruf
KHarr ... Kathryn Harrison
KJF ... Karen Joy Fowler
KK ... Ken Kalfus
LDR ... Louis D. Rubin, Jr.
LKA ... Lee K. Abbott
LM ... Lorrie Moore
LMill ... Lydia Millet
LS ... Lee Smith
MB ... Melissa Bank
MC ... Michael Chabon
MCon ... Michael Connelly
MCunn ... Michael Cunningham
MD ... Margaret Drabble
MG ... Mary Gordon
MGait ... Mary Gaitskill
MGri ... Michael Griffith

ML ... Margot Livesey
MSB ... Madison Smartt Bell
MW ... Meg Wolitzer
NM ... Norman Mailer
PA ... Paul Auster
PC ... Peter Carey
PCam ... Peter Cameron
PCap ... Philip Caputo
PCle ... Pearl Cleage
PE ... Percival Everett
PF ... Paula Fox
PM ... Patrick McGrath
RB ... Russell Banks
RBP ... Robert B. Parker
RFD ... Robb Forman Dew
RP ... Robert Pinsky
RPow ... Richard Powers
RPri ... Reynolds Price
RR ... Roxana Robinson
RW ... Robert Wilson
SA ... Sherman Alexie
SC ... Sandra Cisneros
SCraw ... Stanley Crawford
SK ... Stephen King
SM ... Susan Minot
SMK ... Sue Monk Kidd
SO'N ... Stewart O'Nan
SS ... Scott Spencer
ST ... Scott Turow
SV ... Susan Vreeland
TCB ... T. C. Boyle
TK ... Thomas Keneally
TM ... Thomas Mallon
TP ... Tom Perrotta
TW ... Tom Wolfe
VM ... Valerie Martin
VV ... Vendela Vida
WK ... Walter Kirn
WL ... Wally Lamb

INDEX TO BOOK
DESCRIPTIONS

*Asterisks denote short story collections and other works covered by omnibus descriptions. For example, *The Curtain of Green* by Eudora Welty is folded into the entry "Stories of Eudora Welty."

ACKNOWLEDGMENTS

Thanks to:

- The 365 writers whose books are listed in *The Top Ten*. This book is a wide-eyed fan's note, a floor-touching bow, an awed homage to you, who have given us timeless gifts.

- The 125 writers who demonstrated such warm generosity in contributing their lists to this work. For many it was an agonizing process through which they were sustained and pushed on by their love of literature.

- The 18 writers who displayed erudition, insight, and a gift of brevity to capture hundreds of great books in less than one hundred words to create the brief descriptions: Bruce Allen, Rod Cockshutt, Claire Dederer, John Dicker, Roger Gathman, Denise Gess, Denise Heinze, Marvin Hunt, Charlotte Jackson, Robert Lalasz, Al Maginnes, Erin McGraw, Lydia Millet, Glenn Perkins, Marcy Smith, Donna Seaman, Todd Shy, and Julia Ridley Smith.

- My gifted and gentle editor, Amy Cherry, who believed in

this project from the start, and improved it every step of the way. My eagle-eyed copy editor, JoAnn Simony.

- My agent and pal Mickey Choate.
- My supportive and inspiring colleagues at *The News & Observer,* including Melanie Sill, John Drescher, Dan Barkin, Suzanne Brown, G. D. Gearino, and Dwane Powell.
- My mother, Suzanne Pederson; my sister, Tabitha Zane; and my in-laws, Lewis and Kitty Steel.